Hugs !

Melanie Moulard

x

VESTED INTEREST:ABC CORP BOOK 1

MY
SAVING
GRACE

NEW YORK TIMES AND *USA TODAY* BESTSELLING AUTHOR
MELANIE MORELAND

Dear Reader,

Thank you for selecting MY SAVING GRACE to read. Be sure to sign up for my newsletter for up to date information on new releases, exclusive content and sales at melaniemoreland.com

Before you sign up, add melanie@melaniemoreland.com to your contacts to make sure the email comes right to your inbox!
Always fun - never spam!

My books are available in both paperback and audiobook! I also have personalized signed paperbacks available at melaniemoreland.com.

The Perfect Recipe For **LOVE**
xoxo,
Melanie

My Saving Grace by Melanie Moreland
Copyright © 2020 Moreland Books Inc.
Copyright #1178145
ISBN Ebook 978-1-988610-47-4
Paperback 978-1-988610-48-1
All rights reserved

MORELAND
BOOKS INC.

Edited by
Lisa Hollett—Silently Correcting Your Grammar
Cover design by Karen Hulseman, Feed Your Dreams Designs
Photographer Eric David Battershell of O'Snap Media
Cover Model Christian Petrovich

Quote Permission from Darling Duke by Scarlett Scott @ 2018

Readers with concerns about content or subjects depicted can check out the content advisory on my website: https://melaniemoreland.com/extras/fan-suggestions/content-advisory/

DEDICATION

For my Minions

You know why

Thank you for making me smile

Love you all

PROLOGUE

GRACE

I woke up, my head aching and my limbs heavy. I blinked in the darkness of the room, my mouth feeling like the Sahara Desert. The room was unfamiliar, and it took me a moment to recall I was in a hotel room in Las Vegas.

Why did my head ache so badly?

I searched through my memories of the day before. Finally resolving the mystery of the trademark and copyright fiasco. Spending a carefree afternoon in Vegas. Having fun at the slots, sampling a couple of buffets. Seeing the sights. Then I got a call before we left for the airport to inform me that my plane was canceled due to a mechanical malfunction and the earliest flight I could get out was the next day. It was a long-ass flight with lots of stopovers all over the States before it landed in Canada, but it would at least still get me home before Addi's wedding. I hadn't wanted to come on this trip so close to her nuptials, but I had. Jaxson had asked, and I had said yes. It proved how much of an idiot I was.

The fact that he came to mind as soon as I woke up only solidified that assertion.

What the hell happened to me after that phone call?

I racked my brain, trying to remember, to grasp some minute detail of yesterday, but the one clear memory in my mind was meeting *him* a couple of months ago.

I had interviewed at Smith and Hodges and was offered a position to article with the firm. Articling, as I had learned in law school, was a uniquely Canadian term— basically, I would be a paid intern and benefit from hands-on experience with a mentor. After the interview was done, I was sent to Jaxson Richards's office. His outer office was empty, so I knocked on the door, waiting until he called out for me to enter. He sat behind his massive desk, and the moment our eyes met, my world tilted.

Tall and broad, stern and fierce, he stared at me, rising from his chair. His eyes were like iced fire, the blue vivid and clear. His hair was so dark, it was almost black and brushed to gleaming. His suit fit him perfectly, and as he strode toward me, I caught a glimpse of his powerful thighs, large hands, and wide chest. He held out his hand, a smile tipping up one corner of his full lips and making the cleft in his chin prominent. I had never seen a man as handsome in my life. Considering the caliber of the group of men around me all the time, that was saying something.

"Grace VanRyan, I presume?"

I slipped my hand into his and shook it. The shock that tore through me at his touch startled me. For a moment, I was speechless, my throat dry, the words I needed to say unclear. I shook my head and found my voice, wondering why I was suddenly so nervous.

"Mr. Richards. Yes, I'm Grace." I cleared my throat, my words sounding strangely breathless. "It's a pleasure to meet you. I look forward to our time together."

He tilted his head. "As do I."

He escorted me to the chair across from him and waited until I sat down. It was only then I realized he was still holding my hand. He released his grip and sat down, resting his elbows on his desk. Then he asked me the strangest question.

"Tell me about Grace VanRyan. Besides being an articling law student."

I had expected him to ask about school. What I wanted to get out of my time with the firm. My thoughts on the future. Not to ask about me.

"Nothing much to tell, really. I'm pretty boring."

"I find that hard to believe." He smirked, lifting one eyebrow. "You may be at the beginning of your story, Ms. VanRyan, but I doubt you're boring."

It slipped out before I could stop myself. "Gracie. My friends call me Gracie."

He inclined his head, a crooked smile gracing his lips. "Gracie," he repeated.

He sat back, not pushing the subject any further. He spoke of the firm, his history, and what he expected of me. We discussed some of the cases he was working on.

"Why corporate?" he asked.

"I've always been fascinated with it," I confessed. "My father is in marketing, so he always talked about trademarks and copyrights. I loved it when I went into the office with him, and I always snuck into the legal department and asked a thousand and one questions."

"VanRyan—VanRyan," he repeated. "Richard VanRyan?"

"Yes."

"I know his work."

I smiled, unsure what to say.

He went over the hours, where I would work, and answered all my questions. He beamed at me, the gesture turning his stern face into one of warmth, filled with personality.

"Your enthusiasm is to be commended. I look forward to having you under me."

My eyes widened, and he hastened to correct himself. "Work under me. With me. I have a feeling we'll make quite the team."

I had to push aside the thought of being under him. How his powerful body would feel against mine. The pleasure those large hands could bring. I felt my cheeks flush, and I had to lower my gaze before he noticed. Silence fell, and then he cleared his throat and asked me a few more questions.

I shook my head to clear it, knowing I couldn't have such thoughts about the man who would be my boss, and responded in the proper manner, my mind fixed firmly on business.

Finally, he stood, buttoning his jacket, indicating our time was done.

After confirming my hours, I left, already excited about working with him. About the knowledge I would learn.

I had no idea the greatest lesson I would learn would be heartache.

I curled my body tighter as I tried to tamp down the painful memories.

How the excitement led to agony. How I discovered his charm hid a selfish man intent on his own pleasure. Realizing to my horror, I had fallen in love with someone incapable of returning that love and who had lied to me with his sweet words and gestures. The future I envisioned was nothing but a lie.

The face he showed the world was nothing but a lie.

I had no choice but to work with him every day, hiding my suffering. Wondering how love could become hate. I refused to let him see my inner turmoil. I was determined to finish this articling position, walk away, and never see Jaxson Richards again. I hadn't wanted to come on this trip, but the partners—and Jaxson—had given me no choice.

I groaned as I shifted, the pain in my head changing from a dull ache to a constant pounding. As I moved, I stiffened as I realized the weight on my hip wasn't that of the blanket, but of a hand.

My stomach rolled when reality hit me. Someone was in bed with me. I had slept with a stranger. I got drunk in Vegas and slept with a stranger. How clichéd.

Ignoring the ache in my head, I shot out of bed, yanking the blanket with me. I fumbled around, finding the light and switching it on. I squinted as the pain shot through my temples, and I gasped when I recognized the man lying in the bed beside me. Not looking upset at all, Jaxson pulled himself up into a sitting position and had the nerve to smile at me.

"Not a stranger," he said, letting me know I had spoken my thought out loud. "How are you feeling, darling?"

"What the hell are you doing here?"

"Until a few moments ago, I was sleeping. You must need some Tylenol. Let me get it for you."

"Don't bother. I meant, how the hell did you get into my bed?"

He smirked, lifting one leg up to his chest and reclining back with his hands beneath his head. He looked too handsome and far too comfortable for this situation.

"Since this is my room, you're the one in *my* bed."

I looked around, seeing he was right.

"What the hell happened?"

"I would think that was obvious." He indicated the torn condom wrappers. "We had sex."

I gaped at him. "Why did I have sex with you? I don't like you!"

He leaned forward, his blue eyes bright in the dim light. His smile was wicked, and I wanted to wipe it off his face with my fist. "You *really* liked me last night. At least three times."

We'd had sex three times?

"At least," he confirmed. "I'm not counting the orgasm in the car, and I think I missed one other fuck. Against the wall, I think."

I was stunned. I stared at him, horrified. I had slept with my boss. Again.

"I can't believe I did that," I mumbled, gripping the blanket.

"That's not the only thing you did, darling."

"What could be worse?"

He studied me closely. He indicated my hand gripping the blanket.

"You married me."

A thin, too-tight band encircled my ring finger. He held up his hand, showing me a matching ring.

7

"How about that for clichéd, Mrs. Richards?" He smirked.

The room spun, and my stomach heaved.

The last thing I remembered was his shout before the floor rushed toward me.

Unconsciousness had never been so welcome.

CHAPTER 1

EARLY FALL - GRACE

I woke early, already eager for the day to begin. My first day as an articling student. It felt as if years had passed since my interview at Smith and Hodges, leading up to my starting with them, although it had just been a matter of months. I had been keen to reach that stage of my career and looked forward to putting into practice what I had learned. At my interview, they explained I would work with two lawyers over the course of my year in order to learn more during my time with them. I knew law students were often hired at the end of their stint, but I planned on working with the lawyer at BAM and cutting my teeth there before moving to ABC. Bill held a wealth of knowledge, and I wanted to soak it up before he retired and someone younger took his place.

When Jaxson Richards's name was mentioned at the interview, I was excited.

And after meeting him, I had been doubly anxious.

Jaxson Richards was larger-than-life, and much to my dismay, I couldn't stop thinking about him since our meeting. He was incredibly handsome and confident, and his blue eyes radiated intelligence. Unable to resist, I had checked him out on the internet, my eyes widening at the vast array of articles about him. He was thirty-eight, single, and had been with two other law firms in his career. Each change had moved him to a more prestigious firm, and he had been with Smith and Hodges for five years. Aside from the legal articles and the professional information the company's website held, I came across a lot of pictures of him with women. Beautiful women. When I focused on the dates, I noticed none of them lasted long. I had shaken my head, closing the laptop. He would be my boss, and his personal life was none of my business. I was going to Smith and Hodges to learn everything I could for the next year so I could move ahead with my life. Nothing more.

If only I could convince my head to stop remembering how my hand felt within his.

And now the day I had been waiting for had arrived. The next step in my journey.

I slipped from bed, pushing my feet into my ever-present slippers, and shuffled to the kitchen. I switched on the coffee then headed to the shower. Half an hour later, I sat at my small table, sipping a cup of the hot, fragrant brew. I glanced around my apartment, the space never failing to make me happy.

I lived in a small building, nestled in the downtown core of Toronto. A five-minute walk brought me into the hustle and bustle of the city, but the street I lived on was relatively quiet. It was a two-bedroom place, filled with charm and character. Hardwood floors that squeaked underfoot, plaster walls, tall ceilings, and windows set with leaded glass trim that sparkled in the sunlight and took all my effort to open. The kitchen had real wooden cupboards, and the claw-foot tub in the bathroom was ideal for a long soak. I loved every inch of it.

My father had been horrified by my choice.

"Your uncles own some of the most luxurious apartment complexes in Toronto," he had argued. *"You have your pick. What on earth are you thinking, Gracie-girl?"* he asked as he looked around, askance.

I ran my finger over the chair rail, the wood like silk under my touch. "I like this place."

"Their buildings have security, air conditioning, and modern appliances. There is a high-rise of theirs five blocks that way if you insist on this neighborhood. I'll call Mad Dog right now and arrange it." He pulled his phone from his pocket. *"You can't live here."*

I laid my hand on his arm. "I like this place, Dad. The neighborhood is great. The building is safe. There's a new air conditioner in the bedroom window, and I'll get one of those portable ones in here. I can walk up the three flights of stairs easily." I met his eyes, lifting my eyebrows in silent reminder.

"I'm sure they have places with walk-ups," he huffed.

11

"No. I like this one. The rent is reasonable, and I can walk to the bus or streetcar. There're lots of little shops around. It's close to school."

He ran a hand through his hair. "Money isn't a problem, Gracie."

My mom, who had been quiet until this point, tugged on his arm. "Richard darling, leave Gracie alone. She's an adult, and this is her decision. I agree, this place is charming."

She and I shared a knowing glance between us. My dad was over-protective and hated my independent streak. I had earned a scholarship to go to law school, and he had insisted I concentrate on school and not work, which hadn't sat well with me. I had gotten a part-time job at one of the small coffee shops anyway. The pay wasn't great, but I enjoyed it nonetheless. It gave me a chance simply to be Grace, and I met some amazing people who became friends and made a little money that was mine. My mother understood the importance of that, having had a different upbringing from my dad. He had been displeased, but as usual, supported me in my decision.

I had wavered when it was time to choose my career. I knew how much my father secretly hoped I would join him in the world of marketing. I went to school for two years before I finally admitted the truth. Marketing wasn't my passion. I didn't have the drive or talent my father had. The flair for design Heather possessed. The day I told my parents, they had both been shocked, but my father had insisted I stop following what I thought was his dream and concentrate on my own. He was horrified I had done something I thought would make him happy rather than pursuing my own desires. I took a little time off, did a lot of soul-searching, then registered for the next available opening in the law program in Toronto and never looked back.

I didn't want to live on campus, and I had fallen in love with this place. My dad loved modern, sleek buildings. I preferred old, Victorian ones with character. He loved luxury and all the trappings his wealth brought him. I had been lucky growing up and always appreciated the ease I lived with, never worrying about money, but I never took it for granted. I valued how hard he worked to give us a good life. His ethics helped mold mine, and even though he grumbled over my independent streak, I knew he was proud of me.

My dad had cajoled, pleaded, and even threatened, then accepted my decision. I capitulated to a few of his demands. No walking after dark, a modified security system he would get BAM to install, and twice-a-week check-ins until he was comfortable. Years later, those still happened.

My mom told me a few years after I had moved in that he'd thought I would change my mind, but I never did. I was still in the same space and still loved my little home, much to my dad's chagrin.

As if he knew I was thinking about him, my phone rang. Smiling, I hit speaker.

"Hi, Dad."

His rich baritone filled my apartment. "Hello, Graciegirl. Excited for your first day?"

I chuckled, sipping my coffee. "I am. Nervous too."

"Don't be. They're lucky to have you."

"It's three a.m. in BC, Dad. Are you still awake or up early?"

"Still awake. I wanted to wish you well today, baby girl. Let you know I would be thinking of you and how proud I am."

I smiled at his words. Even across the country, I could feel his love. He was very open with his feelings for us. He and I had always been close. Growing up, he was a hero in my eyes. I still thought so. He was strong and affectionate and had always been a great dad. He was a consummate businessman, his career in the marketing industry legendary. His name was synonymous with excellence, his reputation stellar. He was also known as arrogant and confident—someone you didn't want to go toe-to-toe with. But to us, his family, he was just Dad. Loving, stern, affectionate, and funny. He worshiped my mother, his love for her evident in his gaze and the way he put her first in every decision. Given their rocky start, theirs was an interesting story with a fairy-tale ending.

Hard to live up to.

I realized my dad had said something and was waiting for my response.

"Sorry, Dad. What did you say?"

"I asked if you needed anything."

"No. I'm good."

"You met your boss, right?"

"Yes."

"He has quite the reputation in intellectual property law."

"Yes. He was, ah, pretty intense. Very serious. But I'm excited. He seems as if he wants to teach me. He laid out his expectations very clearly."

"I have no doubt you're up to the challenge, my girl. You can do anything you put your mind to."

"Thanks, Dad."

"If he steps out of line, let me know."

I laughed. "He's older than me, Dad. I highly doubt a law student doing her articling is his speed. Especially me."

"You are far more beautiful than you give yourself credit for. All I'm saying is watch it. Watch all of them."

"They have a very firm nonfraternization clause. I'm not concerned."

He huffed. "Okay, good. Remember the moves I taught you anyway."

"Aiden taught me," I corrected, trying to hide the amusement in my voice.

"I was there. I helped."

"I love you, Dad."

"I love you. Have a great first day."

"I will."

"Gracie?" he murmured before I could hang up.

"Yes?"

"I love you, my baby girl," he repeated. "I'm always here."

"I know, Dad. I love you too."

He hung up, and I knew he would go back to bed and seek out the comfort of my mother's embrace. Despite the gruff businesslike exterior he presented to the world, underneath, he was a softy and his family meant the world to him. I knew if I ever needed him, he would be right there, ready to defend or protect.

I smiled as I got ready for the day.

CHAPTER 2

GRACE

I arrived at the office early, eager to start the next chapter of my life. The building was quiet when I arrived, the security desk staffed by an older man with a wide grin. When I gave my name, he checked the list and nodded, handing me a pass card.

"That will get you around until you meet with HR for a permanent one. The elevator is to the right, and you need to use this to get to your floor."

"Ah, is the staircase open?"

"Six flights of stairs," he informed me.

"I know."

He chuckled. "One of those fitness people, are you?"

I was relieved he came up with that idea. "Yes. It's good exercise."

"End of the hall. You'll need to use the pass card to gain access."

"Great."

I climbed the steps, hoping Jaxson didn't require a lot of errands to the main floor. I entered the hallway and headed to Jaxson's office, somehow not surprised to find the door open. I could hear him moving around in his office as I set down my bag, noticing the new desk and chair in the outer office. I paused in the doorway of his space, watching quietly for a moment. He was studying a sheaf of papers, muttering low under his breath. He held a takeout cup of coffee, the steam wafting in the air as he raised the cup to his full lips, taking a sip. It was impossible not to notice how handsome he was. With the early morning sun coming in the windows, back-lighting him, his stature was imposing. Tall and broad, he stood ramrod straight, intensely focused. Today, he wore a charcoal-gray suit, his shirt snow-white against the dark color. A tie with stripes of purple, gray, and black was a splash of color on his broad chest. His hair gleamed in the sunlight, a slight frown creasing his fore-head as he studied the documents. The cleft in his chin was deep, and the random idea of wanting to dip my tongue into the divot surprised me. I shook my head to clear that strange thought and lifted my hand to knock on the doorframe.

He glanced up, and we both froze. Our eyes locked, his intense blue meeting my softer hue. I felt a sudden change in the air. It became sharp, focused—powerful.

It was as if the rest of the world ceased to exist and there was only him and me left. My heartbeat picked up and my breath caught. He blinked, cocking his head as if to study me.

Then he set back his shoulders and spoke. His voice was detached.

"Ms. VanRyan. Good morning."

I startled at the sudden change but found my voice.

"Mr. Richards."

"You're early."

"I wanted to make a timely start."

"I didn't hear the elevator."

"Oh, I took the stairs."

He dropped his gaze to my feet, taking in the low heels I preferred. His eyes ran lazily up my legs, his perusal slow. I felt a catch in my throat as my body suddenly hummed. It felt as if he were touching me with his gaze, burning his way up my body. I tightened my grip on the doorframe, a subtle shudder running through me. I had dressed carefully this morning, wearing a simple blouse in my favorite color of royal blue and a skirt that fell to my knees. It had small kick pleats that moved as I walked, and I liked how it looked. Professional, yet pretty. I had my hair up, and the only jewelry I wore was a pair of earrings my parents had given me when I graduated. Simple pearls with a tiny diamond accent—

they were my favorite, and I wore them a lot. I had hoped to make a good impression.

He didn't say a word, lifting his coffee cup to his lips and draining the liquid.

Our eyes locked once again, and I swore I saw a smile pull at his mouth as he swallowed.

He crossed the room to his desk, tossing the file on top and the empty coffee cup in the garbage. He cleared his throat, his voice warmer when he spoke.

"Watch out for the third step from the bottom. The edging has a habit of lifting on the right side. I would hate for you to trip."

"Noted." My voice sounded breathless.

He lifted his arm, indicating for me to sit. The movement pulled up his sleeve, and I noticed the heavy watch on his wrist, the glint of silver catching the light.

"Sit, Ms. VanRyan. We have a lot to discuss."

Thirty minutes later, my head was swimming. In the brief moment it took me to sit down, Mr. Richards's voice had changed yet again, and he was back to being cool. He listed his expectations in detail, told me about the cases he was handling, informed me the desk I had seen earlier was for me. "You'll be sharing the space with my assistant, Michael."

"Okay."

"He was away when you were interviewed. You can introduce yourself when he arrives. He'll take you to HR and show you around."

"All right."

"I'll be working you hard, Ms. VanRyan. I have high expectations. The last student I had lasted a month and asked for a different lawyer. Think you can do better?"

I met his eyes. They were intense and serious, with none of the heat from earlier remaining. Maybe I had imagined it. I straightened my shoulders and refused to show him how nervous I felt. "Yes," I stated firmly.

"What makes you so certain?" he asked, cocking his head and studying me.

I couldn't help the smile that pulled at my lips. "Because, as my mother would say, I am my father's daughter. I'm known for being tenacious."

He lifted his eyebrows but remained silent.

"I plan on giving this my all, Mr. Richards. I want to do this. Learn everything I can. I'm not afraid of hard work. I didn't earn the grades I received by being a slacker. I will push and push until I get the job done." I paused. "And not to your satisfaction, but to mine. I guarantee you, whatever your standards are, mine are equal if not higher."

He looked surprised at my words, then nodded as if satisfied. He handed me a stack of files. "Look over these until Michael arrives. There is a kitchen down the hall if you want coffee."

"Could I bring you a cup?"

He shook his head. "You're not my errand girl. You don't need to bring me coffee."

"I was simply being nice. I don't plan on waiting on you."

He chuckled. "Okay then, Ms. VanRyan. A cup would be welcome."

"Why Ms. VanRyan and Mr. Richards?" I asked before I could stop myself. "You called me Grace when we met."

"I'm setting boundaries."

"Does Michael call you Mr. Richards?"

"He has proven himself," he stated, affirming my guess.

"So, I have to earn it is what you are saying."

Something dark passed over his face. "Yes."

"Then I look forward to the challenge."

I walked out and sat down at the small desk in the corner. It was bare except for a lamp and a cup holding some pens. I set down the files, looking up and meeting the gaze of my new boss. The way the desk was situated, he would see me when his door was open. He would be watching me.

I went to get coffee, needing a moment to collect myself. Jaxson, Mr. Richards, whatever I had to call him, had thrown me off and made me jittery. He was hot and cold—one moment warm and personable, the next a polite stranger, making me feel as if I was of no importance. It was a strange feeling. But I was going to have to get used to it. I wasn't going anywhere, and I would prove myself to him and anyone else who questioned my aptitude. Grace VanRyan didn't back away from a challenge. Ever. My father had taught me that lesson all my life.

Even if the blue eyes belonging to the man who issued it made my heart flutter.

I would ignore that part.

When I returned to the office, Michael was at his desk. He was my age, tall, slender, his blond hair slicked back, with a wide smile. He was a good-looking man. He was well dressed, and from the look of his area, neat and organized. His hazel eyes were warm, his handshake firm, and his voice welcoming.

"Grace, I'm Michael. I look forward to working with you."

I shook his hand, responding to his warmth. "You as well, Michael." My gaze skittered to the closed door, then back to him. "First names okay out here?"

He grinned, mischief dancing in his eyes. "Oh, he's doing the Mr. Richards, 'earn the right to call me Jaxson' thing?"

I nodded.

He leaned forward. "He's a bear. A grumpy, growly bear most of the time, but it's all an act. He's a decent guy. Just go with the flow."

Jaxson's door opened, and he strode out, stopping when he saw us. He frowned, taking in our close proximity.

"Coffee break already?"

"Haven't got that far yet," Michael replied easily.

"Move it along, Michael. I have a busy day. I need Ms. VanRyan up to speed ASAP."

"I'm aware of your busy day. I oversee your schedule. I was welcoming Grace to the office." He sniffed. "Someone has to be nice."

Jaxson glared, then handed me a stack of files. "Read these, and we'll discuss after lunch." He looked at Michael. "Show her around. Make sure her schedule allows some study time. Take her to HR and get her settled. IT should have set up a laptop for her. Find it. I need more information on Drake's Manufacturing. The file is thin."

I spoke up. "I can do that. I'm great at research."

Jaxson's blue gaze flickered to me. "Fine. I need it today." He looked back to Michael. "Get her a computer. ASAP."

"I'm sure there is a computer in the library I can use if there isn't one on my desk. It's not a problem. I can work anywhere."

Jaxson spun on his heel, pausing at his door. "I need coffee, Michael." He met my gaze. "And it is a problem. I want you at that desk, not in the library." He paused. "No personal cell phone usage in the office unless you're on a break."

He disappeared, and the words were out before I could stop them. "At my desk so he can watch me and make sure I'm not breaking the rules?" I muttered. "Jeesh."

His head appeared around the doorframe. "Yes. Trust is earned, Ms. VanRyan, not blindly given."

I felt the heat in my cheeks, but I refused to back down. "The same with respect, Mr. Richards."

His eyebrows shot up, but he didn't say anything. His door shut loudly, and I looked at Michael with a grimace. "So much for a good impression."

He grinned. "Girlfriend, I am totally in love with you. Don't tell my husband that, though. The big brute is a jealous bugger." He indicated a framed picture on his desk, and I tried not to laugh. His husband was shorter than him, slightly chubby, and had the sweetest expression I had ever seen. He was looking at Michael in the picture as if he hung the sun.

"I can see that."

Michael chuckled. "Okay, let's get moving before boss man comes back out and starts yelling. I'll take you to HR and get his coffee and blueberry muffins. He eats two every morning. I think the sugar helps him. He's usually not as grumpy afterward."

I made a mental note of that—it might come in handy. Plus the fact that Jaxson Richards had excellent hearing. I would have to remember that and use an inner monologue for my smart remarks. I grinned at Michael. "My dad is always better once he has a bagel in the morning. My mom says he used to be unbearable before he ate."

He grinned as he opened the door and let me walk out first. "You have experience in dealing with high-handed men. That's a good thing."

I had a feeling he was right.

CHAPTER 3

GRACE

I smoothed down my hair, straightened my shoulders, and knocked on Jaxson's door. He had been in and out all day, meeting with people, on the phone, constantly busy. My computer had been delivered, I had filled out all the necessary forms for HR, and I had spent the day going through the files Jaxson placed on my desk and researching Drake's Manufacturing.

"In," he called.

I entered, shutting the door behind myself. I had learned several things today. Mr. Richards was an extremely busy man. Not only did he deal with corporate, but his expertise in copyright and trademark law kept him in constant demand. His files were varied and vast, and he consulted with several of the lawyers on staff. He liked his records a certain way, and he insisted the documentation on all of them done to his specifications. He was meticulous and precise. Stern and unflappable. His mood did get slightly better after he ate his muffins, but I wouldn't call him friendly. He was reserved with some people and downright cold with others. He muttered under his breath a lot. His hearing was uncommonly good, and he liked his door kept open unless he was on a client call. He grimaced a great deal, especially when drinking coffee.

Yet twice I had spied a small glimpse of a different side to him. I heard him inquire about Michael's daughter, Abby, who had a cold, asking if she was feeling better. I gleaned that he had sent her a stuffed animal—which she adored—to brighten her day. He seemed pleased to find out she was doing better and was happy his gift was met with so much enthusiasm. Another time, I had carried in a stack of correspondence while he was on the phone, and he had glanced up as I walked in. I paused, unsure if I should continue, but he waved me in. "I'm on mute."

I placed some of the files he had given me earlier on the edge of his desk. I had answered all his notes and questions, adding in some thoughts, deciding that he seemed to be the sort of man who would like that initiative.

"Sorry to interrupt," I said quietly.

He grinned, suddenly looking mischievous. "Not to worry. He'll drone on for an hour about some new business venture. He does it weekly." He indicated the open file on his desk. "I get a lot of work done while he yammers on."

"And he doesn't catch on?"

"Nope. I interject a few 'hmms' or comments, let him talk himself out of the idea, then he hangs up, and I get Michael to send him a bill. We all win."

I couldn't help smiling at him. He looked almost boyish, amused at his own antics. He smiled back, and my breath caught in my throat. He was devastatingly handsome when he smiled. The sexy divot in the middle of his chin deepened, and the furrows on his forehead smoothed out. The ice in his eyes melted. He was intoxicating, and I wanted to get drunk on that smile. Realizing the wayward turn to my thoughts, I'd had to turn and hurry away before he noticed my response. Luckily, he needed to throw out one of his hmms, so he didn't notice my flustered countenance.

Now, I approached his desk, unsure which man would greet me. He looked more casual this afternoon, his tie loose, and his jacket slung over the back of his chair. He had his sleeves rolled up, exposing his thick forearms, the dusting of hair catching the light. Other than the heavy watch on his wrist, he wore no other jewelry. His hands were large and masculine. I had to tear my gaze away—for some reason, they fascinated me. I noticed he looked tired, but his eyes were calm and steady as he regarded me.

"Ms. VanRyan."

I sat down and handed him the Drake file. "I got all the information you were looking for."

He looked skeptical. "All of it?"

"Yes."

He glanced through the file, nodding slowly. "Good job."

"Thank you."

He tapped the other files on his desk. "Good work on these as well. I saw your notes on the conflict in the Greyson trademark issue. Good catch."

"Thank you," I repeated.

He pursed his lips. "So polite."

"Simply responding to the vibe, sir."

A smirk tugged on his mouth. "I was a bit over the top this morning, wasn't I?"

"I have no idea. It's my first day. Perhaps you're 'over the top' all the time. You're certainly grouchy." My eyes widened in horror when I realized what I had said. Before I could apologize, he chuckled.

"You have trouble keeping your thoughts to yourself, don't you?"

"Not usually."

He paused, then changed the subject. "Michael showed you around? Got all your paperwork done? A company cell phone?"

"Yes." I flashed my pass at him. "I'm official now."

A strange look crossed his face. "Well, good." He tapped the files beside him. "Keep up the good work, and we'll get along fine."

"I'm not a slacker, Mr. Richards. I'll work hard for you."

He pursed his lips, opened his mouth to speak, then stopped. "I'm sure you will. Have a good night, Ms. VanRyan."

My time was obviously up. I stood to go. "You as well."

I left, wondering why I hated to do so.

The week was crazy. I was busy every moment of every day. I did research, completed various tasks for Mr. Richards, sat in on meetings and pored over contracts. I was fascinated with the way he worked. He disliked idle chatter. Hated small talk. He was unfailingly polite with his clients but cut straight to the heart of the matter, keeping all his meetings short and productive.

"Time is money, Ms. VanRyan. I hate wasting both."

He was generous, though, with information. He answered my questions thoroughly and started a new routine of his own in order to help me learn. Every morning, I would find a jotted note on my desk with a hypothetical situation. I would have time to think and plan, and we would discuss it before I left at the end of the day. When I was wrong, he never lost patience, instead explaining where I made my mistake. When I was correct, his praise was sparse, but sincere.

"Well done."

"Excellent thought process."

Once or twice, I earned one of his rare smiles. It made me want to work even harder.

One day, he was late and there was no note. Instead, he called me into his office.

"I've been offered to sit on a board of directors of an outside corporation. Should I consider it?" he asked.

I realized that was today's lesson, and he wanted my first instinctive response—no time for research or preparation.

Lawyers were often asked to sit on the boards of outside corporations. I'd had this discussion once with Bill.

"No."

He lifted an eyebrow, silently telling me to proceed. I mulled the words over in my head, trying to come up with the appropriate response. Since Jaxson liked honesty, I decided to lay it on the line.

"The bottom line is that is a shitload of responsibility with few, if any, perks. More work, more time—plus the legalities, the chance of being sued, and the question of where you owe your responsibilities. Your loyalty. It's simply not worth it unless it is a company you are completely one hundred percent behind. Even then, it's a gamble. Who wants the headache of a bickering board? The egos and whims that do nothing but waste your time? I can't imagine

you being patient enough to put up with that, frankly. You'd tell them to fuck off pretty fast."

For a moment, he said nothing. I saw his lips quirk and he nodded. "Very…eloquent, Grace. All valid points."

I felt my cheeks flush.

He indicated the door. "You can go. Good job."

As I got to the door, he asked me to close it. I swore I heard him laughing as I got to my desk.

I decided to take that as a win.

I was so busy, I never had a chance to use the allotted time to study that the firm allowed. It was an awesome perk, but I was already learning so much. Jaxson was a great teacher. But I knew I had to study. Friday afternoon, he was out at a meeting I wasn't a part of, and Michael was packing up to head home early since Abby had a doctor's appointment for her vaccinations.

"Larry goes to pieces. I think he cries harder than she does," he told me. "I have to go be there and hold the two of them up."

He paused at the door. "Jaxson won't be back. These meetings go all afternoon. You should head home too."

"I thought I might study."

"Oh, good plan. You have your pass. The door locks at six, so make sure you have it with you if you leave the room."

"I will."

After he left, I headed to the library and began to study. It was a comfortable room, with some tables and chairs and plenty of light. I set up my laptop and began. Facts, cases, and figures filled my head. I wrote out key notes, filling page after page on my tablet my dad had given me. It was the best gift he'd ever gotten me. I found writing something out helped me remember things better, and this tablet let me do that, then saved the document in both my written form and a typed format to refer back to. It let me copy images as well. I loved it.

It was the sound of a throat clearing that stopped my endeavors. I looked up to see Mr. Richards standing in front of the table I was working at.

"Ms. VanRyan, what are you doing?"

"Studying."

"It's nine p.m. on a Friday night."

I blinked. It was nine o'clock? The time had flown by. I looked at the books I had spread out around me. The page count on my tablet. I had been busy.

He frowned. "Have you not used your allotted study time?"

"Um, no."

His frown deepened. "I don't expect you to work all evening to get your studying done. You have the time. Use it."

"I was just so busy this week. And the work is fascinating. I'm learning so much—"

He cut me off. "Regardless. The time is to be used for studying. No arguments. Do you understand?"

"Yes."

"Why don't you pack up and head home?"

"Yes, I will."

"I assume you have a parking spot underground? It's late and beginning to rain."

"Oh no, I take the bus. I don't drive."

At his shocked expression, I tried to explain. "I mean, I can drive. I know how, but I don't here in Toronto. It's so crazy with traffic. I take the bus or the streetcar."

"What about the subway?"

I suppressed a shiver simply thinking about that. "No. I don't like the subway."

His gaze pierced through me as if trying to decide if he should question my remark or not. "Fine, Ms. VanRyan. Pack up your things, and I'll drive you home."

"Oh no, it's fine. I'm used to the bus."

"It's late and raining. I will drive you home." His tone brooked no argument. He leaned over the chair, snapping shut the books. "You've worked hard enough. Get your purse and coat. I'll wait at the elevator."

"No!" I exclaimed, standing so fast my chair toppled. "Really, it's no bother. I'll take a cab."

"I will drive you," he said through clenched teeth. "You will be perfectly safe."

"I know that. It's that, ah, I need a few moments, and I don't want to keep you waiting."

He looked perplexed. "I'll wait in the car in the garage and catch up on a few emails, then. How about that?"

I relaxed. "All right. Thank you. I appreciate it."

He left, and I quickly put away the books and grabbed my coat and purse in the office. I ran down the stairs, spotting his car easily since it was the only one left in the private garage. Sleek and sexy, the black Audi was purring. Jaxson sat behind the wheel, his eyes on his phone as I approached, and I tapped the window before getting in.

He frowned as I buckled up the seat belt. "I didn't see you come from the elevator."

"Oh, I took the stairs. After sitting all day, I needed to stretch my legs."

I felt his sidelong glance, but I didn't add anything, and luckily, he let it go. "Where to?" he asked lightly.

"Jamison Street."

"Off St. Clair?"

"Yes."

"My old stomping grounds," he mumbled.

"Really?"

"I lived on Coventry."

"Oh yes. That's only a couple of streets away."

We were quiet for a moment, and I enjoyed the warmth of the car. The leather seats were plush, and the music playing low in the background soothing. And the car smelled like Jaxson. Warm, rich, and distinctive. I liked how he smelled.

Then my stomach grumbled. Loudly.

Jaxson glanced over.

"Sorry," I muttered, embarrassed.

"You didn't eat dinner, did you?"

"I was busy."

"I doubt the apple and wedge of cheese you nibbled at lunch helped either."

I turned my head, gaping. *How did he know what I ate for lunch?*

Before I could ask, he was turning the corner a few blocks from my apartment.

"Do you know Rocking Ramen?"

"I've walked past it."

"You like soup? Noodles?"

"Yes."

He pulled up beside the small building. "Good. It was, and still is, one of my favorites." He shut off the engine, unbuckling his seat belt.

"What are you doing?"

"Feeding you."

"That isn't necessary! I'll eat when I get home."

"Nope. We're eating now."

"Is that wise?"

He looked at me and lifted his eyebrows. "We're getting a bowl of soup, Grace. I'm not suggesting a romp on the table."

My cheeks flushed at his words, and a small part of me pouted. I'd bet that a romp on the table would be far more satisfying. I shook my head. "Now I'm Grace?"

"We can't share a meal and be formal. Besides, you earned it. Now, get out of the car. I'm starving."

With that, he climbed out and shut the door. I had no choice except to follow.

CHAPTER 4

GRACE

There was no doubt Mr. Richards—or Jaxson, as I was now allowed to call him—knew what he liked and also that he liked to be in charge. When we entered the mostly empty little restaurant, he pointed out a table in the corner, told me to go sit, then went to the counter and ordered. He came to the table carrying two Tsingtao beers and a bottle of water. He set them down, indicating the icy cold bottles. "Wasn't sure if you liked Tsingtao."

"I do."

He pushed a bottle my way and lifted his, waiting until I had done the same. We clinked necks, and he lifted the bottle to his mouth, taking a long swallow. I had to look away. How did he make taking a sip of beer look so sexy?

I took a sip from my bottle, the cold liquid hitting my throat. I hummed in appreciation.

"I ordered a large special soup and some crispy spring rolls."

"The special?"

He grinned. "It's awesome. They make their own ramen, and the broth is to die for. Then they add all sorts of vegetables and top it with crispy chicken and pork."

"Sounds delicious."

"It is."

We were quiet, sipping our beer and relaxing. A few moments later, the soup arrived, steaming and fragrant. A plate of spring rolls was set beside it, and smaller bowls placed in front of us.

I inhaled deeply, suddenly starving. Jaxson picked up my bowl, lading in a large portion, adding meat and vegetables. "Eat," he instructed.

I didn't argue. The broth was rich and flavorful, and the spring rolls with the spicy dipping sauce tasty and crisp. The chicken on the top crunched with every bite, and I moaned low in my throat at the deliciousness of the simple fare. I opened my eyes to see Jaxson staring at me, his chopsticks frozen in midair.

"What?"

"I take it you're enjoying it."

"Yes."

"Am I going to get a *When Harry Met Sally* moment?"

For a second, I was confused, then I recalled the moment in the movie when Meg Ryan pretended to have an orgasm in the middle of the restaurant. I began to laugh, and with a wink, Jaxson joined in.

"Not quite that good. Close, but not quite."

He lifted his eyebrows. "I see."

I changed the subject. "How was your meeting?"

He shrugged, slurping some noodles. He chewed and swallowed, wiping his mouth.

"Boring. Once a month, we have these team-building things. I go because it's expected."

"You don't enjoy them?"

He took a long swallow of his beer and studied me. "Frankly, as a rule, Grace, I'm not much of a people person."

I tried to hide my grin and failed. "All people, or lawyer people?"

"All of them."

"Even your friends?"

He shrugged. "My friends think I'm a dick."

"Ah."

He laughed darkly. "Just kidding." His voice dropped. "I don't have many real friends."

I could only blink. From the tone of his voice, I knew he was serious.

"Your family?"

His expression darkened. "I have none."

"Oh."

The silence was uncomfortable, and I knew I had touched on a very personal subject.

"And you don't even like to hang with other lawyers? You don't enjoy the trust-building aspect?"

He snorted. "I wouldn't trust any of them as far as I could throw them. I have zero desire to 'hang' with any of them, as you put it."

"Is it because of your position? I imagine you're hoping for partner?"

He shook his head. "I was offered partner at my last two firms. This offer came with immediate partnership. I turned them all down."

I blinked. "You don't want to be a partner?"

"No. Partnership comes with more responsibilities. It implies a lasting bond. I don't believe in that. Nothing lasts. And the thought of having the hassle of dissolving that partnership when I leave or they want me gone doesn't appeal."

"Maybe that wouldn't happen."

He met my gaze, his eyes serious. "Nothing lasts, Grace. Everything in life shifts. That's why divorce attorneys are in such high demand. Custody cases fill the courts. Business partners are constantly suing one another. Love dies. Friendships end. People move on. It's inevitable."

I was shocked by his words. "I disagree. My family is proof that love lives and thrives. That friendship can be a lifelong bond."

"Then you're one of the lucky few."

"Pardon my bluntness, but that sounds like a lonely life."

"I like your bluntness. But in my opinion, it's a good one. I expect nothing. I want nothing. I owe no one. I rely on no one. I don't have to conform to anyone or worry about anyone's feelings. I live to please myself. I know nothing lasts, so there is no surprise when it ends." He drained his beer. "And everything always ends."

"I have no idea what to say to that statement."

He shook his head. "I've shocked you, little Grace."

"Not shocked, just saddened."

"No need to be sad. That's life." He wiped his mouth. "You finished?"

"Um, yes."

He stood. "Come on, I'll take you home."

In the car, we were silent. His words affected me somehow. He truly believed them. I could see it in his eyes, hear the conviction in his voice.

"Grace?"

I glanced toward the sound of Jaxson's voice.

"We're here."

"Oh." I undid my seat belt. "Thank you for dinner, Jaxson."

"Grace——" He stopped and drew in a long breath.

"Yes?"

"I'm glad your world is different from mine."

Our eyes met in the dimness of the car. Slowly, the air changed. His expression shifted, and his eyes—his brilliant, intense ice-blue eyes melted. They warmed, no longer distant and remote, but gentle. The longer we stared, the more they changed. Ice became fire. Cold became heat. It flared and burned, making my breath catch. I felt the intensity of the moment bearing down on us. Nothing existed outside the car. Nothing mattered except now. Jaxson. His head began to lower just as mine inched forward. I shivered, knowing what was about to happen.

Then a car went by, honking the horn loudly, and the moment exploded, shattering into jagged shards of reality.

Jaxson reared back as if burned. He gripped his steering wheel.

"Thank you for your efforts this week."

It took great determination to get out of the car without tripping. "Thank you for dinner," I repeated, at a loss for any other words.

I shut the door and began to walk away when he lowered the window and leaned over the seat. "Wait."

I bent down. "Yes?"

He shut his eyes, shaking his head. "Nothing. Just—have a good weekend, Gracie."

He drove away.

I watched him go, suddenly realizing what he had called me.

Not Ms. VanRyan. Not Grace. *Gracie.*

Had he even realized it?

Monday morning, there was no sign of the man who'd insisted on driving me home and getting me soup. He was removed and cool, although he did still call me Grace and he didn't correct me when I called him Jaxson the first time.

Michael grinned. "Earned it, did you?" he whispered.

"I guess so."

He high-fived me. "Took me two weeks. You go, girlfriend."

Jaxson reappeared as our hands hit, and he stopped, watching us with narrowed eyes.

Michael grinned at him. "You need something?"

"Make sure Grace's schedule contains her allotted study time. And be sure she uses it." His glare encompassed us both. "I don't want to have to listen to the partners complain I'm ignoring the guidelines set out for articling students."

He turned and went back to his office, the slam of the door echoing.

I cringed, but Michael ignored it. "You heard him," he stated. "Wednesday and Friday, I'm slotting your hours in. For the love of God, take them."

The hypothetical notes still appeared on my desk, although our discussions were far shorter, and a couple of times, all I got was a fast "Good work," as he passed my desk the next morning. I missed those moments with him. Seeing his smile light up his eyes and hearing his low, rich baritone voice say the words. The logical part of me knew it shouldn't matter. He was my boss—nothing more. I barely knew him. But somehow, in some way, it mattered a great deal.

He seemed wound tighter than usual, which made me tense and wary. I was having trouble sleeping and felt tired by the end of the day. At times, I had difficulty concentrating, which was highly unusual for me. It felt as if I were somehow connected to him and his moods were affecting me. It was all very confusing.

Thursday morning, I picked up the notepaper, reading the lesson for the day. It involved trademarks, which was one of my favorite subjects, and I was eager to start on it. Between that and the files on my desk, it was a busy day and time flew by.

In the afternoon, Jaxson's office door was flung open, and he strode out, his face like thunder.

"With me," he snapped, meeting my eyes. "We have to go to the courthouse."

Jaxson had been on a tear all day. He'd argued with one of the partners, his muffled voice carrying his displeasure through the closed doors. He'd yelled at Michael about his calendar, which, when I peeked at it, was as orderly and organized as ever. Usually eating something helped calm him, but today, that didn't work.

He stormed from his office, tossing the sandwich in the wastebasket beside Michael.

"Drowning in mayo, for fuck's sake," he roared. "Are you trying to kill me?"

Michael looked at him then down at the wastebasket. "No, I think you'll do that yourself with your high blood pressure," he stated mildly.

"Get me another one and watch how they make it." He strode back into his office, slamming the door so hard it shook.

"I'll go," I offered. *"I could use the fresh air."*

He shook his head. *"He would freak over that. Trust me. I'll go."* Then he grinned. *"But I think I'll do a little window-shopping while I'm out."*

"You shouldn't push him."

"He deserves to be pushed."

Jaxson came out twice to check where Michael was. Luckily, I was on the phone both times, so I only heard his mutterings and threats about needing a new assistant.

Michael took him his sandwich, telling him the deli had been crazy, and walked back out, shutting the door and Jaxson's diatribe off behind him. He threw me a wink and sat at his desk.

Jaxson hadn't come out of his office again until now.

Michael shot me an apologetic glance, and I grabbed my purse and hurried after Jaxson.

"What is it?"

"The documents you took to the courthouse yesterday appear to be missing."

"What? I handed them right to the clerk exactly as you instructed me." I protested.

"She says differently."

"Jaxson, I took them."

"We're going down there to sort this out. Since it's your error, you're coming with me."

The elevator doors opened, and he stepped in. I realized too late he expected me to join him.

"I'll take the stairs and meet you downstairs."

"We don't have time for that nonsense." He grabbed my arm and dragged me into the elevator, the doors gliding shut behind me before I could protest.

I pushed myself back into the corner and shut my eyes. Seven floors to the basement where the garage was located. It was just seven floors. I began to recite the words in my head I had been taught. *I am safe. I can breathe. I can do this.*

Except the doors opened on the floor below us, and the elevator was suddenly full. Instantly, I felt the heat rise around me. My chest constricted, and I struggled to get enough oxygen to fill my lungs. It didn't help when a child at the front of the crowd pressed every button, causing the elevator to stop every few moments, the jolt causing my stomach to lurch. People in the elevator groaned, and the child's mother chastised him. I wanted to push through the people and escape, but I couldn't get my feet to cooperate. I felt a sheen of moisture on the back of my neck, and I tightened my hand on the rail behind me, keeping my head down and reciting calming words to myself.

Then I felt it. Jaxson's ever-present heat. He was close. Far closer than he had been, somehow moving in next to me. He slid his arm around my waist, drawing me tight to his side. He spoke quietly close to my ear, so only I could hear.

"Hold on to me, Grace. I have you."

He shifted, his hand running up and down my back under my jacket in long, soothing passes. Of its own violation, my hand released itself from the rail and gripped on to his suit jacket, the texture of the fine wool soft under my fingers. I let myself feel him. His warmth. The scent of him, spicy and rich, filled my head. My panic loosened, and I inhaled deeply. Jaxson gripped my hip, guiding me from the now-empty elevator and into the parking garage. He didn't say anything until we reached his car. He unlocked the door and gently pushed me into the passenger seat. He crouched down beside the car.

"Are you okay?"

"I'm sorry," I whispered.

"You have nothing to be sorry for."

"That was embarrassing."

He pursed his lips and shook his head. "You're claustro-phobic," he stated.

"Yes."

"No one but me noticed. You're very good at hiding it."

"I hate it."

He shocked me when he half rose and slid his fingers around the back of my neck. He leaned in close and pressed his lips to my forehead, his mouth lingering. Then he stood and shut the door, rounding the car and sliding into the driver's seat.

"That's why you take the stairs."

"Yes."

"You can't be in an elevator at all?"

"If I prepare myself, I can."

He let out a humorless chuckle. "I didn't exactly give you the chance."

"You didn't know."

He regarded me for a moment then started the car. "I do now. And it won't happen again. I'm sorry, Grace."

His apology surprised me. I had seen him angry. Annoyed. He yelled at people. Ordered them around. I had never once heard him apologize for anything. I let my head fall back into the cool leather headrest. "It's fine."

I was surprised to feel his hand cover mine and squeeze it. "I hate that I caused you discomfort," he murmured.

He stunned me into silence. But for some reason, I gripped his fingers, and his hand stayed with mine all the way to the courthouse.

It felt right having our palms nestled together.

And what that meant, I had no idea.

CHAPTER 5

GRACE

By the time we reached the courthouse, I had recovered except for the lingering embarrassment. I hated showing that weakness to people —and somehow, Jaxson knowing seemed extra hard. As we headed to the clerk's office, I felt his anger returning. He followed me up the steps, and I turned to him, angling my head. "You know, Jaxson, you get further with honey than vinegar."

He glowered. "What does that mean?"

"Simply that, sometimes, yelling isn't the answer."

"Someone lost a file. If it isn't recovered, it jeopardizes the case."

"Terrifying everyone around you isn't the answer."

"I don't terrify people."

"Yes, you do. You yell and glower and make people nervous."

"I don't make you nervous," he pointed out.

I resisted rolling my eyes. "You make *everyone* nervous."

Before he could respond, we reached the office. I paused with my hand on the handle.

"Why don't you let me handle it?"

He narrowed his eyes, looking uncertain. "Fine. You have five minutes, then I'm stepping in."

I rolled my eyes. "Such patience."

"Five minutes," he repeated.

The clerk's office was surprisingly quiet. The woman I had spoken with yesterday came forward, her face paling when she saw Jaxson behind me. I wasn't sure if his reputation preceded him, or if she'd had dealings with him prior to now. I smiled at her reassuringly, explaining why we were there.

She frowned. "I'm certain the file was delivered," she insisted.

"Apparently not," Jaxson snarled.

I turned, glaring, and he shut up but kept glowering. I turned back to the clerk, desperately trying not to notice how attractive Jaxson was when he was upset. His eyes were vivid in his face, his cheeks highlighted with slashes of crimson. His features, set against the dark color of his hair, suited the anger. He was tall and severe, looking sexy in his deep brooding.

"If you could check," I asked.

She disappeared.

I spun on my heel. "You frightened her. My God, you *walked* into the room and *frightened* her."

"I can't help that."

"That wasn't even one minute. You promised five."

He shrugged. "I'm a lawyer. We lie all the time."

My lips quirked. "Stop it."

"Stop what?"

"Being cute."

"No one has ever accused me of being cute before, Ms. VanRyan. I think you're mixing up your words."

"I think you're mixing up my head."

A slow grin appeared on his face. "Is that a fact?"

I shrugged. "No. I'm a lawyer in training. I lie too."

I didn't expect his bark of laughter. If I thought him sexy when he was brooding, amused looked like sin on him. His white teeth flashed, the dimple in his chin deepened, and he looked like a wet dream.

He tapped me on the nose. "Touché, Grace. Touché."

The clerk reappeared, running a hand over her hair to smooth it. "Mr. Richards, I apologize. The file was misplaced but has been delivered. I can't begin to tell you how sorry—"

He cut her off with the wave of his hand. "These things happen. I'm grateful you were able to locate it. Thank you for your assistance, ah…?"

She stared at him, no doubt as much in shock as I was at his change of demeanor. "Ah, Marie. I'm Marie."

"Thank you for your assistance, Marie."

She beamed and handed him a business card. "Here is the confirmation number. If you have any other issues, contact me directly."

"I'll do that. Grace, we need to head back to the office now."

He escorted me out, his hand in the middle of my back. He was quiet as we headed to the car.

"Maybe you're right," he mused. "This honey thing might be worth a shot." He opened my door. "But I think I'll use it sparingly. Wouldn't want people to think I've gone soft."

"Heaven forbid."

Michael approached my desk. "What happened this afternoon?"

I looked up from the file I was studying. "What?"

"He leaves like a bolt of thunder and comes back a kitten."

I chuckled. "I'd hardly call that a kitten." I indicated Jaxson's closed door. "More like a sleeping lion. I'm sure he'll be snarling again soon enough."

"He said thank you to me. Thank you. I've worked for him for over four years, and I think the closest I have gotten to a thank you is a grunt. You must have said something."

"As if he would listen to me."

"He did—whatever you said, girlfriend, keep it up."

I shook my head. Jaxson had been silent in the car as we headed back to the office. More than once, I saw him glance at me out of the corner of his eye, and I waited for him to speak. He never did. He seemed tense, and I sighed internally, wondering why his mood had turned yet again. He blew hot and cold, and I found him diffi-cult to keep up with. At the office, he didn't say a word as I headed for the stairs and he rode the elevator. Jaxson was talking to Michael when I walked in, and other than the occasional glimpse, I hadn't seen or spoken to him.

At five, Michael stood, switching off his light. "I'm out of here."

"Have a good night."

I worked a little longer, then shut the file. This was going to be a complicated case. I had a list of research I would need to start tomorrow. Too many siblings claiming the rights to a logo and trademark, and the copyrights were a mess. That was what often happened when a family company member passed. Documentation was sparse, and siblings began to fight. It was going to be ugly.

I heard the low timbre of Jaxson's voice as I tapped on his door. He must have ended the phone call he had been on, and I opened the door at his bidding. He was at his desk, hanging up the receiver, looking reflective.

"I'm heading off now."

"I need a moment of your time."

"Sure."

"Shut the door, please."

I did and sat in the chair in front of his desk and waited. Jaxson cleared his throat.

"I need to apologize for this afternoon."

I waved my hand. "The elevator thing? It's fine. I try not to draw attention to it."

"I meant for getting too personal. Kissing your forehead, holding your hand."

I felt a frisson of disappointment. I didn't want his apology. He had helped me, and I appreciated it. And to be honest, I had liked it.

"I haven't given it a second thought," I lied. "You helped me as one human to another. We can leave it at that."

He nodded, although he looked upset at my words. I was about to stand when he spoke again.

"Have you had counseling?"

I frowned at the personal question. "Yes."

"Obviously not *good* counseling."

"I *beg* your pardon. I was in therapy for a long time. Considering how bad my condition was to start, the fact that I can even get in an elevator at all is a miracle," I replied, my voice sharp. The kitten had definitely left the building, and the sleeping lion was awake.

"There are new therapies—"

I stood. "I don't need more therapy. What I need is for you to mind your own business and stay out of my personal life."

"But it's not your personal life when it interferes in this office."

"Because I walk up and down stairs?"

"What if we have a client meeting in a high-rise? You going to hoof it up fifty flights of steps, Grace?"

I narrowed my eyes, refusing to let him see what the thought of being in an elevator for fifty stories did to me. "If that were going to happen, I would ask to be given a little time to prepare myself. I would be fine if I were ready."

Maybe not quite fine, but I would handle it.

"How much time would you require?"

"Ten minutes," I spat. "Trust me, Mr. Richards, if it came to that, I wouldn't cause you any embarrassment."

He stood, leaning on his hands, fury emanating from him. "Is that what you think? That I would find you an embarrassment?"

"I have no idea what to think. Once again, you're being an arrogant, overbearing...*jackass*. My inability to be in enclosed spaces is none of your concern."

"*Jackass*, am I? Is that how you talk to your superiors?"

I was furious. His mood swings were hard enough to deal with. I didn't have to listen to his lectures about my personal issues. I stood and hurried to the door, pausing to turn when I got there. "When I'm with one of my *superiors*, I'll remember that and watch my tongue."

I slammed the door behind me.

JAXSON

I blinked at the hurricane Grace VanRyan had turned into. Even her fading footsteps sounded angry. Her snippy words echoed in my head.

When I'm with one of my superiors, I'll remember that and watch my tongue.

A burst of laughter escaped my mouth. She was *ferocious.* And too damn sexy when she was angry.

I stared at the closed door, completely impressed. She'd slammed it so hard, the wall shook.

For a little thing, she was strong—and unknowingly, she pushed my buttons.

What was it about that woman that made me react the way I did? I had spent all afternoon worried—about her. I didn't worry about anyone except myself.

It shouldn't matter if she was claustrophobic. Despite what I said, it didn't affect my life. If we had a meeting and she chose to take the stairs, as long as she was on time, I shouldn't care.

Except I did.

Instead of working, I spent the hours googling claustrophobia. I called an acquaintance who was a therapist and picked his brain. Spoke to my doctor. I took notes and tried to find a way to help.

For an articling student. One who hadn't asked for my help, nor seemed to want it. A woman who would be out of my life in a few months and I would probably never see again. It—*she*—shouldn't matter that much to me. But she did.

I had no idea why. All I knew was when I felt Grace's sudden shift in the elevator and I glanced over and saw the sheer panic on her face, something in me snapped. She was struggling to hide her turmoil, but her ashen skin and the way she had shrunken in on herself deflated the anger that had been burning inside me and replaced it with an intense need to help her. One of the things I found so attractive about Grace was her self-assured confidence. She wasn't arrogant or egotistical but sure of herself and forthright. I admired that greatly. The woman in the elevator was terrified and trying desperately to keep herself under control. I was certain if she gripped the rail any tighter, it would bend under the force. When I shifted closer, the way she had allowed me to comfort her pleased me. The need I *had* to comfort her shocked me. She let me hold her, lead her to my car. I had kissed her forehead, the act of tenderness unexpected but so natural when it came to her. I had held her hand in the car, the feel of her warm palm resting within mine too good to pull away. None of it was appropriate behavior as her boss, but I found I didn't give a damn about that.

She had fascinated me the first day I met her. Her beautiful hair, vibrant, warm blue eyes that shone with intelligence. Her outward poise. Small in stature, she projected a much larger image, her presence demanding attention. It wasn't only for her beauty. She had a lovely speaking voice, soft and feminine, but she utilized it well. She was smart and articulate, and I enjoyed talking to her. She wasn't given to gestures, instead only using her hands occasionally to emphasize her point. My normal questions when interviewing a law student went out the window. I wanted to know more about Grace VanRyan. What made her tick. It had taken all of my control to stop myself from asking too much and returning to the business at hand—namely her employment with the firm. After she left, I had cursed myself for my lack of control and decided it was a momentary lapse that wouldn't happen again. She was an articling student, therefore, an employee of the law firm, which had a strict nonfraternization policy. Add in the fact that at thirty-eight, I was ten years older than she was. And her boss.

It had been a blip.

Except, as soon as she walked in on her first day, my world shifted once again, and she was in my orbit.

And I had no idea how to stop it. How to curb the reactions and feelings she brought forth in me.

The way I responded to finding her in the library late on a Friday night, studying, shocked me. To ensure she got home safely was paramount. The smart thing would have been to put her in a cab and carry on with my life. Instead, I drove her home, took her to dinner, and thoroughly enjoyed the time I spent with her until the subject turned personal and serious. Her look of incredulous disbelief when I expressed my thoughts on life had made me surprisingly uncomfortable. Her earnest protests about real love and friendship were heartfelt, although I knew them to be untrue in my life. I hadn't lied when I told her I was glad her world was different from mine. She deserved the best. The moment in the car stayed in my memory. How the subtle scent of her filled the interior of the vehicle. How right it felt having her beside me. How desperately I wanted to feel her mouth underneath mine. To kiss her. Taste her. It went against everything in me. I was her boss. Older than she was. More experienced. When the moment was broken, I was grateful we hadn't crossed that line. That I hadn't let one moment of weakness ruin my life.

Yet, she remained. Always in my thoughts, my gaze lingering on her far too long as she sat at her desk, busy working. I started closing my door more, simply to stop myself from acting like a lovestruck idiot. It had been the one place the desk would fit, but it wasn't until the first morning that I realized how clear a view I had of her.

She was sitting at her desk, talking to Michael, her focus on him.

Mine was on her.

The overhead light showed glimmers of red in her dark hair. She had her chin propped up in her hand, and she was smiling at something Michael said. She held a pen in one hand, tapping it slowly on her desk. Her long, sexy leg swung in time with the pen. I was captivated by her.

I had been ever since.

And today, I had planned on apologizing to her about kissing her, holding her hand. Explain I had been concerned but shouldn't have crossed that line. Instead, I tried in the worst way possible to get her to open up about her fear and came across as judgmental and demeaning. I angered her, and instead of an apology, we sniped at each other, Grace refusing to back down in the face of my ire.

She gave as good as she got—if not better.

I scrubbed my face. I hadn't counted on this attraction. This odd sense of need to look after her. I had dealt with many articling students before, both male and female, with no reaction. Fellow female lawyers who were intelligent and beautiful without batting an eye.

But Grace VanRyan was singularly unique. She captivated me in a sense I hadn't yet grasped.

And that terrified me more than anything.

CHAPTER 6

GRACE

I barely slept at all. I gave up at five and got up, sitting on the sofa with a cup of coffee in my hand. All I could think about was the fact that I had told off my boss. Twice. Jaxson Richards didn't strike me as the kind of man that would accept that very well. I had a feeling I would be reassigned to a different lawyer right away. I dropped my head down in defeat. I had wanted to work with him. He was brilliant, even if he was difficult to handle.

Last night, I had walked home, too upset to sit on the bus. In the time I had been working for Jaxson, I had already learned so much. He was amazing to observe. He had a quirk I wasn't sure most people noticed. His intense gaze took in every detail, and his mind absorbed every minute element. He recalled names, facts, numbers that others could not. He had no need to reference notes, his brain recalling the necessary information easily. Yet he never called attention to that fact, shuffling papers, appearing lost in thought as if mulling over words in his head. I saw it because of how closely I watched him.

He fascinated me. More than I wanted to admit. More than any man had ever captured my attention until now. He was a force unto himself. Terse and sharp with most people in the office, he seemed unapproachable at times. He didn't suffer fools easily and got impatient fast. Yet, there was still something that drew me to him. I didn't understand my attraction, except to know it was something I could never act on. I highly doubted I would ever have the chance anyway. Jaxson was older and more experienced than I was. From gossip I had heard, and what I found on the internet, he had a reputation as a monogamous dater—but he never stayed with anyone very long. And he was my boss.

Still, I found myself thinking about him too much. How handsome he was. The sexy divot in his chin I wanted to kiss. The way his chest filled out a suit. How his shoulders looked under the taut material. How he almost kissed me last Friday.

And his hands. I couldn't believe how sexy I found his hands and arms. I had never noticed details like that on any other man until now. Large, wide palms. Long, thick, yet strangely elegant fingers. He wore a heavy silver watch on his wrist that caught the light. I found his forearms appealing when he would roll up his sleeves, and I could see the muscles bunching and flexing. More than once, I had to look away as I fantasized about those fingers touching me, his muscles working as he stroked my skin, bringing me pleasure.

All thoughts I needed to keep at bay. He was unattainable. And I wasn't his type.

I looked down at the notepad on the arm of the sofa and smiled as I saw the date I had scribbled down while on the phone the night before. Addi Ridge had called to remind me of a cake tasting I was to attend with her that was coming up soon. She was the daughter of my dad's friend, Bentley Ridge, and was marrying her best friend, Brayden Riley, right before Christmas. My sister Heather and I were both part of her wedding party. We had all grown up together, and although I was a little older than Addi, we had always been close. Despite the fact that I had lived in BC and she lived here in Toronto, our families were so entwined, I saw her a lot, and we'd spoken and texted every day for as long as I could recall. I spent summer vacations here, most Christmases and other holidays, our families blending and forming our own little world. It wasn't a surprise when she and Brayden got together, and they had never once faltered in their devotion to each other. It was going to be a magical day, and I was looking forward to being part of it.

"How goes the articling?" she asked.

"Oh, it's, ah, great."

"Gracie, what's wrong?"

"Nothing," I lied, running a hand over my aching head. "It's been a day. A file got lost at the courthouse, and it took a lot to sort it out. I'm tired, that's all."

"What's your boss like?"

I couldn't tell her the truth. That he was arrogant, rude, sweet, and sexy. That he haunted my dreams and, at times, made my days a living nightmare.

"Intense." Was my reply. "Brilliant, but he has a temper. He yells a lot. His assistant is a saint."

I was telling the truth. Michael never reacted to Jaxson's moods. He carried on and did his job, ignoring the tirades and demands.

She chuckled. "Sounds like a young version of your dad."

I chuckled. My mom and dad had said they met when Mom worked at the same place Dad did before he went to The Gavin Group, where he still worked to this day. As I got older, I noticed my dad always became evasive and seemed uncomfortable when one of us would ask about their beginning. Finally, I asked my mom, and she told me the truth about how their relationship began. The arrogant, nasty man my father had been. The way he basically forced her to marry him. How they got to know each other and fell in love. The drastic change in my father. She had confided how he was known as "The Dick" in the marketing world and how often he yelled in the office, his arrogance knowing no limits. It was hard to picture my loving, protective father as anything but the almost-perfect man I thought he was, but my mom also told me of his past and what had shaped him. How she'd seen the pain behind the mask he wore and how deeply she fell in love with him. Then she winked.

"Don't tell him you know. He will tell you his own version one day, although he'll leave some parts out. He would be horrified if he thought his Gracie knew everything about his past. He couldn't handle it if you thought less of him."

I had assured her I would stay quiet, but eventually, we all knew at least the basics of the story, and we liked to tease my dad on occasion. I never divulged how much I knew, but somehow, it made my dad even dearer to me, knowing how much he overcame to be the man he was now.

"A bit, I think. Hard to deal with at times, but it's not forever. I am enjoying learning, though."

"Good. Okay, gotta go. See you soon!"

The cake tasting was something to look forward to. I missed seeing Addi these days, but between the wedding and her crazy schedule overseeing ABC Corp., and my articling job and studying for the bar, there never seemed to be time.

With a sigh, I realized it might be for the best. She knew me too well, and I wasn't sure if I could hide my jumbled feelings for Jaxson from her. I found them confusing, so there was no way I could make her understand them.

With a start, I returned to the present and grimaced as I sipped my now-cold coffee. I stood and went to the kitchen to dump it in the sink and get ready for work. I had to brave the lion this morning, and I had a feeling he was going to be in a foul mood. I hoped I could smooth the waters and not be transferred to another lawyer so soon. I would be known as being difficult, and I didn't want that reputation following me.

I stepped into the shower, sighing as the hot water poured over my tense shoulders. I would have to apologize. Groveling was a small price to pay for my future. I had to put on my big-girl panties, swallow my pride, and say I was sorry.

I hoped he gave me the chance.

It was cold out, so I dressed in pants and wore my favorite blouse. It was girlie, with lacy sleeves and a draped neckline in a deep blue. I added a soft shawl in grays and blues. I had noticed the office was always cool and Michael told me Jaxson preferred it that way, so I made sure to keep a sweater or shawl with me. When I got to work, I waved at Milt, the security guard, and headed up the stairs. I was relieved to see Michael already at his desk, busy with files.

"Hey," he greeted me.

"Hi." I cast my glance at Jaxson's closed door. "How are things?"

He rolled his eyes. "The lion is in his den."

"No kitten today?" I asked, trying to sound lighthearted.

"One with rabies, maybe."

I grimaced. "Oh."

"He wants to see you when you're ready." He paused, lowering his voice. "You might want coffee first."

I tried not to whimper. If he was in a foul mood already, the day was going to be hell. I straightened my shoulders and tucked my shawl close. "Already had two cups. I'm good." Then I knocked on the door, waiting until I heard Jaxson's terse "In."

I swallowed and opened the door, wondering what my fate would be.

JAXSON

I heard Gracie's voice outside my door, and I steeled myself to remain impassive. I was determined to go forward and keep things professional. I would apologize properly for yesterday, and hopefully, we would move past the day. Past the last week, even. I didn't want to lose her as an articling student. She was smart and clever, often adding insight when discussing a case that others would have missed. She obviously studied hard and was a good student. She was eager to learn, soaking up everything I showed her, her questions intelligent and her work ethic strong. She would be an asset to any firm. Over our dinner together, I had been surprised to discover her relationship with the BAM Corporation and her plans to join them, then the newer branch of the company. They would be lucky to have her. It also explained her advanced thinking. She'd had hands-on experience few other law students would have access to, and she'd made the most of it. My admiration of her grew the more I got to know her.

"In," I called, ready to face her and stop this craziness. She was my articling student; I was her boss. Simple. I could do this.

Except, she stepped inside my office, and all I could see was her. Her long, beautiful hair cascading over her shoulders. A pretty blouse in blue setting off her coloring. A shawl draped around her shoulders that looked soft and made her sexy in an artless way. And her gaze.

My eyes had often been described as ice-blue and as cold as winter. Gracie's eyes were warm and wide, the blue irises so vivid, they reminded me of the ocean on a clear, sun-filled day. Inviting and fluid. I wanted to drown in them.

For a moment, our eyes held. I noticed she looked tired, and I frowned, inclining my head and studying her. I disliked seeing her tired, especially given the fact that I was certain I was to blame for her lack of rest.

Soft color diffused her cheeks, and she shut the door, sitting across from me. "Mr. Richards," she began.

I held up my hand. "Jaxson. I'm still Jaxson. And you're Grace. All right?"

Her tense posture relaxed. "I would like to apologize."

Again, I stopped her. "Grace, can we move forward? Yesterday was a shitshow of epic proportions. I overstepped, you spoke your mind. We both regret it. Can we leave it at that?"

"I was rude."

"And so was I. In fact—"

A knock on the door interrupted us, and Michael stuck his head in. "Sorry. Sabrina Wells insists on me interrupting you. She needs to speak to you right away."

I tamped down my impatience. "Give me one minute."

Sabrina Wells was another lawyer in the office. She was nothing short of a raging bitch, and I steered clear of her as much as possible. She was demanding, impatient, and tiresome to deal with. I often wondered if handling ugly divorces all the time had made her that way, or if it was simply her natural inclination. Unfortunately, I was unable to avoid dealing with her all the time. She was a known troublemaker and liked to throw her weight around whenever she could. I suspected the main reason she was kept on was her incredibly high billings.

I looked at Grace. "We can finish this later. I have meetings most of the day."

She stood, looking anxious.

"Take the day and use the library. Study for the bar. I've kept you so busy, you haven't used your allotted time."

"I've been studying in the evening."

The words were out before I could stop them. "Your boyfriend doesn't object to all the hours you spend on your studies?"

A rueful smile crossed her lips. "No boyfriend to worry about."

"Ah," I mumbled, feeling an odd sense of relief at her words and still wondering why I asked. "All right. I'll deal with Sabrina, and you have a good day. We'll talk again later."

She nodded and walked out, barely clearing the doorway when Sabrina strode in, shutting the door so fast, I was sure Grace felt the rush of the action. I lifted an eyebrow, studying Sabrina.

Her hair was blond, slicked back into an elegant knot at the nape of her neck. Her suit was no doubt designer, her heels high, and her makeup expertly applied. She was attractive, deadly, and cold. She wore a permanent scowl on her face I was sure some men found inviting, perhaps challenging. I did not.

"Jaxson."

I cocked my head. "Sabrina. What is so urgent you need to interrupt my meeting with my articling student?"

She approached my desk, sinking into the chair Grace had vacated. I couldn't help but compare the two visitors. One soft, pretty, and anxious. The other hard, cold, and determined. It was like comparing a rabbit to a viper.

"The divorce case I'm handling involves a company. Both are claiming they own the rights to the logo. The wife, my client, insists she came up with the concept and wants compensation added to the settlement. Her ex says he created the concept and refuses. There seem to be some gray areas around the copyright ownership."

I shook my head. "You could have emailed me. In fact, I need you to do so, and I'll look into it once I have all the particulars."

A coy leer crossed her thin lips that were skillfully made up to look fuller. "But then I couldn't see you. I thought perhaps we could have dinner and discuss the case."

"No."

She laughed, the sound somehow unpleasant. "Jaxson," she purred. "I would make it worth your while."

I tried not to roll my eyes. She had attempted on numerous occasions to invite me to dinner, to meet after hours, even blatantly offering a hotel room for a night. No matter how often I said no, it didn't seem to matter. She made no secret of her desire to sleep with me.

"No strings, no personal feelings," she had assured me.

"Not interested, thank you. Have you read the nonfraternization policy?"

She shook her head, speaking to me as if I were a child. "No one has to know, Jaxson. I'm not looking for a relationship. Just a good fuck on occasion." She arched her eyebrow. "I'm always up for that."

I regarded her disdainfully. I didn't find her attractive, and I wasn't interested. I also didn't dip my pen in the company inkwell. That never ended well. After seeing a colleague lose his entire life because of a bad decision, I had been quite happy to read the rather dated and long nonfraternization document. Not, apparently, that Sabrina cared about it. But the bottom line was that I was not, in any way, attracted to her.

"No, Sabrina. Send me the details. I'll look it over."

A flash of anger emanated from her brown eyes. "You're making a mistake."

My own anger piqued. "I have said no, and I mean it. I'm not into sneaking around and risking my career over a piece of ass. I'm not going to change my mind, so drop it. I have a busy day. Send the file particulars, and I will look it over for you and send my advice. Good day."

Her eyes narrowed. "Too good for me, are you?"

"Yes, frankly, I am. I have no desire to bed a snake," I snapped, my patience reaching its limit. I was tired of every interaction with her coming down to this point. I didn't care if she made trouble for me; I was weary of these encounters. "I'm a busy man, Sabrina, with little time for games. You've taken up enough of my time."

She stood, obviously furious. Rejection didn't sit well with her. Her eyes shot daggers at me. "You'll regret it."

"I'm sure I will."

She left, leaving my door open in her wake. I rubbed a hand over my eyes, already exhausted. I glanced up to see Grace watching me, her expression worried. I lifted one shoulder in a silent dismissive gesture and rolled my eyes. She grinned before dropping her focus back to the file she'd been looking over.

Michael appeared in the doorway, blocking my view. "Should I have the office fumigated?"

I chuckled. "Might not be a bad idea."

"Your first meeting is in the boardroom. You're booked solid all day, including a meeting in the judge's chambers at three about the Dorset trademark."

I stood. "Right." I grabbed the first file of the day and headed to the door, stopping before I left the office. "Grace."

She looked up. "Yes?"

"I have a meeting at three you should attend. The Dorset case. The judge is granting us a chance to argue in his chambers—perhaps prevent a trial. I want you to sit in. Great experience."

"All right."

"All right. I'll touch base later."

GRACE

Later that afternoon, I watched Jaxson argue, his words and thoughts clear. The other lawyer wasn't as well prepared, and the judge agreed that Jaxson's client had proven his claim superseded the other one and advised the other party not to proceed with a trial. It had been interesting and inspiring to watch Jaxson in his element. He was articulate, calm, and nothing short of brilliant, and I sat, my rapt attention focused on him. I didn't take notes, knowing I would never forget a word he had said.

He had been kind today, meeting me at his car, not questioning the stairs. He was cool and distant—the very epitome of a boss. When the meeting was over, he stopped to talk to a colleague in the hall, and the lawyer for the other side approached me.

"You're new," he stated, eyeing me up and down, his leer making me want to cringe.

"Can I help you?" I asked, keeping my voice polite but cool.

"Yeah, you can. I want to buy you a drink."

"No thank you."

He stepped closer—far too close for my liking. He had struck me as sleazy earlier, and up close, even more so. He was decent-looking but had an unpleasant scowl on his face. I'd had the feeling he was the sort of lawyer that liked to coast along in his career—taking the easy cases, ones he could make a lot of money on, without really caring about the outcome.

"Come on. One drink."

"I said no."

"I'll make it worth your while."

I was about to tell him where to go, when Jaxson was beside me. "Grace. We need to head back to the office."

I felt relief. "Of course."

The jerk-off didn't take the hint. In fact, he edged closer, his hand hovering in the air as if he was going to touch me.

"I was asking your girl out for a drink, Richards. Give me a minute."

Jaxson glanced at me, his eyes cold. "You interested?"

"*No*," I stated for both their benefits.

Jaxson took my elbow. "My *girl* said no, Franklin. So, fuck off."

We left Mr. Franklin gaping after us. I tried not to giggle at his shocked expression as I hurried to keep up with Jaxson. He pushed open the stairway door and began to descend to the parking lot. I shook off his grip. "Slow down—I'm going to fall!"

He snarled out a reply. "Keep up."

At the bottom, I stopped. "What is your problem?"

He whirled around in the semidarkness of the stairwell, his face like thunder.

"You need to keep your personal life outside office hours."

"What?" I gasped.

"You can't date other lawyers—especially those on the opposing side."

"I wasn't planning to!"

The sound of footsteps heading our way made me realize how close we were standing.

"We'll continue this at the office."

"Yes, we will," I snapped.

I stewed the rest of the afternoon. I couldn't keep up with him. One minute, he was fine. The next, he was breathing fire. I hadn't done anything wrong, yet it seemed I made him angry. Even though I wanted to learn from him, perhaps it wasn't going to work. We were like chalk and cheese.

Finally, Michael left, waving goodbye. "Have a great weekend, Grace."

"You too."

"Don't stay too late."

"Wasn't planning on it."

After he left, I locked Jaxson's outer door and approached his private office. I rolled my shoulders, knowing what was going to happen would determine my future.

I knocked and went in after he bellowed for me to enter. He was obviously still angry.

I sat down across from him, each of us eyeing the other irately.

"What is your problem?" I repeated my earlier question.

He didn't waste any time getting to the point. "Did you want to go for a drink with him, Grace?"

"No!"

"He was standing awfully close."

"And I was trying to step back when you showed up. In fact, I would have told him off before you rushed in to save the day."

"He kept looking at you during the meeting."

I hadn't noticed. All my attention was on Jaxson. "He can look all he wants. I'm not interested."

He drummed his long fingers on the desk. I tried not to stare at them.

"It's your outfit," he announced.

"What the hell is wrong with my outfit?"

"It's too damn sexy."

I gaped at him. "It's pants. I'm wearing *pants*, for God's sake."

"Your blouse. It's too…too much."

I glanced down. Nothing was showing, my collarbone barely visible. The neckline was modest, the sleeves long, and I was wearing a shawl.

"*You* are being ridiculous. The lawyer, that Sabrina woman who came in here this morning, was showing more skin than I am. There is nothing wrong with what I'm wearing."

"Do not compare yourself to her."

An irrational flash of jealousy hit me. "She's out of my league is what you're saying?"

He glared. "Don't push it."

I threw up my hands. "I give up. Why don't you write me a list of what I can wear, who I can talk to, and what I should think, Jaxson?"

"Don't be stupid."

"*Stupid?* This from the man who thinks wearing pants is overtly sexy."

"They are," he insisted.

"Don't be an ass," I hissed before I could stop myself. "You're acting like an idiot, and you're being irrational."

"You're pushing my buttons."

"*Your* buttons? You're the one with the over-the-top reaction here. You're being a jackass—again."

"Fond of that word, are you?"

"It suits you."

"Shrew," he replied.

"What did you call me?"

"You heard me. You're a shrew. I was trying to help you earlier."

I was done with this insanity. The man was clearly deranged.

I stood. "For the record, he came over to me. I said no—twice. If you hadn't shown up, I would have walked away or, if I had to, pushed him away. I can take care of myself, Jaxson. My father taught me how to throw a punch if required, so I don't need you to rescue me, and I don't appreciate your overreactions. My outfit is perfectly acceptable, and you are, in fact, a jackass."

"Is that so?"

"Yes." I drew in a deep breath. "In fact, if this is your way of having a discussion, you can stuff it, Mr. Richards."

I turned and headed to the door.

The next thing I knew, Jaxson was behind me, spinning me around and crowding me against the wall, his body hot and unyielding.

"Jesus," he spat. "Gracie, you drive me crazy."

"What?" I asked, confused.

"I keep fucking this up." He hung his head. "You get close, and I lose all common sense. I do things I would never do—say things I shouldn't."

I stayed silent, letting him ramble. I liked the way it felt with him pressed up against me. I could feel his strength and his anger. Both were addictive somehow, and I wasn't afraid of either. The irritation I had been feeling started to be replaced by a different sort of buzz. One of longing.

"*Jesus*," he uttered. "I keep doing this. Last week, spending time with you outside the office. Yesterday, kissing you in the car. Holding your hand. As your boss, I shouldn't do any of that. Or pass judgment on your life. I didn't intend that to happen. And today." He groaned. "Seeing him beside you, chatting you up. I wanted to punch him in the face. What is it about you that messes up my head?"

I frowned. "I don't understand."

His intense blue eyes met mine. "I didn't mean to start an argument, Grace—yesterday or today. You're right, there is nothing wrong with your outfit. You're beautiful. And yesterday, my words were born of hating to think of you living in fear—of anything. I wanted to help. But I know it didn't come across that way."

His confession disarmed me.

"I apologize for both—my rudeness and my inappropriateness in the car yesterday."

We were so close, I could feel every solid inch of him. His scent filled my head—citrusy, musky—heady. He was tense, his muscles bunching, his jaw working as our eyes locked and held.

"I liked the car," I whispered, the words torn from me before I could stop them.

He rested his forehead to mine with a low groan. "Don't tell me that, Gracie."

His breath washed over me. Mint and coffee. I could taste it. Taste him. I wanted to taste more.

"I liked the way you told him off today. You made me feel protected."

"Fuck," he mumbled, his eyes locked on my mouth.

"I like how you feel this close to me."

He groaned again, the sound low and desperate.

Exactly the way I was feeling.

"Jaxson," I murmured.

"What are you doing to me?" he replied, sliding his hand along my shoulder and up my neck, cupping my cheek. "You make me want things I can't have."

"Like what?"

"Like feeling your lips underneath mine. Tasting your mouth. Knowing if the heat of it is as addictive as I think it would be."

"Find out, then."

He crashed his lips to mine.

And I was lost.

CHAPTER 7

JAXSON

Her mouth.

Good God, her mouth. One taste of her and I knew I would never have enough. Her lips were soft and warm underneath mine. They opened for me as I pulled her close, and our mouths fused together, as if made to be that way. She draped her arms around my neck, and without a thought, I slid my hands under her ass and lifted her. She wrapped her legs around me, drawing me tight to her body. For a tiny woman, her legs seemed to go on forever—especially in those cursed pants that showed off her spectacular ass to perfection. The ass I was now cupping, stroking, and palming. Gracie moaned, the sound low in her throat as I kissed her deeper, all rational thought long gone. Our tongues glided together, discovering, tasting, going deeper—claiming and possessive, both of us lost to the passion that sizzled around us.

I delved my fingers under the waistband of her pants, up under her silky blouse, feeling the delicate ridges and dips of her spine. The soft warmth of her skin. I used my other hand to fist her beautiful hair, the thick strands smooth and rich on my fingers. I broke from her mouth, running my lips down her throat, up the column of her neck, tugging her earlobe into my mouth and sucking.

"We need to stop," I mumbled, finding my voice.

"No," she replied, cupping my jaw and bringing my face back to hers. "Never."

I stumbled blindly to my chair, sitting down, Gracie now in my lap, straddling my thighs. Her heat pressed down on me. My cock was rock hard, aching, demanding to get closer to her. I groaned while she undulated over me as I fisted her hair and kissed her harder. I slid my hand back under her blouse, trailing my fingers over her, gliding them to her breast, and running a circle over her nipple with my thumb. The nub peaked under my touch, and Gracie moved restlessly over me, her whimper an erotic sound. I found the button and zipper of her waistband, tugging open the material and slipping in my hand. Gracie gasped, rising slightly in the chair, her legs parting farther. I cupped her, teasing her with my finger, groaning as I discovered her. She was slick and warm. Responsive. She threw back her head as I stroked her clit, kissing and biting my way up and down her throat.

"Jesus, Gracie. You're so wet for me."

She bucked against my hand, a breathless plea falling from her lips. "Jaxson."

She was beautiful on my lap, her head back, her hair flowing over my knees. Her mouth was open, her tongue pressing on her bottom lip. I needed that tongue on mine again. I grabbed the back of her neck, bringing her mouth back to me. I slid one finger, then two inside her, pressing my thumb on her clit. I moved them in tandem, speeding up as she began to shake and whimper.

"Come for me, Gracie. Come all over my hand."

I covered her mouth as she broke. Her body locked down, her muscles fluttering, tightening on my fingers as she came. She cried out, and I swallowed the sounds, keeping them for myself alone, gentling my touch and drawing out her orgasm.

I had never seen such a captivating sight. It was one I wanted to see over and over again.

She shuddered, and I stopped my teasing, cupping her briefly before pulling out my hand. I engulfed her in my arms, letting her rest her head against my chest. Our breathing was ragged, the sounds filling the room. I stroked my hand over her hair, the tenderness she inspired in me raging suddenly. I tightened my arms around her, wanting to stay that way forever. When she lifted her head, I held my breath, fearing what I would see in her eyes.

Accusation? Regret?

But she smiled, her blue eyes so filled with warmth, my chest ached.

"Hi," she whispered.

"Hello," I whispered back.

Another smile curled the edge of her lips as she shifted. I grimaced as she brushed against my erection, and she frowned.

"Ignore it. It'll go away."

At least, it would once I got into the bathroom and took care of it. I was rock hard and aching.

She pushed against my chest, and I shook my head.

"No, baby. Don't go."

She leaned up, kissing my mouth, running her tongue along my lips. "I'm not."

She slid off my lap and, in a fluid movement, sank to her knees in front of me, reaching for my belt.

"No," I protested, even as I lifted my hips, letting her tug down my pants, freeing my cock. "Gracie, I didn't expect…" I swallowed as she took me in her hand. "You don't have…" I groaned as she ran her fingers over my weeping cock. "Baby, you can't—" I let my head fall back as pleasure tore through me when she sucked me into her mouth. I was lost as she tugged on my thighs, and I pushed forward to the edge of the chair. She rose on her knees, taking me deeper into her throat. She lifted her eyes, meeting mine, the intensity of her gaze making me shudder. Sexy wasn't the right word to describe the vision. On her knees, my cock in her mouth, her eyes focused on me as she sucked, licked, and teased. Her hands moved restlessly on my thighs, and I covered them with mine.

"You look so perfect with my cock in your mouth, Gracie. I've never seen anything so sexy."

She swallowed around me, and I was done. Pleasure, hot and pulsating, ran through me. I came hard, groaning her name, spilling down her throat. I wove my fingers into her hair, gasping and shaking until I was spent. Slowly, she withdrew and rested her head on my thigh as I ran my hand over her tresses.

When she lifted her head, our eyes locked. She grinned, but I saw the worry in her eyes. "How clichéd was that?" she murmured. "Blowing your boss in his office."

I tugged her off her knees and back to my lap. I held her tight. "Don't. What happened wasn't clichéd or tawdry."

"What was it?" she asked.

"The start of something." I pressed a kiss to her head.

"The start of us?" she asked.

I frowned. "I don't believe in happily ever afters, Grace. I think everything comes to an end. I told you that before."

She pursed her lips but didn't argue.

"The start of us for now?" I offered.

"Well, I guess we started *for now* with a bang, then," she muttered.

I began to laugh, thrilled she joined in. I kissed her head. "I guess we did."

I drove her home, following her inside her cozy apartment and looking around with unabashed curiosity. Her home was charming—filled with antiques and comfortable furniture. Bookcases overflowing with novels, pictures everywhere, and her scent saturating the space. Floral, light, and alluring. Two large windows butted against each other in the corner of the room, giving a good view of the street and the park across from the building. Gracie had a large chair in front of them, and a pile of books lay on the table beside the chair. More books filled the shelves under the windows. A blanket was thrown over the back of the chair, and a pair of glasses sat on the pile of books. An empty mug sat beside them. I could imagine her curled up, reading, sipping coffee, and relaxing.

She came from the kitchen and handed me a glass of wine. I leaned down and kissed her forehead, and we settled on the sofa, her knees touching mine as we faced each other.

"I love your space. It's so you."

She smiled. "Thanks."

"Given who your family is, I'm surprised you live here, though," I confessed. "Even I live in a BAM building."

She took a sip of her wine. "Trust me, my dad wasn't happy about my choice. Neither were any of my uncles. But most of their inventory is high-rises, which I wasn't interested in. The few older, low-rise buildings Uncle Bent has were too far away from where I wanted to be." She paused, looking embarrassed. "I-I don't like the subway. I need to be close to the buses and streetcars or near enough to walk."

Given her claustrophobia, her explanation made sense. "I see."

"I liked this place. I liked the location, the access, the fact that there was a little park across the road. Reid came in and wired up the place, Aiden made sure the locks were to his satisfaction, and I moved in. I think they thought I would change my mind, but I've lived here the whole time I've been in Toronto. I like my neighbors, I have a guest room for my parents or siblings if they come to visit, and I'm happy here." She took another sip of wine. "It's light and open."

"That's important to you. The light." I had noticed how she always gravitated toward a window. Kept a light on by her desk.

"Yes."

I picked up her hand, rubbing her fingers between mine. "Have you always been like this? The fear, I mean?"

She grimaced. "No."

"Can you tell me?"

She lifted her eyebrows. "Pretty personal stuff for so early in our, ah, relationship."

I met her gaze, raising my eyebrows to match hers. "So was my cock in your mouth. I think we're good."

She gaped at me, then laughed. "Touché, Mr. Richards."

"Tell me," I encouraged. "I want to understand."

She blew out a breath, becoming serious. "I was about six. I went to a friend's place for a birthday party—Lana was her name. There were lots of us little girls running around. We were playing hide-and-seek inside the house, and Lana's cousin told me she had the best place to hide. She was a couple years older than me, and I followed her out back. There was an old shed at the back of the property, and inside was a trap door in the floor where they used to store stuff." Gracie swallowed, looking down. "She lifted the door and I got in, but instead of her joining me, she slammed it shut and ran off."

"Jesus."

"I couldn't get out. Lana's mom was busy with everyone, and it took a while before they noticed I was missing."

I moved closer, sliding my hand up and down her arm, feeling the tension radiating from her.

"They looked for me inside, but no one thought about the shed so far from the house. Lana's mom called my parents and the police."

"And her cousin said nothing?"

"Not at first. She was jealous that Lana liked me better and wanted me out of the way. I don't think she realized when she slammed the door, it jammed, and then when I didn't show up, she got frightened and said nothing. Finally, she admitted to them we'd gone outside and where she'd left me."

"How long were you trapped?"

She frowned, worrying her lip. "It felt like forever, although it was only a few hours, I think? I lost track of time. It was dark and damp. The smell of the decaying dirt all around me is something I'll never forget. I was so scared—I kept calling and trying to get out." She held up her hand, and for the first time, I noticed the scar across the palm. "I cut myself trying to escape. It never really healed."

I captured her hand and kissed it, holding it tight to my torso. The thought of her as a child, alone, terrified, and trapped, did something to my chest. The thought of what could have happened if she hadn't been found in time echoed in my head. It made me crazy.

Her focus became dim as she lost herself in memories. "I moved from scared to terrified, and I was crying and cold. I remember curling up on the floor, trying to get warm and wishing for my dad. He would fix it. He would find me. I knew it. Then I heard it—his voice. My *dad's* voice, yelling, calling my name. Telling me he was coming. I sat up and cried for him as loud as I could, hitting the wood above me. And suddenly, the door opened, and he was there with a police officer." She shuddered. "He lifted me out and held me so tight I could barely breathe. He was crying." Her voice dropped. "I had never heard him cry that way."

"He was terrified he had lost you."

She nodded. "I don't remember a lot after. My mom was there, I was in a blanket, my dad was yelling. The police asked a lot of questions. Lana's mom was crying. Finally, they took me home." She met my eyes. "I had nightmares for weeks—months, even. I couldn't sleep without the light. And it took a long time and counseling before I could be in a place without windows."

I lifted her hand to my mouth. "Gracie, my darling— how awful. What happened to the cousin?"

"I have no idea—my parents told me she would never come near me again. Lana never saw her either, from what I understood. Our friendship sort of fizzled out. Her parents felt terrible, and my father never got over his anger. It wasn't a good combination. I heard they had moved, so we didn't even see each other at school anymore."

"Your father is very protective of you."

A small grin played on her lips. "You have no idea." Then she sighed. "So, elevators and closed, dark spaces are still an issue. I'm better than I was. I can actually get in an elevator now as long as I prepare myself. Walk-in closets are okay as long as there is a light and an open door. But I will never be completely comfortable in small spaces."

"I understand." I drew in a deep breath. "I'm sorry for pushing you yesterday."

"You didn't know."

"I do now. Going forward, I will do better."

For a moment, there was silence. "Will we be going forward?" she asked quietly.

That was the million-dollar question. "Gracie," I began.

Her gaze met mine. "Jaxson."

"I broke every rule there is in the company the past while. Every rule I have ever abided by in my professional career."

"Do you regret it?" she asked.

"No. Not a single bit."

"So, it wasn't just a thing?"

"You think I'm the sort of man who lets his student blow him and walks away?" I asked.

She sighed. "Jaxson, we were both caught up in the moment. I'm a big girl. I get that."

I held up my hand, stopping her. "No. That is not what happened. You captivated me the moment you walked into my office, Gracie. I have been fighting against the attraction ever since. Tonight was me giving in." I frowned in worry. "Was that all tonight was to you? A passing moment?"

"No. Not at all." She glanced away, suddenly shy. "I'm not that woman, Jaxson. I don't sleep with my boss. I don't give blow jobs in the office." Color saturated her cheeks.

"I don't have relationships with people I work with." I paused. "Or anyone else."

She looked startled. "I—"

I took her hand, lifting it to my mouth. "You're different, Gracie."

"I am?"

"Yes. How, why, and what happens in the future, I have no idea, but all I know is you're different. But I can't promise you anything. Can you accept that?"

"I can. But, Jaxson, how is this going to work?" She fretted. "The nonfraternization policy at the office." Her eyes widened. "I could be let go. You could be fired."

"No one is going to find out. We would have to be careful. Especially right now while we work together."

"So, we hide."

"We're circumspect."

"I'm your dirty little secret."

"No. You're nothing of the sort. You are far too special to ever be that." I ran a hand through my hair in vexation. "Don't ever refer to yourself that way. Do you understand me?"

She traced her finger over my cheek. "What am I, then?"

I sighed, leaning into her touch. "This is all new to me, Gracie. I have never acted this way. Felt this way. I need some time to figure it all out."

"How do you feel?"

"Out of control. I spin in circles when you're close."

She edged closer, our bodies pressing together. "I feel dizzy when I'm near you."

I pulled her onto my lap. "Then we'll hold each other up."

She grinned up at me. "I've been here before."

"I plan on you being there a lot." I palmed her ass. "You fit perfectly."

She laid her head on my shoulder, and I rested my chin on her head. "There are a hundred and one reasons we shouldn't be together. We're opposites. We're at two different points in our lives. My course is set, and you're just beginning yours. I'm too old for you. Too cynical and jaded."

"You forgot opinionated. Fussy. And domineering."

My lips quirked. "That too."

"You hate pants."

I chuckled. "I don't hate pants." I stroked her curves. "Do you have any idea how amazing your ass looks in these pants? I've had a perpetual hard-on all day. Between the pants and the sexy lace on your blouse, I was a goner."

"Ah, that's why you were so cranky."

"Shut it."

She lifted up her head. "Okay. So, you're old and cranky but like my ass. What else?"

I groaned. "I'm your boss."

"That's the crux of it, isn't it?"

"It is. It should stop me in my tracks. I knew before you left my office the first day I was in trouble. I should have asked to have you with Lynn first and given myself time to build up my defenses."

"Would that have helped?"

"No."

"So, what do we do?"

"I have no idea. Except I do know this. I'm powerless to stay away from you, Grace."

"I feel the same way."

I bent my head, meeting her lips. "Then we figure it out together."

CHAPTER 8

JAXSON

I didn't want to leave her, and I was pleased to find out Gracie loved Chinese food as much as I did, so we ordered in dinner. We sat on the sofa, sharing containers, eating with chopsticks, and talking. I loved listening to her voice. I discovered in the office when I was upset or angry, locating her voice, hearing the tone, seemed to calm me. If she was busy and quiet, I found excuses to ask her questions, simply to listen to her.

She told me about growing up, the BAM Compound, her best friend/cousin's upcoming wedding, and a multitude of other funny stories. I made sure to stay clear of anything else too heavy tonight. She had already shared something painful, and I didn't want her upset again. I indicated the bookshelves under the windows.

"You like to read."

She nodded enthusiastically around a mouthful of noodles. "My mom got me into it. She always read to us as kids, and as I got older, I read to my siblings." She grinned. "My dad did too, but he liked to use voices and make us laugh."

"You're very close to him."

"I am. He's always been there for me—for all of us—but we have a special bond."

I went back to the original topic. "I would have taken you for a Kindle girl."

"Oh, I have one. It's great for travel and on the bus, but at home, I like books. I like holding them, the feel of the pages." She paused. "Do you read?"

I winked. "It's helpful in my line of work. Contracts and all."

She threw back her head in laughter. "Cheeky. I mean do you like to read in your spare time? Books?"

I stroked my chin, looking thoughtful. "Is porn included?"

"I am going to give you a facer if you're not careful."

I frowned in confusion. "A facer? Is that like a different word for a blow job? Because I'm all for it." I waggled my eyebrows for effect, and she rewarded me with a loud giggle-snort, covering her mouth, which made me laugh.

"No, a facer is not a blow job. It's an, ah, expression I read a lot in books. It means punch you in the face."

"I've never heard of that expression."

Soft color diffused her cheeks. "You probably don't read the sorts of books I do. I, ah, have a thing."

The way she was blushing and her hesitant words piqued my interest. "A *thing*, Gracie VanRyan? What sort of thing?" I leaned closer, grinning. "Do you read, like, dino-porn?" I tickled her under the chin. "I hear *that's* a thing."

She slapped my hand away. "No. I like historical romance."

I couldn't help but tease her. "Historical? As in dukes and rakes?"

Her color deepened. "Yes. Especially dukes and rakes. I love losing myself in that world."

"I see. I suppose I fall under the category of rake."

"Yes, you do."

"Hmm." I set aside my container and chopsticks, wiping my mouth. She watched me as I took her chopsticks, never breaking eye contact as I licked the last of the sauce from the ends and tossed them into the container with mine. She gasped as I hauled her onto my lap and kissed her. Long. Slow. With intent. She tasted of soy sauce and spice. Grace.

Perfection.

"What are you doing?" she murmured.

"Keeping up my reputation."

She wound her arms around my neck. "I thought maybe you were showing me a different kind of facer."

"If that's a challenge, Gracie, I accept."

GRACE

Nothing in my life prepared me for Jaxson Richards. The logical part of my brain screamed at me that what was happening was wrong. But being in his arms felt so right. It didn't matter he was older, jaded, grumpy, or my boss. I didn't care about anything except the feeling of his mouth on mine, the way his heat soaked into my body as he held me tight, or the ache deep inside me I needed him to ease.

I didn't have a lot of experience, but I'd dated. My parents had been fairly strict—especially my dad—and the fact was that, growing up, I spent most of my summers here in Ontario with my extended family. Unlike Addi, my soul mate wasn't among them. They were my cousins, my friends, and that was all. Back in BC, I hung with friends, mostly in groups, rarely starting a relationship, knowing I'd been gone every summer and over a lot of holidays. Plus, the fact that there was never anyone I was very interested in. I had shared a kiss or two with a few boys and I went steady once, and that was about it. When I left BC and came to Toronto, I met a few men, even had a longtime boyfriend, but it ended mutually. We both agreed our lives were headed in different directions and wished each other well. He had been my first, and since we'd broken up, I had only had a relationship with one other man.

Neither of them set me aflame the way Jaxson did. I had never desired a man the way I did him.

He set me on my bed, his mouth leaving mine. "Tell me to go, Gracie," he begged, his voice low and raspy in my ear. "Tell me to stop."

I grabbed his shirt, dragging him back to my mouth. "No."

His kiss was carnal. Deep, possessive, and addictive. It felt as if he was claiming me. I kissed him back with equal ardor, claiming him as well.

"If I don't stop, I'm going to be inside you." His muffled declaration made me shiver. "Once I do, that's it. We can't go back."

I nipped his ear. "I don't want to go back. I want your hands on me, Jaxson. I want you inside me. I'm aching for you."

He groaned, and seconds later, we were both naked. The sounds of rending material, carelessly discarded clothing, filled the room. He stood, gazing down at me as I looked at him in wonder. His arms bulged, his torso taut and that tantalizing vee prominent. His thick cock jutted out, and I recalled the way he tasted, how he felt in my mouth. I wanted to feel him in a totally different way.

"Birth control," he suddenly announced.

"Covered."

"Condoms."

I indicated the nightstand. "In the drawer."

He lifted one eyebrow.

"Addi gave them to me as a joke. She is constantly bugging me about getting laid." I stretched my arms over my head, thrusting out my breasts. "She'll be thrilled when I tell her I used them."

"We can't—"

I shook my head, a flutter of sadness going through me. "I won't tell her who you are, Jaxson."

He paused with a frown. "Gracie—"

"Don't." I held out my arms. "Make me yours."

The next moment, I forgot everything else as his mouth molded to mine. His hands, the sexy hands that fascinated me so, smoothed and glided over my body. His touch was equal parts tender and possessive. He followed his touch with his mouth, his tongue tracing a path as he murmured his thoughts out loud.

"You are so beautiful," he whispered.

"You have a tiny mole." He kissed a spot on my inner thigh. "Right here. I'm going to think about this mole when I see you in the office. Every day."

He sucked my nipples, grazing them with his teeth. "Your breasts are perfect. Look how they fit in my hands." I gasped as he bit down gently then blew on my sensitive nipples. "Perfect."

He slipped his hand between my legs with a groan. "So ready for me, Gracie. God, you feel so good. I want to feel all of you."

My body was on fire, every part of me burning. I wanted him. I couldn't stop touching him—feeling the way his muscles rippled on his back as he moved. The strength in his shoulders. The way the coarse hair scattered on his chest rubbed my breasts, abrading my nipples. How his erection felt, hot and heavy on my skin. I wrapped my legs around his hips.

"Feel me, Jaxson. Fuck me."

He captured my mouth as he sank inside me, inch by inch, slowly thrusting until we were joined so tightly that we were one. I shuddered at the feeling of him consuming me, the heat and girth of him filling me up so completely, I knew I would never be the same again. No one else would ever feel this good.

He began to move, his low grunts and groans filling the room. He kissed me hard, licked at my neck, nibbled my shoulder, returned to my mouth. I gasped and shivered, moved with him, absorbed his powerful strokes, the pleasure radiating through me. His body was covered with a sheen of sweat, his frame shaking with the effort of his movements. My headboard creaked, the sheets shifted, and the pillows beside me fell to the floor. I gripped his skin, kissed his head as he buried his face into my neck, wrapped my legs tighter as my orgasm hit me, exploding with a ferocity I had never experienced. I cried out his name, flinging back my head as he stiffened, his orgasm melding with mine. We soared, peaked, and ebbed, and then finally, we both collapsed, our ragged breathing replacing the moans and cries of passion we had shared.

His weight pressed me deep into the mattress, and for a moment, I held him, needing to feel him as close as possible. He lifted his head, his eyes warm and soft. He smiled, the divot in his chin deepening, and I smiled back, touching it with my finger.

"I like this. It's cute."

"I'm never cute."

"You are at times. When you relax and are simply Jaxson. You're funny, sweet, and cute. Sexy, too."

He ran his finger over my lips and kissed me. "And when I'm not relaxed?"

"You're still sexy. But intense. You're more standoffish, I suppose."

He rolled away, leaving the bed and going into my bathroom. He came back, the condom gone, and slid back into bed, dragging me close. I rested my head on his chest and sighed in contentment as he ran his fingers through my hair.

"I've had to learn to be standoffish. It's how I've survived life."

I peeked up, seeing his frown. "I'm sorry."

"I don't really want to get into my past right now, Gracie."

"All right." I laid my head back down, stroking his chest in lazy circles.

"Do you want me to go?" he asked.

"No."

For a moment, the room was silent. It felt right, having him here. Being in his arms. I felt safe and protected. I knew he was holding back, but I hoped in time he would confide in me. I had told him about what happened to me as a child. Outside my family and the counselor I went to, few people knew. People rarely noticed. In most cases, it was easy to "forget" something and tell them I would meet them. They would leave, and I would prepare myself to get on an elevator. Or in rare cases, I could suffer through a short ride if I had to. These days, the explanation of "I'll take the stairs," was accepted more readily. They assumed I was a health nut. I had learned many ways to disguise my fear. I had come a long way over the years, but I had accepted that perhaps I would never fully recover from the trauma and had instead learned coping techniques.

Jaxson had noticed immediately. He was observant and clever. He had also been as closely attuned to me as I was to him—something I hadn't experienced with anyone else.

He brushed his lips across my crown.

"I don't believe in forever, Grace. I don't think there is one. People come and go from our lives, and that is the way of the world. Everyone had a use, and when it's done, it's done."

I pushed myself up on my elbow. "I don't believe that. Love exists. Forever exists."

He shook his head, smiling sadly. "I won't argue with you because that is how it is in your world. You are one of the lucky ones. But in my world, in my life, everything has a time limit."

"Even me?"

He gentled his voice. "Even you. Once your articling is done and you leave the firm, your path will take you away and onto new things."

"How can you say that after what we experienced? Dismiss whatever this is between us?"

"It's called lust, Gracie," he stated firmly. He tucked a strand of hair behind my ears. "It's intense for both of us, but that's all it is. You deserve the world. A man who can love you completely and fully. Give you everything. I'm not that man, Grace. I don't have it to give you. All I have to give you is my body and a limited amount of time." He touched my chin. "If you can accept that, you have me. If not, I understand."

He believed what he said. He honestly felt that way, but he was so wrong. I had seen the man he hid behind the cold exterior. I felt his passion. His care. He told me he had spent hours researching claustrophobia to try to help me. Someone who didn't care wouldn't do that. He had spent so many years denying his feelings, he couldn't recognize them. I was convinced of that fact. I had to be patient and let him figure it out. Figure us out.

Good thing I had lots of time and patience to give him. I would prove to him that he was wrong.

I leaned up and kissed him. He groaned as I slid my tongue into his mouth, silently giving him his answer.

I could only hope, in the end, my instincts were right.

CHAPTER 9

GRACE

The next morning, Jaxson sipped his coffee, looking at me over the rim. "Gracie," he began, a frown on his lips.

"Don't. Don't say you regret last night."

"No. I don't. Not even close. But I want to go home."

I felt a frisson of hurt in my chest. "Oh."

He shook his head. "That came out wrong. I want to go home and get clean clothes. Your toothbrush and shower were appreciated, but I don't want to spend the weekend in my suit."

"What about your birthday suit?" I teased. "I'm good with that."

I liked looking at him naked. He was incredibly fit, and I enjoyed watching him move.

He leaned back in his chair with a smirk. He was wearing his dress pants but nothing else. His pecs and thick arms were on display, his pants hanging low on his hips. Even his bare feet were sexy, the skin smooth, the toenails tidy. He admitted to having a fondness for pedicures and manicures.

"I like my hands to look good, and once I had a pedicure, I was hooked. I like my feet smooth," he confessed. "I suck with nail clippers and constantly had ingrown toenails. Now I'm good."

I enjoyed them as well, so I understood his pleasure. It was nice to see a man confident enough with himself to admit it, though.

"You liked my birthday suit a bunch last night."

"I did."

"I was hoping you liked it enough you would want to spend some more time with me. Like all weekend." He eyed me intently. "I'm not ready to give you up yet."

"I'd like that."

He leaned forward, resting his elbows on the table, looking earnest.

"I want to get a few things, and I'd like you to come with me."

"Okay."

"Gracie, I live in a high-rise. The twenty-third floor."

"Oh. Right—you said a BAM building."

"Yes." He sighed and settled back in the chair. "You stay here, and I'll go. I'll come back as quickly as I can."

"No, I'll come."

"Are you sure?"

"Yes. As long as I can prepare, I can do it."

He reached for my hand. "You can have as much time as you need."

I felt a ripple of nerves flow through me, but I nodded. "Okay."

He squeezed my fingers. "I'll be right there with you, Gracie. Promise."

At his building, I peeked in the elevator, pleased to see it was larger than many and well lit. The doors shut as I stepped back into the hall, taking a final moment to collect my thoughts. Jaxson stood beside me, silent and patient. With a long exhale, I pressed the button, and the doors slid open once again.

"Fast," I observed.

"It's early, and yes, it is a fast elevator. We'll be in and out before you know it," he encouraged.

I stepped in, my heart rate picking up as it always did. Jaxson looked at me, concerned. "Okay?" he asked, his finger hovering over the control panel. "We can do the stairs."

I reached past him and pressed his floor. The doors shut, and I stepped back against the rail without a word. Jaxson stepped in front of me, cupping my face. He leaned close and brushed his lips over mine. "You're amazing."

His touch helped. It centered me, and I gripped his wrists, holding them tight. "Jaxson," I breathed.

He kissed me again, sweeping his tongue inside and deepening the kiss. Instantly, my focus was on him. His touch. His taste. He surrounded me, and with a shiver, I lost myself to him. I was shocked when the doors opened again and he drew me out of the elevator. My rapid heartbeat had nothing to do with panic and everything to do with the man grinning at me.

"That was easier than normal."

He winked. "I guess I need to be your elevator service guy. Like a guide dog, but with hands."

Relief made me giddy. "Will you wear a collar and a lead?"

He wrapped his arm around my waist, tucking me close. "For you, Gracie, I think I would." His eyes darkened. "Maybe we could find a use for them other places."

I laughed. This man. This crazy, unbelievable man. He was so amazing and didn't even realize what he had just done.

Or what he was doing to my heart.

His apartment was a decent size for Toronto. Tastefully equipped with heavy, masculine furniture in neutral colors. He told me to wander around as he headed to his kitchen. There was a small office, a nice bedroom with an en-suite, and his living room had a good view of downtown. With fall surrounding us, the leaves were changing color, and it looked pretty. I headed to the kitchen to find him pouring boiling water into a French press. He took two mugs from the cupboard.

"I need real coffee."

"My Keurig isn't real?"

"Not like this. I buy the beans freshly roasted and grind them myself." He made a face. "I drink the swill at the office because I have to, but here at home, I like the real stuff." He inhaled. "Rich, bold, *perfect* coffee."

"So, you're a coffee snob."

"Yes." He winked. "Once you taste this, you will be too."

He disappeared and returned a few moments later, dressed in a long-sleeved Henley and jeans. The dark gray of his shirt set off his blue eyes, the sleeves tight on his arms. His jeans hugged his ass, and suddenly, I realized what he meant about my pants. He looked indecent. As if he knew what I was thinking, he winked as he slowly depressed the plunger. The aroma in the room intensified, and I inhaled in appreciation.

I took the mug he offered and sipped. Bold, rich, delicious coffee hit my tongue. The flavor was outstanding, the brew every bit as good as he claimed.

"Divine," I said. "Oh my God, that is so good."

"I told you."

I took another sip. "How am I ever going to go back to the other stuff now?"

He laughed and bent, kissing my forehead. "I got you, baby. I'll feed your addiction."

"What if I'm addicted to more than just your coffee?" I asked.

He edged closer. "Now that, I wholeheartedly approve of." He cupped my cheek and kissed me. "Come sit with me."

"Do I get more coffee?"

"Gracie, my darling, you can have just about anything you want." He winked. "Even my coffee."

Happily, I followed him to the sofa.

We spent a few hours at his apartment. I drank more of his delicious coffee, he packed a small bag, and we headed back to my place. He didn't even wait until the elevator door opened, instead kissing me in the hall, wrapping his arm around my waist, and lifting me into the elevator effortlessly. His mouth never left mine until we were back in the parking garage.

"What if someone else got on the elevator?" I asked weakly.

He looked at me askance. "I can't kiss them too, Gracie. One at a time."

I laughed at his silliness and hugged his arm as we headed to the car.

"I would keep kissing you. I don't care."

I liked his response more than I should.

We dropped his bag at my place, and he informed me we needed to go shopping. I laughed as he pulled me into his favorite coffee place, insisting on purchasing a French press and some of his beloved beans.

"I need one at your place," he insisted. "You have to admit, it's far superior."

"It takes longer."

He kissed the end of my nose. "Good things are worth waiting for." He smiled and added quietly, "You certainly were."

My heart sang at his words.

Monday morning, I was anxious as I arrived at the office. I wasn't sure what to expect. I knew Jaxson and I had agreed to keep our relationship under wraps, but how would he act? How would I react to him? The weekend had been almost magical. We shopped and had lunch at a little place he loved that served wood-fired pizzas. It was small and tucked off the beaten path, so we weren't worried about being seen. He was surprisingly affectionate, given the cool demeanor he showed the world. He held my hand, kissed my cheek, often tucked a stray strand of hair behind my ear. The time passed too quickly. We watched movies, took walks, ate takeout. I cooked him breakfast. I baked cookies, which he loved.

"These are awesome. Foster care rarely includes homemade cookies," he confessed. "I was always jealous when I heard other kids talk about them. I was lucky to get a packaged one once in a while."

I wondered if he knew he had let something slip out about his past and the fact that he'd been in foster care. I wanted to ask him questions, but I knew him well enough already to know he would tell me when he was ready and I shouldn't push. I swore, though, that I would bake him cookies frequently.

We made love. Often. In the shower, in my bed, on the sofa. In the kitchen. On the floor of the kitchen.

One of the things he had picked up when we were shopping was a box of condoms.

"Your cousin only got average. Not a good fit." He leered at me with a grin. I tried not to laugh, but I failed. I couldn't argue. He was far more than average.

I paused outside the office door and rolled my shoulders. Jaxson had left last night, kissing me long and hard before he did. I had hoped he would call or text, but I hadn't heard from him. I wasn't sure what that meant after the weekend we'd spent together, but I tried not to make too much of it. He was no doubt busy getting ready for the week ahead.

I entered the office. Jaxson was leaning on Michael's desk, his tablet in hand. They were going through his schedule, the same way they did every Monday morning. Michael smiled widely at me.

"Hey, Grace! How was your weekend?" That was his standard greeting.

Jaxson looked at me, his expression neutral. His voice was cool. "Grace. Good morning."

There was nothing unusual. Nothing out of the ordinary, yet I felt flushed. Nervous. Anxious.

Longing for his touch.

I forced a smile, hoping I looked casual. "Jaxson." I directed my gaze at Michael. "Same old, same old. How about you?"

"You know me. Living the high life. All glamour and sparkle."

I winked at him, his mood infectious. I knew he'd spent his weekend at home with his longtime husband, Larry, and their darling two-year-old daughter. He doted on them both.

"Abby keeping you on your toes?"

He grinned. "Big-time. She got into a package of glitter Larry had hidden, and let's just say——"

"Can we save the personal chatter for breaks?" Jaxson snarled. "I have a busy week."

Michael wasn't at all put out. "You don't give us breaks."

"Whatever."

Michael handed him a sheet of paper. "Here it is—all printed out the way you like. I updated your phone and computer. Try to stick to it this time."

Jaxson grabbed the paper, looking it over. I headed to my desk, trying not to notice the fact that all I could smell was him as I went by. Delicious, masculine, and sexy. I could feel the heat of his body as I edged past him, rolling my eyes behind his back in Michael's direction.

Grumpy-ass man.

"Give Grace a copy." Jaxson turned to me. "I need research on some of this."

"Of course."

"I want you at the meetings too. I need your assistance. I have some motions I want filed, and there is a stack of paperwork on my desk you can take care of."

"Absolutely."

He strode into his office, shutting the door. I tried not to be hurt. I knew we had to stay hidden. I was aware he couldn't show anything but professionalism around me. I had told myself all that, yet it still rankled a little. A smile wouldn't have hurt.

Unless, maybe the weekend hadn't meant as much to him as it had to me? Worry niggled at me. I knew his reputation. Lots of women. Brief relationships.

I took the paper Michael brought over. He shook his head. "He's in a mood today."

"So it would seem."

"Ignore him. I do. He'll smooth out."

I couldn't help but ask, "It doesn't bother you? The yelling or the rudeness?"

He shrugged. "I learned not to let it. I figured out it wasn't about me. It has everything to do with him. I do my job." He patted my shoulder. "He's a complicated man, Grace. But he's not a bad one. Ignore it and do your job."

I nodded and switched on my laptop. Ignoring it and doing my job had been easier last week when all Jaxson

Richards had been was my boss. It was hard not to take his mood personally when my mind was wondering if I was the cause for it.

And for the first time since we had crossed that line, I felt the pang of regret.

CHAPTER 10

GRACE

Jaxson's office felt as if it had a revolving door all day. People were in and out, and our interactions were brief and professional. I worked on the files he gave me, read through the contracts, and went to the courthouse to file the necessary documents. I arrived back at the office, encountering Michael heading out the front door.

"Where are you off to?"

He held up a manila envelope. "Jaxson wants these hand-delivered today."

"I can take them."

"No, the office is about two blocks from my place, so I'm taking them and not coming back. I forwarded the phone to the main reception. They'll handle it the rest of the day. His Majesty okayed it."

"Is he still in a mood?"

"Actually, I think he's calmed down. He went out for a little while and seemed better when he got back. I think he snuck in a treat. I swear the sugar helps him."

I chuckled. He always did seem better when he ate something—especially something sweet.

"Okay. I'll head up and finish the day."

I entered the office, feeling apprehensive. Jaxson's door was open, and he was on the phone. I sat down, noting another pile of work had appeared. One thing was for sure—I was never bored. I glanced up, surprised to see Jaxson's gaze fixed on me. Our eyes locked across the room, and I felt my chest constrict. His gaze was pure heat. A banked fire that lit one within me. Memories of his mouth, his hands, his body on mine, filled my head. Longing swept through me. It took everything in me to break the powerful connection and look down. My hands shook as I opened the top file, staring at it blindly. The power Jaxson had over me to reduce me to this quivering mass of need frightened me. Then I heard it. His voice calling one word.

"Gracie."

I looked up. No longer on the phone, he was leaning on his desk, watching me. Once again, I felt the pull of his gaze.

"In my office," he stated, then paused. "And shut the door. Please."

I stood and crossed the floor, the pull getting stronger the closer I got to him. I stopped a foot away.

"You needed something?" I asked, hating the underlying tremor in my voice.

"Yes, I do." There was a beat of silence. "I need you."

He reached out and hauled me to his chest. His mouth covered mine before I could stop it. Except I didn't want to stop it. I grasped the back of his neck, kissing him back furiously. Our tongues tangled and dueled. Our lips were pressed together so tightly I thought we'd draw blood. He held me so close I could barely breathe. Anyone could walk in and see us. I didn't care. I needed his mouth on mine more than I needed anything else. This articling position. My next breath. He broke away, ghosting his lips down my neck, pushing away the collar of my shirt with his nose and nipping at the skin he uncovered.

I gasped as he licked the skin, soothing the burn. "Jaxson," I murmured. "The office."

"I can lock the door from my computer." He paused. "You can open the door anytime though, Gracie. You're free to go. But we're safe."

I was always safe with him. I knew that. "I don't want to go," I breathed out.

He took control again, kissing, caressing, holding me. He tasted of coffee and sugar, and I knew he'd been snacking. His scent surrounded me. His heat warmed me. His closeness brought comfort. His mouth brought desire.

Then reality hit, and I pulled back, staring up at him.

"You've ignored me all day."

"I had to."

"You never called or texted. Not once."

He ran a finger over my cheek, tucking a curl behind my ear. "The company monitors all cell phones and emails, Gracie. I couldn't risk you."

"Oh." I hadn't thought about that.

"I went out and got myself a personal cell. Now, I can call and text you."

"You didn't have one before?"

He shrugged. "No need. I rarely make personal calls." He smiled and tapped my nose. "Until now."

I felt a tug of sadness, but I returned his smile.

"Michael said you went out. That was why?"

"Yes. I couldn't ask him to get it for me. He'd figure it out. I will not risk your reputation."

"Why would you care? You said you don't care about—"

He tapped my mouth with his finger. "Forget what I said. I do care, Gracie. I care more than I should."

Then his mouth was on mine again.

A couple of weeks later, Michael perched on the edge of my desk. "What are you doing about a costume?"

I looked up, confused. "Costume?"

"It's Halloween in a couple of weeks. The office does dress-up. Did you not read the memo?"

I blinked. Halloween? I had been at the firm for six weeks. Where did the time go?

"I don't think I saw it. They really dress up? Even the lawyers?"

He grinned. "The ones not in court that day. And some of them do once they come back to the office. Departments carve pumpkins, and they get judged by the partners. The prizes are awesome. Last year, I won third place, and Larry and I had an amazing dinner out."

"Wow." I wouldn't have suspected that about the firm. It seemed well run and the partners nice people, but I didn't think they'd be into costumes and pumpkins. "I haven't even thought about it."

"You need to. And we need to plan a pumpkin."

My gaze drifted to Jaxson's closed door. "Do *all* the lawyers dress up?" I asked with my eyebrows raised. I couldn't begin to imagine Jaxson dressing up.

He chuckled. "Last year, he took off his tie and said he was dressed as a casual lawyer. The year before, he held a cigar between his lips and said he was a smoking lawyer."

I bit my lip to stop laughing. "Maybe this year, he'll hold a book and say he is a reading lawyer."

"That's not a bad idea," Jaxson mused as he walked into the office. "I was going to drape a bathrobe over my shoulders and say I was a sleeping lawyer."

The laughter spilled over, and I covered my mouth.

Michael stood. "You could try, Jaxson. The top prize is a hotel package for the weekend. Maybe a break would do you some good." He walked over to his desk. "It would certainly do me some good."

Jaxson met my eye with a subtle wink and walked to his office. "I'll see what I can do, Michael."

"I won't hold my breath."

I bent my head, pretending to read the words in front of me, but as usual, when Jaxson was close, I was distracted. I knew if I looked up, his eyes would be on me. Watching. Absorbing everything about me. Almost caressing me with his glance. I didn't dare risk it.

We walked a tightrope these days. Boss and student by day. Passionate lovers after hours and on weekends. At times, it was hard to separate the two. One glance from Jaxson could set me aflame. A smart remark from me turned him into a raging madman, although he was often that way, so few people noticed except me. This was a different type of anger. His eyes would darken, his gaze became even more intense than usual, and the sexual tension ramped up so high, my body responded of its own accord. It was dangerous, crazy, and delicious.

At times, I didn't recognize myself. Grace VanRyan, the cool, unflappable girl who always thought everything through. The one who toed the line and followed the rules. I was dependable and quiet. Confident with my place and the direction my life was headed in. I had my future mapped out. Finish law school, article, study for the bar, then join ABC Corp. and work with the lawyer at BAM, learning and soaking up as much knowledge as I could, while taking extra courses on trademarks and copyrights to hone my skills. A personal life, including love, was part of the distant future.

Until Jaxson entered the picture.

He consumed me. Sex with him was unlike anything I had experienced until now, and our appetites for each other were voracious. Our conversations were long and varied. It felt to me as if his views on the future were changing. Softening. Now had become next week. Next week was often referred to as later. I could envision him as part of my life.

Michael's voice interrupted my musings. "Grace."

I glanced up. "Sorry?"

"I have those documents ready to head to the court-house." He held up a file.

"Oh, right." I stood and took the file, then returned to my desk to grab my coat. It was getting chilly these days, late fall swirling around us.

"Think about a costume," Michael urged.

"She needs to be thinking about studying," Jaxson griped, walking from his office. "Far more important."

"Everyone needs to have fun, Jaxson. You should try it," Michael responded.

"I have fun," Jaxson snarled.

"Berating me and bossing Grace around is not what I consider fun," Michael shot back.

I tried not to laugh as I picked up my purse. "You could wear a bear hat and be yourself," I teased, meeting Jaxson's eyes. "Not too far a stretch."

"I'm going to fire both of you," he retorted.

"Whatever." Michael sniffed. "Good luck."

I left the office smiling. Jaxson liked Michael a great deal and was good to him, but it was something only the two of them knew about. Michael complained about him, Jaxson glowered at Michael, and they were both fine with it. As with everything personal, Jaxson hid his emotions.

I walked to the courthouse, my breath hanging in the air. I would have to change my fall coat for a winter one soon. Last night after coming home from the cake tasting with Addi, there had been frost on the ground—

early for Toronto, but not unheard of. Brayden had driven us out to the winery where the wedding was to take place, and I was excited to see the spot where they would get married. The winery was owned by ABC and had been one of Addi's visions. It had been extensively remodeled, and it was spectacular. The various cakes had been delicious, and in the end, they had decided on a simple white cake, light and flavorful, with rich butter-cream frosting. They also added a variety of different cakes for the midnight buffet to please everyone's palate. I had brought home several pieces. Jaxson had been waiting for me and took great delight in sampling many of them. Then sampling me. He had texted me a few times while I was with Addi and Brayden, but they were too wrapped up in each other and the wedding to notice, which I was grateful for. That was a conversation I didn't want to have with Addi. She'd ask too many questions I didn't have answers for. She would be shocked at my relationship with Jaxson and worried, and I wanted her to concentrate on the upcoming nuptials, not the fact that I was sleeping with my boss. Although I was certain it was more for both of us, I wasn't ready to divulge anything. It was too personal, too new, and if I was honest, too overwhelming.

I arrived at the courthouse and put all other thoughts out of my mind.

Halloween arrived, the city blanketed in its first dusting of snow. I arrived at the office early, changing into my costume in the washroom. Michael and I had planned it all out, deciding to coordinate our costumes and double our chances to win a prize. I stood back, looking at my reflection in the mirror. I had my hair done up in a twist, a few tendrils escaping. I was dressed as a lady from the late 1800s. I had found the dress in a thrift shop—it was an old costume from a defunct theater company, and I loved it. Deep burgundy satin and velvet whispered against my skin as I moved. The skirt was wide and layered with lace, the waist pin-tucked and the sleeves three-quarters long. The neckline was plunging but had lace trim to give the illusion of modesty. Luckily, it had a built-in corset and a hidden back zipper. Otherwise, I'd never be able to get into it on my own. I added some low-heeled boots that were comfortable, and since the skirt was long, you couldn't see anything but the tips, so they worked. I felt like a heroine in one of the historical novels I loved to read. I smoothed my hand down the skirt, wondering what Jaxson would think. If he would even react.

I walked into the office and clapped my hands in glee. Michael was dressed in a costume of a scholar from the same time period as my dress. His dark breeches and waistcoat fit his slim build. He'd slicked back his hair and wore wire-rimmed glasses. His tie was a simple length of black material, tied in the fashion of the day. He struck a pose beside his desk, clutching a heavy tome and looking serious. He'd brought in a few props, including some old lanterns and candlesticks and more old books, giving his area the look of a studious law clerk.

"Oh my God, you look perfect," I enthused.

He grinned and pushed up the glasses sliding down his nose. "You look stunning. That dress was a find."

I curtsied low. "Thank you, kind sir." I grinned. "The office looks great!"

"I bet we're going to win."

"Of course we are." Jaxson's voice startled me, and I turned, gaping at him.

For a moment, the office was silent. Three sets of eyes roved and assessed. Two were shocked, unable to believe what they were seeing.

Jaxson stood in front of us, dressed in the elegant, fashionable garb of the late 1800s—matching the theme Michael and I had planned perfectly. From his breeches to his cravat, including his scowling countenance, he was the textbook specimen of a broody duke. The cut of his claret-colored tailcoat clung to his broad shoulders. A stylish waistcoat hugged his torso. His black boots were polished to a high gloss. The navy of his breeches was set off by the snowy white of his shirt, and the color was echoed in his cravat. The haughty set of his shoulders and chin made him my own personal fantasy come to life. He carried a walking stick. He looked sexy, elegant, and powerful. He took my breath away.

Jaxson's eyes took in my outfit. They lingered on the neckline, following the deep vee softened by the lace. I saw the flare of heat in his eyes before he grinned. "My lady," he intoned with a deep bow.

I held back my giggle. "Your Grace." I dipped into another curtsy.

"Should I ask how you managed to fit that on a bus?" He indicated my wide skirt.

I returned his grin, feeling giddy. I couldn't believe he had dressed up. That he had kept his costume secret. It was so authentic; he must have worked hard to get it all together. And I knew, somehow, he had done it for me.

"I changed here."

"Good plan." He turned to Michael. "Turn down the lights and give the place a little more ambiance. Fire up those lanterns. Light the pumpkins."

Michael blinked. "Okay."

Jaxson rubbed his hands together. "I brought candy to give out."

Michael's shocked expression said it all. "You brought candy," he repeated.

"Yes. None of the other offices planned that. I checked. And no one else had a theme. We're taking all the prizes this year."

Michael and I exchanged a glance. He looked at Jaxson. "Have you been drinking?"

Jaxson drew back his shoulders. "Nope. I just want to win."

He turned and walked into his office, the tails of his coat lifting and showing off the spectacular ass his breeches were hugging.

Once again, I understood his dislike of my pants.

CHAPTER 11

GRACE

Michael was beaming as he donned his coat. "Great haul."

I chuckled. We had won for best team-work, best office, and Jaxson won best costume. He had acted the part of a duke all day, his language in keeping with his character. The office was busy with people coming in to see our costumes and admire them. I think they were all shocked over the fact that Jaxson had participated. Their expressions were amusing.

"Are you sure you don't want this?" Michael asked, holding out the certificate for dinner.

I shook my head. "I'm not a sushi lover, and I know you are. You and Larry go and enjoy."

"You could have my spa day," he offered halfheartedly.

"I have one of my own. I'm good."

He glanced at Jaxson's door. "I wonder if he'll use the hotel package."

I shrugged. "I would think so."

"I wonder who he'll use it with," he mused. "I can never keep up with his women."

I tamped down the stirrings of jealousy. I hated thinking of him with anyone else. I had never felt so possessive of a man until now. The thought of him touching someone else, kissing them, taking them away for a weekend, made me see red. I had to duck my head and collect myself.

"No idea," I mumbled.

"Well, enjoy the wine," he said, buttoning up his coat.

I had won third place for best costume. The wine basket was filled with tempting treats and some interesting-looking vintages I was looking forward to trying.

"I will. See you tomorrow."

He left, and the low hum of Jaxson's voice ended in his office. I glanced up to find him leaning back in his chair, studying me.

"My lady," he quipped. "A moment of your time."

I stood, the silken swish of my skirts brushing against my legs. I sat carefully in front of his desk, the material bunching around me.

"You should have won first prize." Jaxson traced a finger over his lips. "You are stunning."

"I didn't have the wow factor."

"The wow factor?"

I winked. "Everyone was so shocked you dressed up, you have to add in that factor to the equation." I paused. "Why did you? Dress up, I mean?"

He tugged on the cravat, loosening it around his neck. "I overheard you and Michael planning. You sounded so excited, I guess I wanted to be part of that excitement."

His words tugged at my heart. "You made my day."

"That dress made my year." He waggled his eyebrows. "Are you completely historically accurate? Are there stockings and garters, a chemise, and stays all hidden under that satin?"

"How do you know all that?"

He grinned so widely his eyes crinkled and the divot in his chin deepened. A matching dimple, rare and small, appeared to the left side of his mouth. It only happened when he was totally at ease and happy.

"I checked out a few of your books, Gracie." He tutted, shaking his finger. "They are quite risqué for a lady such as yourself."

I felt my cheeks darken. "When did you read them?"

"I was bored waiting for you the night you were out eating cake. I picked up one you were reading." He paused, another wide grin appearing. "I got hooked. I've been reading on my Kindle."

"Oh," I breathed out. "Tell me, Your Grace," I teased. "Have you on smalls under your fine attire?"

Slowly, he shook his head.

My grin matched his. "Nor do I."

He leaned forward, tapping a button on his computer. I heard the soft click of the outer door. He licked his lips, eyeing me lewdly, and spoke in a low, raspy voice.

"Now, you tell me, your ladyship, is that sweet cunny of yours wet for me? Is your pearl aching for my touch?"

"Yes."

He held out his hand. "Then come to me, my wench, and I'll cure the ache."

"I can't be a lady and a wench," I protested, even as I stood.

He winked as he pulled me down on his lap. "You can in my story." His lips hovered over mine. "And I promise you the most satisfying of all endings." He slid his hand under the full skirt, skimming over my legs, pushing them apart. "You are going to spend on my fingers, my tongue, and my cock. You good with that?"

"Oh God, yes. Yes, yes, yes."

Two weeks passed, the time simply disappearing. My days were busy and productive, Jaxson teaching me constantly, entrusting me with more tasks. He was at my place many nights, and we spent most weekends together. He had looked pleased when I offered him a key, pulling me in for a deep kiss as he folded his hand around the shiny metal. He told me he liked the warmth of my place more than the modern edge to his apartment. And although he assured me he had no issues with distracting me in the elevator, he let me know he hated to see how tense I became, knowing we would be stepping inside one.

"I dislike seeing you upset, Gracie," he murmured, stroking my cheek. "The anxiety you feel bothers me so much. I'm not used to feeling empathy like that toward another person," he admitted.

I saw a side to him that no one else did. That no one had ever seen, he assured me. He was funny and sweet. Caring. He worried about me constantly. His intense gaze took in everything, and I often looked up from my work to find his eyes focused on me. Silent conversations happened. Longing, lust, desire flowed between our desks.

And love.

Against everything in me, I had fallen in love with Jaxson Richards. He was nothing like the type of man I thought I would lose my heart to, yet he was perfect for me.

Older, stern, and seemingly unapproachable, the man I knew was vastly different from the reputation he carried with him. He still held back, not yet prepared to share his life or story with me, and I did my best to remain patient. To let him know I was there when he was ready. I hadn't told him yet that I was in love with him, unsure how he would react, but I planned on telling him soon. I hoped he would reciprocate my feelings, although I knew saying them would be harder for him.

Wednesday night, he had a late meeting, and he called when he was finally home.

"Hey," I answered the phone with a sigh, wishing he had come here instead of heading to his place.

"Hello, darling."

It thrilled me when he called me that. Every time, I had the same reaction. He didn't use the term often, but it meant a lot when he did.

"How was the meeting?"

"Tedious. This is going to be a mystery to unravel. The layers in this corporation are multiple and murky. There have been too many gray areas allowed in the past, and now it's a mess. I've never seen so many trademarks and copyrights mixed together and improperly recorded. Neither side is willing to budge. The money is too important to them."

"I'll help."

I could feel his smile. "I know." He huffed out a long exhale of air. "I'm too tired to head over. I'd be no good to you tonight."

I laughed quietly. "Jaxson, you know I don't expect all-night sex marathons all the time."

"But you like them," he replied.

"I like sex with you, but if you came over and wanted to crawl into bed and sleep, I'd be good with that too. I like being with you."

He was silent for a moment, and I let him ponder those words. He was used to one sort of relationship. One that was exactly what he described. Sex. Physical release and nothing else. He was still learning his way through quiet nights, moments spent in each other's presence that were filled with conversation, laughter, soft moments of sharing.

"I like being with you as well," he finally stated.

"Well, that's a good thing."

"This weekend," he asked, "do you have plans?"

"No."

"Good. We're going away."

"Away?"

"Well, sort of. That prize I won at Halloween was for a dinner and one-night stay at the new Bradford Hotel.

Very luxurious. I added a second night, and we're going. I upgraded to a suite."

"Oh, that sounds wonderful."

"You, me, and a whole lot of nakedness," he teased.

"Even better."

"Ah, the suites are on the top few floors. Thirty-five stories. I checked today—the elevators are big and bright. I'll distract you. Are you up for that?"

His words and worry touched me. For a man who insisted he didn't care for other people, he worried far too much about me.

"Yes. At least, I'll try."

"Okay. Friday morning, I'll swing past your place and grab your bag. We can meet in the lobby of the hotel that afternoon."

I hesitated and sighed. "Okay."

"I don't like it either, Gracie, but it has to be this way for now."

"I know," I agreed sadly. He was correct, but at times it hit me. The alternative, however, was far worse. I couldn't imagine Jaxson not in my life.

He yawned, making me laugh.

"I'll see you in the morning."

"I'll make it up," he vowed seriously.

I wasn't sure if he meant not being here or hiding our relationship. I didn't ask either—it was late, and we were both tired.

"Goodnight, Jaxson."

"Sweet dreams, Gracie."

He hung up, and I stared at the phone. I hated the fact that our relationship was shrouded in secrecy. I knew why it was necessary, but I still disliked it.

We were always careful. At the office, we never arrived or left together. At meetings, we sat across from, not beside each other. I usually remained silent, speaking only when asked. I took copious notes for Jaxson and myself, using each meeting as a learning tool. Soaking up the language and nuances of the legal world. We never ate lunch together and kept all our interactions professional. He rarely closed the door when I was in his office so as not to alert Michael to anything.

When we ventured out together, we stuck to small places close to my apartment. We bought groceries and cooked at home. Jaxson loved to cook, and I enjoyed watching him in the kitchen. Precise, organized, and meticulous, he cooked the way he practiced law—with passion and drive. Part of me, the logical part, knew what we were doing was wrong. Sneaking around wasn't the way a relationship worked. But the larger part of me, the part that was entwined with Jaxson, didn't care. The Grace I thought I was fell away. He was all I saw. He was all I wanted. I didn't think about my future, his unshared past, or how we got to where we were. All I wanted or needed was to be in his arms at the end of the day. To make love with him and lose myself. I never felt as much like *me* as when I was with him. He saw through my outward shell and into the real Grace. He knew my fears. He appreciated my intellect. He challenged me. Our discussions were lively and intelligent. He had a wicked sense of humor and made me laugh. I knew I helped him relax. To let him simply be Jaxson. Together, we somehow made sense. I couldn't explain it. I had no idea how my friends and family would react to us as a couple. What my parents would think. Especially my overprotective father. It was hard hiding my feelings and relationship from him, but I knew that was a line I didn't dare cross. Instead, I filled our weekly phone calls with what I had learned, funny stories about Michael, and if I mentioned going anywhere, I let my dad think it was with a girlfriend or alone.

A small part of me wondered if we would ever get to that stage of being open. If Jaxson would ever be comfortable enough, confident enough in us, to present our relationship to the world.

Although Jaxson encouraged me to ask questions, there were two that had never passed my lips. His past and our future.

The unknown responses frightened me too much to risk it, risk us, just yet.

With a sigh, I stood and headed to my bedroom. I had a feeling without Jaxson beside me, sleep would be elusive.

CHAPTER 12

GRACE

F riday afternoon around four, Jaxson strode from his office, tugging on his overcoat. The thick material clung to him, showing off his broad shoulders and wide chest. The heavy fabric hung past his knees. I loved how it suited him, the dark navy color looking good against his skin and hair.

"Michael, I'm out. I have a meeting."

"There's nothing in your calendar."

"It came up earlier. I forgot to jot it in. It's personal." He lifted his hand in a quick wave. "Both of you can leave early. Have a good weekend."

He left, shutting the door behind him, the scent of his cologne remaining behind.

Michael snorted. "Well, that dry spell is over."

"I beg your pardon?"

He busied himself, shutting down his computer, tidying his desk. "*Personal* means he's off with someone. Which means he's found a new lover."

My stomach clenched at those words, which was irrational. The lover was me. Michael didn't know that, though, and he didn't know I wasn't new. But I was curious.

"What makes you think he was in a dry spell?"

He frowned as he tugged on his coat. "He's been different. Restless. Edgy. The way he always gets when he's between, ah, company. It's been getting worse."

"Really? I thought he was that way all the time."

He laughed, switching off his light. "Well, there is that, but he's been different." He stopped in front of my desk. "I've worked for him longer, so I probably know him a little better."

I had to hide my smile. "You're right."

He grinned. "Girl, he told us to head home. What are you doing still sitting there? Let the weekend commence!" His eyes danced. "You got big plans?"

I had no idea what made me say it. "Just spending some time with my boyfriend."

"I didn't know you had a boyfriend."

"I've only been seeing him a few weeks," I hedged. "It's been casual."

"Ooh, and now it's not?"

I shrugged. "Maybe."

He huffed a sigh. "Thank God I'm past that. Dating is too hard. Larry and I are gonna take Abby for her first swimming lesson, and we have his mother coming for dinner on Sunday. Talk about a nightmare. The one thing she approves of is Abby."

I had to laugh. Michael loved sharing his scary mother-in-law stories, although I had a feeling he secretly adored her. "You have fun."

"Oh, I will. You too. You can tell me all about it next week. I'll live vicariously through you."

"I doubt there'll be much to tell. We're both pretty laid-back."

"Damn. You and Jaxson are both too tight-lipped about your personal lives. I never have any fun." He winked. "Although I bet that man is the opposite. Anything but laid-back, if you catch my drift."

"Um, that's our boss," I mumbled, feeling heat flush my cheeks. Jaxson was definitively not laid-back when it came to sex.

Michael's laughter followed him out the door. I slowly tidied up my area, finishing the last few notes on the file I was working on. Jaxson was right—it was an unholy mess. Every time I thought I was making an inroad, another mystery popped up. How it had gotten to this state, I had no idea.

I stood and switched off the light, tugging on my coat. I was going to walk to the hotel and text Jaxson once I arrived. He would meet me down in the lobby and ride up with me in the elevator. I had to admit, I wondered if the fluttering in my stomach was as much nerves at the thought of the elevator as they were the thought of spending the weekend with Jaxson. I planned on telling him how I was feeling. How much I loved him. I hoped that he would realize I meant it and would feel safe enough to talk to me about his life. That we could figure out how to navigate our future. Because I knew, without a doubt, I wanted him there with me. Forever.

My phone buzzed in my pocket as I hurried toward the hotel. I smiled as I answered my sister's call, using her old nickname.

"Hey, Hedda."

She laughed. "Hey, big sis. What are you up to?"

"Um, meeting a friend for drinks," I fibbed smoothly, hating the fact that I would lie to my sister, but knowing it was necessary.

"I won't keep you long. I have no idea what to get Addi and Bray for a wedding gift. Reed is useless with ideas."

"Hey!" he shouted in the background. "I make up for it with bedroom ideas, babe."

I had to laugh. Reed was always cracking jokes, making me laugh. I was certain all the time he spent with Aiden as a kid influenced his odd sense of humor. Heather adored him beyond reason, and they made a great couple.

"I know," I agreed. "Hard to think of something. I know they asked for donations to their favorite shelter in lieu of gifts, which I plan to do, but I want to get them something."

"Me too. Wanna get together tomorrow and do a little shopping? Maybe we can find something and do lunch. I haven't seen you for a few weeks. We need to catch up."

A tremor of guilt went through me. I hadn't seen my sister because I'd been too busy with Jaxson. And now I had to refuse her yet again.

"Sorry, kiddo. I'm working. We have a really intense case and a deadline."

"All weekend?" she asked, sounding disappointed.

"Yeah." I swallowed down the guilt. "How about we meet on Tuesday night for dinner? We can do some shopping after?"

"Okay, that works. Addi called earlier to remind me of the dress fittings on Monday. I'm sure she'll be calling you too."

"You're probably right. We can firm everything up Monday night."

"You want to drive with me? I can pick you up after work."

"Perfect."

"Okay, see you at six?"

"Sounds great."

She hung up, and I arrived at the hotel. I thanked the doorman as he opened the heavy glass door with a flourish. I stepped inside the welcome warmth of the lobby, looking around curiously. Opulent. Decadent. Those were two words that came to mind. Soft music played. A bar was situated in the far corner, the muted sounds of voices drifting across the lobby. Large, deep chairs and sofas were scattered around. The scent of flowers and pine filled the area. I pulled off my gloves, rubbing my hands together. It had turned colder outside, and my walk hadn't been as pleasant as I hoped, aside from the call from my sister. Jaxson would be annoyed that I hadn't taken a cab, so I decided I would wait a few moments before calling him to let him know I was here and warm up. But as I approached a seating area, I saw him. He sat on the other side of the lobby, a drink on the table beside him. He was still in his suit, his tie in place, a newspaper on his lap. As I watched, he lifted the drink to his lips, and his gaze met mine. The arrogant, slightly bored expression left his face as our eyes locked, and a smile played on his lips, the cleft in his chin deepening. I headed his way, slowly tucking my gloves into my pocket, our gazes never leaving each other. It felt as if I hadn't seen him in weeks, not a couple of hours.

The longing, the need to touch him, to feel his mouth on mine was paramount. His hooded gaze told me he was feeling the same way I was, his look of desire blazing my way, making my breath catch.

Then a woman stepped in front of me. "Jaxson? Is that you?"

I stopped, instinctually veering away and taking a seat to the side. I casually unbuttoned my coat, watching surreptitiously as Jaxson spoke with the older woman. He had risen from his chair and shaken her hand, then did the same when the man I assumed was her husband joined her.

"What are you doing here?" she asked.

"Meeting a client," he stated smoothly. "He's staying here but running behind. I thought I'd have a drink and catch up on emails while I wait."

"Oh, do join us for a drink."

"He'll be here any moment."

"I won't take no for an answer. He can meet you at the bar."

"Perhaps another time."

She crooked her arm around his. "You always put us off. One drink. We're heading out to meet friends, so it will be quick, but I must insist."

"Fine."

As they moved past me, he spoke again, while typing on his phone. "It will have to be a fast one. I hate keeping people waiting."

I glanced up from my phone I had pulled from my pocket. A text flashed with a set of numbers.

Jaxson: *3040*

For a moment, I frowned, then a waiter appeared by my elbow. "Drink, madame?"

"Yes, please. A dirty martini. Extra dirty."

I waited until it arrived and signed the bill with the room number Jaxson had sent. I sipped the cocktail in appreciation and scrolled through my phone. The anticipation I had been feeling was flat now, reality biting me in the ass. I was something to be hidden. Even though I knew it was necessary for both our sakes, it still rankled.

My phone buzzed, and I saw Addi's name. I answered, grateful for the distraction.

"Hey, you."

"Hi, yourself. Am I catching you at a bad time?"

I took another sip of my drink, tugging an olive off the stick and chewing it. "No, waiting on a friend. Just having a martini."

"A dirty one?"

"Yep."

"Bad day?"

I chuckled. "What makes you say that?"

"Because you only drink dirty martinis when you're pissed off. Tough day at the office?"

"That's part of it."

"What's the other part?" She paused. "Man trouble?"

I didn't want to get into it with her, but I still felt like talking. "You could say that."

Her voice got too excited. Too inquisitive. "Are you seeing someone?"

I cursed myself. I couldn't say anything to her. She'd ask a million questions. Call my sister, who would call back to pump me. Heather would tell my mom, who would say something to my dad...and *that* was a phone call I had no desire to receive.

"No, some jerk in the office. You know the ego of lawyers. Sometimes the God complex is strong in them."

Disappointment saturated her tone. "Oh. Is he hassling you?"

I looked down, brushing off my skirt. "No, being an asshole."

Pant legs and shiny shoes appeared in my line of vision. I looked up to see Jaxson in front of me, his mouth set in a scowl of displeasure.

"Upstairs," he snapped. "Now."

157

I frowned. "Listen, Addi, can I call you back? My friend is walking in."

"Sure. I wanted to remind you that Cami says the final fitting is Monday."

"Yes, Heather is picking me up. I'll be there." I hung up and picked up my martini. "Your friends gone?"

"I said upstairs."

"I'm not finished my drink."

He took the glass from my hand, draining it in one long swallow. "Now, you are."

I glared at him. "I was enjoying that."

He leaned down, his eyes like ice. "I said *now*."

I stood and petulantly plucked the skewer of olives from the glass, popping them in my mouth. They were the best damn part, and I wasn't leaving them. I followed Jaxson, chewing the salty vodka-soaked bits of heaven and swallowing them. The area by the elevator was busy, and we stood back, waiting for it to thin out.

"God complex?" he hissed at me, staring straight ahead. "Asshole? That's what you think of me?"

"I was just venting to a friend." I couldn't explain to him why I had used those terms. I should never have mentioned anything to Addi at all.

"I didn't expect to see anyone, for fuck's sake," he snarled.

"And I didn't expect to have to sit in a lobby waiting like a hooker for her next job," I snapped back.

He gripped my elbow. "Stop it."

I shook off his grip. "You stop it."

He glowered at me. "You knew going in this was going to be difficult, Grace. We talked about it. You said you understood. Then the first time we're tested, you resort to calling me names?" He shook his head. "I didn't want to go have a drink with them. I wanted to be with *you*. I didn't have much of a fucking choice."

His words struck me, and I heard the underlying hurt in his voice. He was right—on all counts. Shame filled me, but before I could speak, a man pushed past us, hurrying to join the lineup waiting for the elevator.

The last group entered the elevator, and the lobby was clear enough that I could see inside. It was well lit, the walls white marble. As elevators went, it was fairly large, and now that the lobby wasn't so busy, it shouldn't be overly full. Jaxson stood next to me, his anger simmering but still patient. He didn't rush me, instead letting me make the decision. I inhaled deeply, centering my breathing, concentrating on the air moving in and out of my lungs. Our unexpectedly sharp words had thrown me, my reaction had been unusual, and I felt off-kilter. I needed to focus to get on the elevator and get out of the public eye so Jaxson and I could clear the air.

"Ready?" Jaxson's voice was strained and low. Although he was angry, he was being tolerant.

"Yes."

He pushed the button, and a moment later, the doors opened, another large group stepping out. I moved to the side to let them pass, the action separating us farther. I curled my hands into fists as I stepped inside, heading directly to the back corner. Another couple entered, followed by a family. A man in a heavy overcoat brushed past Jaxson, pushing his floor with an impatient jab of his finger. I began to panic until I saw Jaxson beginning to cross the threshold. Then I heard it. A voice calling loudly. "Sir! Mr. Richards! You left your phone!"

Looking startled, Jaxson turned. He held up his hand to the man at the front of the elevator. "Hold the door, please." Then he stepped away to accept the cell phone being handed to him.

The man in the elevator snorted, jabbing at the control panel. "Catch the next one. I don't have all day."

And to my abject horror, the doors slid shut.

CHAPTER 13

GRACE

I looked down, the pattern in the carpet spinning before my eyes. I hadn't prepared properly. I thought Jaxson would be with me. I was already upset over our fight, and the usual panic set in fast. I began to chant in my head, the calming words barely keeping me under control. The walls seemed to close in around me, the air becoming thicker. The sound of Jaxson's shouted curse as the doors had shut echoed in my head. I concentrated on the timbre of his voice bouncing around in my mind. I kept my breathing slow, focusing on one leaf in the carpet. The green was heavily embossed, the detail rich and vivid on the ivory background. I concentrated on that leaf as the doors slid open and people got off, until I realized I was alone in the elevator, and I had no idea what floor it was on. I dared to lift my eyes, horrified to see it had gone past the thirtieth floor and I was headed up to the top floor alone. I managed to peel my hand off the railing and press my floor, then crushed myself back against the wall. I felt the beads of sweat soak the back of my neck as I struggled to remain calm. One couple got on to head back down, and I prayed no one else would call the elevator. After what felt like an eternity, the doors opened, and I found the strength to push myself off the railing and stumble into the hall. I caught sight of myself in the mirror hanging across from the elevator. I was pale and I looked frantic. My legs were shaking, and I grabbed at the table in front of the mirror, sucking in much-needed oxygen. Rushed, heavy footsteps headed my way, and suddenly, Jaxson was there.

"Gracie," he breathed. "Fuck." He wrapped his arms around me, pulling me close. I gulped in his familiar scent. Sank into his warmth. Let him lead me down the corridor, the endless parade of doors going past. We stopped in front of a set of double doors, and Jaxson swiped a card and dragged me inside. He directed me to a sofa, pushing me down gently, pulling off my coat, rubbing my arms, murmuring hushing noises. I heard a strange sound and realized it was me. My ragged breathing was loud in the silent room, and I clapped a hand over my mouth. He knelt in front of me, pushing my hair off my face. "I'm so sorry. Damn it, baby, I'm sorry."

I met his eyes. All I saw were concern and worry, his earlier anger gone. "Jaxson, what you overheard—I was upset and venting, but I shouldn't—"

He cut me off, pressing a finger to my mouth. "It's okay, Gracie. I understand." He gathered me into his arms, settling on the sofa, and I relaxed against him, my breathing slowing, my fear dissipating, and the usual embarrassment settling in.

"I'm fine. I'm so sorry."

"You have nothing to be sorry for. That asshole could have waited five seconds. If I see him in the lobby, he's getting a facer."

His use of the term hit me, making me laugh. "You can't do that," I sighed, resting my head on his shoulder. "You'll have to go to jail, and you're too pretty to be in jail."

He chuckled, pressing a kiss to my head. "Not the start to the weekend I had planned. I was sure by now we'd be on to round two."

I knew he was trying to lighten the mood, wanting to tease me.

"Round two? You're pretty sure of yourself."

"The God complex in me, I suppose," he stated dryly. "All us asshole lawyers have one."

"Oh God, Jaxson," I whispered. "I didn't mean it."

"But you said it. Why are you angry with me?"

"I'm not. I mean, I was—a little. Not mad. Annoyed is a better word. And I know it's silly."

"Tell me anyway."

"I felt—" I huffed, trying to find the right word "—dirty and frustrated, I suppose. Unable to stand beside you, having to pretend I didn't know you. Sitting in a hotel waiting for my lover, unable to even go upstairs by myself. I hated watching you walk away. I hated feeling like I wasn't good enough."

"Don't say that," he snapped. "Stop thinking that way."

"You asked. I was being honest."

Our eyes locked, the tension between us beginning to build again.

"You are worth more than I can say. But for now, we have to be careful. I was trying to protect us."

"Which makes me a secret. Makes us a secret."

He pressed his forehead to mine. "I hate this. I don't get enough time with you, and I don't want to spend it arguing. I know it's hard at times, Grace, but for now, that is how it has to be. One day, it will be different. We'll move on, and this time will be just a blip."

His words surprised me. It was the first glimpse I had that he was thinking of a future with me. I cupped his cheek. "I'm sorry. Between the woman dragging you away and the elevator, I'm tense and jumpy." I ran circles on his cheek with my fingers. "I didn't mean to say you were an asshole."

"And the God complex?" he asked dryly, lifting one eyebrow.

MY SAVING GRACE

"Um…"

He chuckled. "I have been accused of that before. The asshole part, too."

"I didn't mean—"

He cut me off with a swift kiss. "It's fine, Gracie. You had every right to be annoyed. I knew you were upset as I walked across the lobby. You have no idea how incredible you looked, sitting there sipping a dirty martini, your legs crossed and swinging, looking perturbed. You were a fucking siren. Even pissed at me, you were sexy. I wasn't the only one looking either."

"Whatever. I wasn't looking back."

"I know. You didn't even notice. You have no idea how astonishing you are."

I had no response.

He kissed my nose. "I think, darling, we just had our first fight."

I felt tears threatening, but he shook his head. "No crying. We're both under pressure, and it happened. It's all good." He pressed a kiss to my forehead. "I'm more concerned about how you're feeling after what happened in the elevator."

"I'm tense," I admitted. "It always lingers."

I ran a hand over my head. "I hate that what is an everyday, normal thing for people turns into such a

165

MELANIE MORELAND

dramatic event for me. I hate you have to deal with it because of me."

"We all have our elevators, Gracie."

I looked up. "Will you ever tell me yours?"

He stood, taking me with him. "Not tonight. All I want is to figure out how to get you un-tense." He walked into a luxurious bathroom, the marble gleaming under the lights. A massive tub was in the corner. "How about a soak, and we'll order dinner in tonight? No risk of anyone interrupting us then."

"I'd like that."

He set me on my feet. "Good."

"Will you join me?"

He bent and took my mouth, kissing me hungrily. He pulled me against him, his tongue gliding along mine, his hands tight on my waist. He was breathing hard as he pulled away. "Yes. You get in and soak. I'll arrange dinner. Wine?"

"Yes."

"Okay. I'll get a bottle sent up now, and you can have a glass in the tub. I'll be in soon and, ah, wash your back."

"Thank you."

"Anything for you, Gracie. All you have to do is ask."

He turned and walked away. My eyes followed him, my heart wondering if he meant that. When I told him I loved him and asked for him to love me in return, would he still feel the same way?

With a sigh, I turned and began to fill the tub. I couldn't help but wonder if the disastrous start to the weekend was a sign. I shook my head as I began to unbutton my blouse.

I was being silly.

I woke up Saturday morning with Jaxson wrapped around me. One leg was thrust between mine, his arm curved around my waist, holding me close, his large hand cradling my breast. His face was buried in my neck, his warm breath drifting over my skin. Awake, he was warm; asleep, he was an inferno. He had told me he didn't sleep well, yet the nights he was with me, he slept deeply. I was thrilled to bring him enough peace that he could rest.

I shifted a little, recalling last night. The tub and wine had taken the edge off. Jaxson's thorough lovemaking had finished relaxing me. We ordered room service and spent the evening on the deep sofas, sipping wine, staying close. He had recovered his good mood, and I was relaxed. I climbed on his lap, kissing him as he delved his hands under the fluffy robe, his erection pressing against me. I rode him to a shattering orgasm, calling out his name as I came around him.

And now I could feel his cock pressing into my back, awake long before he was. Carefully, I rolled, Jaxson groaning under his breath in protest as I moved away. I studied him in the dim light—his hair tousled and messy from the shower we took before going to bed. His features were relaxed, the stern expression gone as he slumbered. He looked younger, his lips pursed in sleep. The dimple in his chin was prominent. I loved to kiss it, tap it with my finger, tease him about the fact that it could hold a dime easily. He always pretended to be annoyed, but I knew he wasn't. The amused glint in his eyes gave it away.

I lightly ran my hand down his chest, smiling as his muscles contracted under my touch. He groaned low, rolling to his back, still asleep. The blanket tented with his erection, and unable to resist, I pulled back the material, looking at his erect cock. Thick, the perfect length, it was hard and jutting eagerly from his hips. It was so swollen the head was almost purple, and the slit glistened, beckoning me. He moved restlessly in his sleep and breathed my name, making me grin. Carefully, I eased down, hovering over him, then took him in my mouth. His hips surged upward as I licked his shaft, a loud groan splitting the silence of the room. I took him deeper, and his hand flew to my hair as he woke.

"Gracie," he groaned. "What—oh my God, Gracie—"

I sucked, using my tongue as I moved over him. He gasped in pleasure, fisting my hair. "That feels so good, baby. Don't stop. Please don't stop."

I teased and licked, cupped his balls, and swallowed around him. He cried out, his hips moving, low curses, words of praise, pleas of enjoyment filling the room. Jaxson was very vocal during sex. I loved hearing him pant my name, beg for me, tell me what he wanted.

"I'm coming, Gracie. I'm going to come down your throat. You going to take it?" he rasped, his fists tightening in my hair.

I sucked harder and he fell. Gasping, straining, desperate to go deeper. I swallowed as he exploded, the heady feeling of power that came from the intimate act flowing through me. I loved seeing him succumb. Watching him fall apart at my touch.

He collapsed, and I slowly released him, kissing his crown. I lifted my head, meeting his eyes in the muted light.

"Good morning."

He dragged me up his torso, kissing me. "It certainly is."

I snuggled close. "I woke up, and he was already poking me in the back. I thought I'd give him a little relief."

He chuckled. "Horny bugger can never get enough of you." He traced my lips. "Or this spectacular mouth."

I kissed his finger, then playfully bit it. I gasped in surprise as he suddenly rolled, pinning me under him.

"I think, my beautiful Gracie, I need to return the favor. Except you need to come twice."

"Twice?" I asked breathlessly.

He slid his hand between us, his voice low and raspy. "Already so wet. Sucking my cock turns you on, doesn't it?"

"Yes," I admitted. Anything to do with this man turned me on.

"You need this. You need me."

I whimpered as he slipped his fingers inside. "Yes."

CHAPTER 14

GRACE

The day that started so well seemed to unravel as the hours went by. We had breakfast in the hotel room, then Jaxson told me he wanted to go shopping. "I hear there's a great spot about an hour from here. A bunch of little shops that just opened up— like a Christmas village. I know it's early, but this is the first weekend."

"That sounds like fun." I shook my head. "And it's never too early to shop for Christmas. I pick up things all year."

A strange look crossed his face. "I have never bought a Christmas gift."

"Ever?"

"Well, I give Michael a gift card every year. So, I suppose that counts."

I didn't know how to reply. A gift card wasn't the same as shopping for gifts. I waited, hoping he would elaborate. Tell me something of his past. But he remained silent.

"I guess this will be a new experience for you, then," I prodded gently.

"I guess so." He stood and headed to the bedroom. "We should get ready and go."

I followed him, wondering if he would ever open up.

I was tense waiting for the elevator, but with Jaxson's arm firmly around my waist, I stepped in. There were other people in the small space, and he drew me as close as possible, letting me rest my head against his shoulder as he murmured soothing noises in my ear. I remained calm, but I was grateful when we could step out and into the underground parking garage. The drive took longer than an hour, but the scenery was nice, although Jaxson was quiet for the most part. The festive area was easy to find. The stores were all small, home-based businesses selling their wares, and I enjoyed walking around and looking. I purchased a few items, including a lovely set of handblown glasses for my dad for Christmas. He and Maddox would make use of them with their shared love of a good whiskey or scotch. My dad would love them.

I noticed that although we were far from Toronto, Jaxson seemed apprehensive. His gaze swept the crowd often, and his posture was stiff. He wasn't as affectionate as usual. His hand would graze mine but not hold it. He walked a couple of steps in front of me or behind me. He kept his sunglasses on all the time. I suggested coffee at the little outdoor café, and I had no doubt he hesitated before agreeing. I went inside and got the hot beverages, inhaling deeply at the rich aroma. I was sure Jaxson would approve of the brew. I added a couple of their homemade pastries and carried them outside. Jaxson was at a small table in the corner of the fenced-off area, facing the crowd. I stifled a sigh, knowing he was watching in case anyone recognized him. It occurred to me we should have remained in the hotel. He would have been more relaxed, and I wouldn't feel so worried. Guilty that I was causing him more stress. Why he had suggested this outing when it caused him so much anxiety, I had no idea. I sat down, sliding the coffee and pastry his way.

He took a sip, then another. "This is good."

"The owner told me she grinds the beans herself. I thought you would approve. Coffee snob."

A ghost of a smile tugged on his lips. "I simply know what I like." He picked up the pastry and bit down. "Delicious."

I nodded around my mouthful of the buttery treat. The lemon and pastry were perfectly cooked and balanced.

We were quiet as we sipped and munched.

"We should head back," I murmured.

"You can't be finished yet. There are stalls you haven't seen."

"I would rather be in the hotel with a relaxed Jaxson than be here with you so nervous and worried we might be seen together."

He set down his cup. "I'm that obvious?"

"Yes."

"I wanted to give you a nice day. I thought you'd enjoy this place. I heard you telling Michael how much you love the holidays and finding unique gifts." He paused, his voice frustrated. "I guess last night spooked me more than I thought." He reached under the table, finding my hand. "I'm sorry, Gracie. I'm not good company today, am I?"

"No." I squeezed his fingers. "But I understand. I doubt we'll run into someone from the firm up here, though. At least not today. It's just opened, and word isn't out there yet."

"Then we push on."

"Really, I would rather head back to the hotel. I got a few things, and like I said, I am almost done."

He drained his coffee and stood. "I'm going to ask the owner a couple of questions."

I watched him leave, wondering what I would give him for Christmas. Were there rules when it came to a situation such as ours? Did I buy him a gift? From what he said, I shouldn't expect one from him. But that didn't mean I couldn't find him something meaningful that he would like.

Except what would it be? I would have to think long and hard to come up with the perfect gift.

He came out of the shop, a bag of coffee in hand. "Let's keep shopping." He paused. "Please."

I stood. "Okay."

An hour later, I was ready to give up. Jaxson seemed to get edgier as time went along. He no longer even pretended to walk by my side, instead seemingly six or seven steps behind me at all times. He insisted on carrying the bags, and I had a feeling it was the perfect excuse not to hold my hand. His anxiety seeped into me, and I was done. I made one final purchase of a lovely live edge charcuterie board for Addi and Brayden. The wood carver was going to imprint it with their initials and send it to me within a week, so I would have it in plenty of time for their wedding. They loved that style of "grazing," as Brayden called it, and I knew they would love this board. Heather and I could go to one of their favorite stores and fill a bag with all sorts of delicacies for them to serve with the board. It was the perfect gift for them.

"Ready to go?" I asked, forcing a bright smile.

"You haven't finished."

"Yes, I have. I found lots of great things. I'm ready to go back to the hotel."

"I wanted you to have a nice day," he huffed. "I ruined that too, didn't I?"

"Too?" I questioned.

"Last night was a write-off, and now today."

I faced him fully. "I thought we moved past last night. As for today, aside from your anxiety, it has been lovely. I appreciate your bringing me here and letting me shop. I liked spending time with you, so just shut up. Now I want to go back to the hotel and use that big tub again."

"We have dinner reservations."

"Cancel them. We can eat in the suite."

"I wanted to take you to dinner."

"I would rather enjoy a meal in private than have jumpy Jaxson across the table."

"Jumpy Jaxson?"

"You're like a cat on a hot tin roof. Let's accept that it's too hard to be in public and go back to the hotel and enjoy the last few hours we have of the weekend." I winked, trying to make him relax. "Jumpy Jaxson can jump me in private."

He traced a finger down my cheek. "I'm sorry."

"No. No apologies. We need to go forward." I held his hand to my cheek, wishing he would snap out of his mood.

"Then we go to dinner as planned."

I gave in. After all, the restaurant was in the hotel on the twentieth floor.

What could possibly happen?

"Tell me about your cousin," he asked over dinner.

I smiled at him across the table. He was in a deep-gray suit, his shirt snow-white, with a tie of silver and ice-blue that matched his eyes. He was more relaxed than he had been all day. I wasn't sure if it was the wine, the fact that our table was tucked away and private, or if it had been the marathon sex we'd had when we got back to the hotel. Or a combination of all three. Whatever it was, he was charming and sexy, his dark hair hanging over his forehead and his posture relaxed.

"Addi? We grew up in different provinces, but we've been best friends as long as I can remember. I'm older than her, but just by a couple of years. It never made any difference, just like being in different cities. We talked and FaceTimed every day. Spent all our holidays together. She's marrying Brayden Riley—another 'adopted' cousin. I adore him as well. They're made for each other."

"And they're getting married at Christmas?"

"Yes. Addi is president of ABC Corp., and a couple years ago, she found a run-down winery in Port Albany. The company bought it and rebuilt it. She dreamed of getting married there, and now it's happening. She's amazing. She sees potential in places others write off."

"You plan on working there when you pass the bar," he stated, refilling our glasses with the rich red wine.

"I plan on spending time there and at BAM, learning from Bill. He's retiring, and I want to pick his brain."

"You have no interest in working for BAM?"

"No, I want to work for ABC. With my cousins. BAM is too big for me to take on. Our company is young, and I know I can grow with it. Hopefully, whomever Uncle Bent hires to replace Bill will be willing to guide me some as well."

He steepled his fingers, gazing at me. "I see."

"Addi found an odd piece of unused land last year. Ronan and the boys—Aiden's sons—drew up plans, and ABC is going to be situated in Port Albany. I'll be working from there once the building is complete. In fact, Bentley, Aiden, and Maddox are thinking of moving some of the BAM operation out that way as well. They need more space, and Toronto is so expensive and real estate is harder to acquire."

He frowned. "So, you're moving?"

"Eventually, yes."

"You never said anything."

"I wasn't sure if you were interested in the future that far down the road, Jaxson."

He pursed his lips but didn't say anything.

"It's not for a while."

"Where will you live?"

I explained about the BAM Compound. "There is lots of room for more houses. I can live in my parents' place while I decide. They're only there for holidays usually."

"So, your future is all mapped out."

A few weeks ago, I would have agreed with him. But that was before he came into my life. Before he became so important to me. Before I fell in love with him.

"No future is set in stone," I said.

He didn't reply, instead picking up his glass and taking a sip.

"Did I tell you how exquisite you are tonight?" he asked, his voice pitched low.

I blinked at the change of subject. "You said I was lovely."

"That was an understatement. You take my breath away, Gracie."

I felt the color rise in my cheeks at his words. I had worn my favorite dress. Deep red, it had a layered bodice that hugged my torso and a flared skirt that ended at my knees. The neckline dropped off my shoulders, leaving them bare. I wore no jewelry except my usual earrings. I wore heels, which made my legs seem longer than they were, and I had swept my hair up in an elegant French braid, leaving my neck bare. Jaxson's gaze kept traveling over my chest and neck. I could almost feel the heat of his stare touching my skin, and I knew when we got to the room, I would feel his mouth there. It made me shift in my seat a little.

He smiled as if he knew what I was thinking.

I cleared my throat, looking out the window. "The lights look pretty up here."

"Beautiful," he stated.

I glanced over, seeing he was staring at me. I rolled my eyes, and he chuckled.

"Finish your meal, Grace. You need your strength."

I picked up my fork, my appetite for food already satisfied. Another hunger was taking its place. And from the look on Jaxson's face, he was in total agreement.

The elevator arrived, the doors opening smoothly. I stepped in and turned into Jaxson's body. He wrapped his arms around me, holding me tight. We were the only ones in the elevator as the door shut. Jaxson tipped up my chin, his mouth settling over mine, and he kissed me. His intense need was in that kiss, and I lost myself to it. To him. The nerves from the elevator faded away. The fight yesterday, his mood earlier—neither mattered. All that mattered was his mouth. His arms. His closeness. I had never wanted to be that close to a man.

The noise of the door opening broke us apart. Jaxson didn't release me, but he stepped back to allow the group of partygoers to enter. It was obvious they had been drinking, the sounds of their merriment filling the small space. I nestled into Jaxson's arms, my face turned away from the door, facing the large mirror on the back wall. I remained calm, the heat of Jaxson's body grounding me. The partygoers rode up a couple floors, but as they stepped off, one particularly drunk guy ran his hand up the panel, winking at Jaxson.

"A little more time with your woman," he slurred, laughing.

Jaxson cursed, and I shut my eyes. The lurch of the elevator always added to my stress, and we now had more floors of stopping until we got off.

"Hold tight," Jaxson muttered, pressing his lips to my crown. He ran his hands up and down my back in soothing passes. We stopped every floor, the doors opening and shutting. On one floor, as the doors opened, there was the beat of noise, the sound of something odd coming from the hall. Jaxson's body jerked as if he'd been hit, but the doors closed with no one having stepped in with us. Jaxson tensed, his entire frame going stiff, but he didn't speak. His mouth never lifted from my head, his hold on me tightening, his hand pressing my head closer to his chest. When the door opened on our floor, he swept me into his arms and carried me down the hall, still kissing me. In the suite, he carried me to the bedroom. He laid me on the bed, staring down at me. His gaze was tormented. Filled with longing, lust, and pain. Pain I didn't understand. Pain I wanted to erase.

I held out my arms. "I love you, Jaxson."

For a moment, he was frozen. Then he crawled onto the mattress, hovering over me.

"You shouldn't."

"But I do."

He stared down at me, the pain still clouding his eyes. Then they closed, hiding the emotion from me.

"I'll take it," he whispered. "For however long it is, I'll take it."

"Forever," I replied.

"There is only now, Grace. Forever doesn't exist." He covered my mouth with his and kissed me.

I wanted to protest, to tell him there was forever, but I knew not to argue. I would prove it to him. We had time, and I would show him what forever looked like.

But for now, I was lost with him.

Exactly where I wanted to be.

CHAPTER 15

GRACE

Sunday, I woke up, tired and sore. Jaxson had been relentless all night. He was all over me, barely giving me time to recover before he would start again. It was an endless circle of pleasure, and I was as caught up in the vortex as him. I blinked in the late-morning light and turned my head, meeting Jaxson's blue gaze. He looked exhausted, and the odd pain I had seen the night before still lingered.

I cupped his cheek, stroking along his jawline. "What is it?"

"You are so beautiful."

I smiled but shook my head. "Jaxson, what's wrong?"

"Nothing is wrong. I like looking at you."

"You seem worried."

"I'm fine. Your phone has been buzzing the last little while, though. You might want to answer it."

I groaned, covering my eyes with my arm. "What time is it?"

"Just after eleven. I arranged for a late check-out."

"The buzzing would be my dad. He calls every Sunday, and we have 'breakfast' together. I forgot to tell him I wouldn't be around." I flung back the blanket, shivering as the cool air hit my skin. I was forgetting a lot of things these days, it seemed. I grabbed the fluffy white robe and picked up my phone, seeing I had missed four FaceTime requests from my dad plus three messages. I quickly texted him.

> **Grace:** *Dad—sorry. Working on a case in the office. My phone was in my purse. I forgot. Will call when I get home? Love you lots. Gxxx*

His reply came fast.

> **Richard:** *Gracie – I was worried. Spoke to Heather, who said you had a big case. Glad you're okay. We'll do coffee this afternoon instead. Call when you get home and tell your boss you need a day off. Love you, baby girl. xxx*

I sighed, scrubbing my face. I hated lying to the people I loved. Not being able to share with them about something so important to me. I had always confided in my dad and Heather, but I knew I couldn't this time.

Jaxson handed me a cup of coffee. "You all right?"

"Yes." I faced him, deciding to be honest. "I hate lying to them."

He had an odd look on his face. "You won't be for much longer."

I sipped my coffee, waiting for him to elaborate. To tell me he loved me too and we would work this out. Instead, he bent and kissed my forehead. "I'm going to grab a shower. I'll take you home, and you can call your dad."

I watched him walk away, an unsettled feeling coming over me. I expected him to call over his shoulder and tell me to join him. To tease me about what he would do to me in the shower. But he didn't. In fact, he closed the bathroom door, leaving me alone.

The feeling grabbed hold, almost choking me.

Something was wrong.

Jaxson seemed fine when he came out of the shower, a towel draped around his waist. He teased me about moving slow, pushed me toward the bathroom, telling me we had another hour to check out. I showered and dressed, finding him sitting on the sofa, staring at his phone. I felt his anger from the doorway, the deep frown on his face expressing his emotion clearly.

"Jaxson?"

He glanced up, smoothing out his expression. "You ready?" he asked, standing, sliding his phone into his pocket.

"Is everything all right?"

"Yes."

"Who was on the phone? You looked angry."

"No, simply concentrating. The office."

"Can I help?"

He approached me, a tender expression replacing the anger. He lifted up my face and kissed me gently. "No, but thank you. This is something I have to handle on my own."

Our eyes met and held. He hid his feelings well, but I saw the turmoil he was concealing.

"Tell me," I whispered.

He stepped back. "It's fine, Grace. It doesn't concern you. Now, get your bag and we'll head out. You have calls to make, and I have some things to take care of."

He walked away, and the feeling that still simmered below the surface once again rose up, cutting off my breathing. I knew without a doubt he was lying to me.

The question was, about what?

"You look stressed. Are you okay?" My dad's voice was worried, his shrewd hazel gaze seeing too much. Jaxson had dropped me off, stating he had things he needed to take care of. He had kissed me gently, cupping my face.

"I'll call later, Grace."

I didn't fail to notice he had been calling me Grace all day. Not Gracie. He had dismissed me earlier, brushing off my offers of help. He'd been quiet and outwardly calm, but his body was anything but. He held me too tight in the elevator, his arms like a vise around my waist. His grip on my hand was just shy of painful. He was holding in his anger, and he refused to share with me. He refused to share so much of his life with me. I didn't understand what was happening or how to get him to open up to me.

I cupped my jaw in my hand and smiled into the screen, hoping it looked natural.

"I'm fine, Dad."

He narrowed his eyes, the crinkles at the corners only making him more handsome. He was a good-looking man, the silver at his temples adding to his attractiveness, not taking it away. When I was growing up as a teenager, older girls at my school would make comments about my dad when he would pick me up, calling him a DILF. It upset me at the time, but now it made me laugh, remembering his horror when he found out. After that, my mom picked me up more often than he did, and he always remained in the car. My mom thought he was the sexiest man in the world and had no problem telling him or any of their kids that, making us all groan. He had no problem flaunting the fact that she thought that way. They were a wonderful couple, especially given their rocky start. I was lucky to have them as parents, although at times, my dad was a little over the top with his protectiveness.

"What is so important about this case that you're working all weekend? Heather says she hasn't seen you in weeks, and Bent mentioned Addi said the same thing when I spoke to the BAM boys the other day. What's going on?"

I took a sip of my coffee to buy a little time. "First off, both Heather and Addi are busy too. Second, not only am I articling, I'm studying for the bar too. As for this case, it's a mess. Five siblings, all of whom hated lawyers, so they insisted on doing everything on their own, as did their father, who started the company. Contracts, copyrights, trademarks. Except most of what they did was wrong, the copyrights are in a bunch of wrong names, trademarks weren't properly registered." I rolled my eyes with a long exhale. "How they went this long before something major happening is a mystery. Now, one brother died, and his wife is claiming she owns a chunk of the company and the copyrights. The others disagree, and one of them finally decided to hire a lawyer to sort it out. I've been tracing hundreds of copyrights, trademarks—it's a complicated, ugly mess. We're up against a deadline since some of the copyrights are set to expire."

"Is your boss helping at all or leaving it all to you?"

"Of course he is. So is another staff member. The biggest problem is one of the siblings, a sister, claims to have some of the most important documents needed but refuses to hand them over to anyone resembling a lawyer. She calls them all useless, lying wastes of space. She lives in Las Vegas and refuses to cooperate."

"Sounds like a real mess."

"It is." I chuckled. "Every time my boss calls and tries to talk to her, she hangs up on him, after calling him every name in the book. He's started taking notes on some of the unique words and phrases she uses to describe lawyers. He thinks he'll write a book."

My dad threw back his head in laughter. "He sounds like he and I would get along well."

"He is brilliant. I'm learning a lot."

"Is he treating you well?"

I was glad my father was hundreds of miles away and I could control my facial expressions. I shrugged. "He's my boss. I get along well with his PA, Michael. We work well together. And before you can ask, he has a husband and a daughter. We're friends."

My dad studied me. "You look tired, Gracie."

"You said I looked stressed. Which is it, Dad?" I teased. "You, of all people, know you need to make sure your language is correct."

He smirked, one corner of his mouth lifting higher. But I was saved from the inquisition when my mom appeared, sitting down on my dad's lap. Her gentle expression warmed my heart. She was a great mom—loving and giving. She had always been there for me, and I adored her. We all did—especially my dad. Even now, watching how he encircled her waist with his arm, drawing her close, kissing her cheek as she joined in on our call, made me smile.

"Hello, my Katy," he murmured. "I was just asking our daughter why she looked so tired."

My mom rolled her eyes. "Because she's in her twenties, burning the candle at both ends, VanRyan. Exactly the way you used to before you got old and soft."

"I'll show you soft later, woman," he growled.

I laughed. "Ew. Enough, you two. I'm tired because I've been working and studying hard. And frankly, this case keeps my mind engaged even at night, so I haven't been sleeping as well as usual. I plan on a nice nap this afternoon. No work."

My mom's eyes lit up. "Have a soak in the tub. Try those lavender salts I sent you. You'll sleep like a baby."

"Talk about false advertising," Dad snorted. "Babies hate sleep. They're up all the time. What they should say is you'll sleep like a parent of a six-month-old who's had colic and has been taken out of the house by a helpful grandparent."

Both Mom and I spoke up. "Not as catchy." Then we all laughed. Dad had said that line a thousand times.

"Try them," she urged.

I couldn't tell her having a bath would remind me of earlier this weekend when I was soaking in that massive tub with Jaxson. Being held by his strong arms. Feeling completely happy to be alone with him and enjoying the quiet. I wasn't able to tell her the real reason for my stress. I couldn't tell anyone.

"I will," I promised.

Mom asked a few more questions, and we chatted about the wedding and the fact that I would see them soon. "I'm looking forward to Christmas," she exclaimed. "The girls and I have so much planned!"

I smiled at her excitement. We were part of a huge extended family, and we spent most of our Christmases in Port Albany. Mom and all the BAM wives spent weeks cooking, baking, and decorating every year, and every year it was wonderful. This year would be doubly crazy with the wedding. "Me too," I said.

"Will you have time off?"

"Yes. I had explained to the partners about the wedding when they interviewed me, so I have the vacation time I'm allowed booked already. I'll come down before the wedding and stay until after New Year's."

"Wonderful. We arrive the week before." Mom stood. "We'll see you soon, dearest girl. I love you."

"Love you too."

Dad watched her walk away with a small grin on his face, then he turned back to the screen. He leaned close, resting his arms on the table. "If you need anything, baby girl, I'm right here."

"I know, Dad."

"I mean it, Gracie. I know life is crazy for you, but I don't like to see you so worn-out. Anything you need, I'm right here. Or I can be there in a few hours. You just say the word."

Unexpected tears filled my eyes. My emotions were raw today after the ups and downs of the weekend with Jaxson, and the niggle of worry I was feeling deep in my stomach.

"Gracie?" Dad sounded shocked. "Are you crying?"

I wiped my eyes. "You caught me off guard, Dad. I'm so grateful to have you in my corner."

"I always will be."

"I know," I sniffed. "I love you."

His voice became quiet. "I love you, Gracie-girl. You're my little miracle, and you always will be." He met my eyes, the distance between us fading away. "You're sure you're okay?"

"I'm fine. It's the case, the wedding, and Christmas. You know how I get."

He chuckled. "Tenderhearted like your mom. She saw a Hallmark commercial the other day, and I found her in the pantry, weeping."

"Yep. Just like her."

"Okay. I'll drop it. But I'm here."

"Thanks, Dad."

There was a quiet knock on my door around six, startling me. Before I could get up from my chair, I heard the sound of a key being turned, and Jaxson's face peered around the edge of the open door.

"Hey," he greeted, his eyes wary. "Can I come in?"

"Of course."

He slipped in, shutting the door behind him. He had a brown bag in one hand, which he held up.

"Have you eaten?"

"No."

He shrugged off his coat and kicked off his shoes. He was wearing my favorite Henley—the blue setting off his eyes. He placed the bag on the table and crossed the room, bending down and meeting my eyes as he braced his arms on the chair.

"I wondered if I'd find you in your spot. Curled up and reading." He smiled, although it didn't reach his eyes. "When I think of you, it's often of you sitting right here, looking like this."

"Like this?" I asked lightly.

"Content and happy, a book on your lap, a cup of tea beside you. You always drink tea when reading, never coffee."

"They drink tea in historicals more than coffee. I'm keeping in the mood."

He pressed his lips to my forehead. "Well, break out of the mood for a bit and eat noodles with me. I went to Rocking Ramen."

"Okay."

He nodded and stood. "Stay there. I'll bring the food over."

I watched him carefully. He seemed like Jaxson, except for the tautness in his shoulders, the stiff way he was moving. As if he were holding himself in.

He brought over the bag, setting it on the table. He went to the kitchen, returning with bowls and some utensils. He set out the soup and spring rolls, ladling the hot, steaming broth into bowls and adding all the accompaniments they had sent. He handed me the bowl. "Eat."

We were quiet for a moment, enjoying the flavorful soup. He held out the spring rolls, and I took one, munching on it.

"What did you do today?" he asked.

"A little grocery shopping, some laundry. Not much."

"Did you talk to your dad?"

"Yes." I finished my spring roll. "How was your day?"

He sighed and set down his bowl. "I'm sorry I had to leave so fast. Sometimes I get called in to consult on another lawyer's case. This one is, ah, very delicate and personal. I couldn't include you."

"Someone at the firm."

His mouth pinched and his fists clenched. "Yes. It's fucking bullshit," he spat, then stopped, shutting his eyes. "I can't say anything else."

"I understand."

He studied me, and I noticed how dull his eyes looked. "Thank you." He paused. "I wasn't sure you'd let me in tonight or agree to have supper with me."

"Still, you came," I replied.

"I was worried you were upset and you wouldn't eat. I wanted to make sure you did."

His quiet care warmed my chest, easing some of the ache. Whatever was happening with the other lawyer at the office had to be bad, and he was clearly distressed over it. It explained the sudden shift in him this morning. He had switched into business mode.

"Of course I would let you in, Jaxson. I was confused but not angry."

"What if you were angry at me? What then? Would you listen or walk away?"

I frowned. "If I were that angry, I would hope I would listen and give you a chance to explain." I lifted my shoulder. "My mom has always said I am the most forgiving person in the world. I don't get mad often, and I'm quick to let things go."

He picked up his soup. "I'm not surprised." He paused. "Can I stay, Gracie?"

"If you want to."

"I do. Please."

I reached out my hand, and he took it. "Yes."

CHAPTER 16

GRACE

When I woke up Monday morning, Jaxson was gone. It wasn't unusual since he always went home and changed, but it was only four. He had left earlier than usual. He had been quiet most of the night. Reflective. We sat together on the sofa, and he had me read a few paragraphs aloud to him, laughing under his breath about the new dashing, arrogant duke I was reading. I paused while reading the physical description of my newest crush.

"None compare to how handsome you were when you dressed up on Halloween."

He chuckled.

"You slipped into that role so well. The haughty duke hiding his true nature, smitten with one look from the heroine. You often have a lot of the same traits."

He was clearly amused. "Is that a fact?"

"Yes. The Duke of Bainbridge, for example. Arrogant and cold to those around him, but different with his new wife."

He cocked his head, trying not to laugh at my description.

"Is that how you see me?"

"I think so."

"And this duke of yours, is he forever to remain cold?"

I sighed. "No. That is the wonderful part. When he admits his love." I flipped through the well-read pages. "'Of course, I love her. What man could not fall in love with her? She is bold and beautiful, witty and wonderful. She is fearless and determined. I stand in awe of her,'" I read, enthused. "And that is only when he is telling his brother. It gets even better when he declares his love to her."

"I know how he feels. I am in awe of you, Gracie," he said quietly, his eyes meeting mine. For a moment, there was a beat of silence, then he cleared his throat and studied the spine of the book, "Scarlett Scott. She's one of your favorites?"

"Yes—my top one, in fact. I adore her. We're starting a book club at ABC and BAM. We're going to start reading together and discussing. I suggested the Heart's Temptation series to start."

He shook his head. "I fear for the men of BAM and ABC."

I waggled my eyebrows. "Count yourself included."

He stood, swinging me up in his arms and carrying me to the bedroom, his mouth on mine the whole way. I recalled how different our lovemaking was. Jaxson was quiet, intense. His passion was a slow-burning ember simmering along my skin. He was gentle and slow, drawing out my pleasure, keeping me on the edge until I was begging for him. He kissed me endlessly, his lips never far from mine. He held me tightly after, stroking his hand through my hair, whispering my name. I was almost asleep when I heard his low voice.

"Say it, Gracie. I need to hear it."

"I love you," I whispered.

He pressed a kiss to my head and held me tighter. He didn't respond, but I knew it would take time. He held me until I fell asleep in his arms.

I realized it was the first time he'd ever left without kissing me goodbye. The only night I could think of in our relationship he hadn't woken me in the darkness to make love before the morning.

He'd been different all evening.

But at least he'd been here. Nothing else mattered as long as we were together.

Laughter rang out in Cami's large studio in Port Albany. It felt good to forget about everything else and concentrate on Addi and the wedding. Seeing how happy she was bolstered my spirits, and I was able to join in on the merriment. Married to my uncle Aiden, Cami Callaghan was a talented designer. The open space of her loft echoed with mirth. Wide-planked wooden floors, golden and warm with age, creaked as we moved around, waiting for our turn to be checked over by Cami's critical eyes. The whitewashed walls held bolts of fabric in all colors, like rainbows painted in bright hues. Her workstation held no fewer than three computer screens, a large drafting board, and hundreds of pieces of paper. Cami loved to draw her designs, often struck by inspiration and needing to get the lines down on paper. She used computer software as well, but she preferred how her visions flowed onto paper under her favorite brand of pencil. Aiden made sure she always had some at the ready. He was inordinately proud of his wife and all she had accomplished. Her small design company was sought after, and she kept her client list short. Brides and elegant gowns were her specialty, although I had a few of her day dresses in my closet as well.

I sipped my champagne, watching as Heather turned slowly for Cami, the pretty ivory of her dress highlighting her coloring. The dress was simple but perfect. With a heart-shaped neck and jagged hemline that swirled around her legs, it suited her personality. Cami nodded and clapped her hands. "Perfect." She grinned. "That's three down. Gracie, your turn."

I stepped up to the platform, looking in the mirror. My dress was a soft, delicate gold color. The neckline was scooped, the lacy sleeves hanging off my shoulders. The bodice was formfitting, and the skirt hung from my waist in a long swath of material. A deceptively simple dress, the material flowed and draped. As I walked, the skirt parted to form a sort of train behind me, showing off the deeper gold lining underneath. I felt like a princess in it.

Except Cami frowned. She pinched in the waist with her fingers. "Gracie, you've lost weight. It's too loose."

I pursed my lips in vexation. I knew I had lost a little. Between work, Jaxson, and my worries the last little while, I hadn't been eating as well as usual.

"Sorry. I'm so busy I forget."

She looked at my reflection, concern written across her face. "Are you all right?"

"I'm fine," I protested, not liking how everyone seemed to be looking. "I've just been so busy."

Cami picked up her pins as Heather approached me. She stood next to me, eyeing me critically. Before she could say anything, I held up my hand. "Don't say it."

"I was going to say you look okay—tired maybe, but okay."

"Hours of research on this case, is all," I said. "It's a monster. Plus, studying for the bar. All I seem to do is read. And not the fun kind. Instead of dukes and rakes, it's all facts, figures, and legal stuff."

That changed the subject, and everyone started talking about the book club idea. I suggested the first series, and we agreed to start in January once the wedding was over, this case was done, and life had returned to something resembling normal.

Cami made her adjustments and met my gaze. "Try to remember to eat, Gracie. Aiden could recommend some protein drinks that would give you the right supplements and calories."

"I'll call him."

She smirked. "I already did. He is going to drop some off to you tomorrow morning before you leave with Heather to go to work."

I had to smile. There was no doubt he would drop them off, give me a lecture, and finish off with one of his tight bear hugs.

"Thanks, Cami."

She winked. "It's what we do. Family, you know." She stepped back. "Okay, you're done. Don't lose any more."

"I'll try." I had my mother's slight frame and her habit of losing weight when stressed. Heather was more like my dad, slightly taller, with a slim, athletic build. We resembled my mom, although Heather had my dad's hazel eyes that seemed to see everything. She was more outgoing than I was, her exuberance in embracing life evident. Her boyfriend, Reed, suited her well, his teasing nature meshing with hers. She had been filled with news, happily chatting in the car as we drove to Port Albany.

"Reed will drive you home if you want," she offered. "But I assumed you'd stay the night and drive in with me in the morning."

"That was my plan."

I knew we'd be having champagne while trying on dresses, and I wouldn't want her to drive after or for Reed to have to make the trip in and out when I could stay in the guest room at her place. She and Reed had one of the newer houses in the BAM Compound, set up close to the woodlands. They loved to hike and picked the spot for the farther distance to the water and the close proximity to the trails. Heather preferred woods to water, although she loved the view. Swimming wasn't her thing, but hiking was. I always thought it was because she could grab a pencil from her backpack and sketch, whereas while in the water, she couldn't.

Luckily, she'd been too busy talking to ask me too many questions. It had been a strange day with Jaxson running cold again. He'd barely spoken to me except about the case we were working on. He shouted in anger after Helen Fraser, the sister of the Fraser siblings in Las Vegas, hung up on him again, refusing to help. He stormed from his office, slamming out the door, muttering about getting a summons and forcing her to cooperate. He was calmer when he returned, but there was still no personal contact. He often sent a text during the day or a short message to let me know he saw me. He would comment on my outfit or hair, or send a line saying something sweet.

Good job, Gracie.
You're beautiful.
I can't wait until tonight.

But my personal phone stayed silent all day. He knew I was going to Port Albany tonight and that I would be staying over. I had frowned when Michael updated his calendar and I saw he had meetings that ran late into the evening both tonight and on Tuesday. That meant Wednesday would be the first chance I would have to talk to him, see him. It felt like an eternity. I was surprised how much his presence filled my life, even if we had to remain hidden. My apartment seemed empty without him there. My life felt brighter when he was with me.

I changed back into my regular clothes, and we sat around chatting, enjoying one another's company. Sitting beside Heather, I felt a moment of sadness as I watched Cami hug her daughter, Ava. Maddox's wife and Brayden's mom, Dee, chatted with his sister, Shelby. Emmy was married to Bentley, and she sat between her daughters, Addi and Chloe. I missed my mom, and I was looking forward to seeing her soon. She gave the best hugs, and I needed one of them. I needed her guidance, even if I couldn't tell her everything. Maybe I could tell her enough that she would be able to help me. Heather and I exchanged a glance, and I knew she was having the same wistful thoughts of our mom. I wrapped my arm around her shoulder, kissing her head. She grinned and elbowed me in the side, teasing me for being sentimental, but I knew she liked it. I adored my adopted aunts and uncles, and was close to my "cousins." I knew my family was unusual, but it worked for us.

Back at Heather's, I got ready for bed, sliding into the cool sheets. I stared at the ceiling, startled when my phone chimed with a message.

Jaxson: *I hope your evening went well.*

I replied.

Grace: *Yes. Dresses are lovely. Meeting productive?*

Jaxson: *Can't be as lovely as the woman wearing it. Meeting went fine. Appointment at courthouse on Wed at 3. Need you with me.*

That little tidbit made me happy. It meant I would be with him most of the afternoon and he would no doubt come home with me.

Grace: *Okay*, I sent back.

Jaxson: *Sleep well.*

I waited, but nothing else came through. I sighed as I rolled to my side. Something big was happening at the office that he hadn't yet shared with me. I knew there was a chance he never would, given that it had to involve someone at the firm. His door had been shut a lot, and I heard the deep timbre of his voice on the phone a great deal of the time. I needed to be patient and understand the fine line he was walking. That we both were. We could discuss it on Wednesday in private.

The client stood and shook Jaxson's hand. "Thanks, Jaxson. You made this much easier than I expected."

Jaxson waved him off. "You had all the ammunition. It only had to be sorted. You can thank Ms. VanRyan for her efforts."

I smiled as Mr. Waters turned to me. "Thank you, Grace."

"You're welcome. I'm glad things worked out."

He nodded. "Now everything is settled, I can retire, knowing the company is in the right hands." He slipped on his coat. "You'll send the bill to my assistant?"

Jaxson smirked. "Of course. It will arrive promptly."

Mr. Waters chuckled. "I would expect nothing less."

He left, and I gathered up the file as Jaxson jotted down some last-minute notes. My stomach clenched as I watched him, his bold script filling up the page. He'd been stranger than normal the past two days. Not cold, not angry.

Indifferent.

There had been no more texts. No contact at all. In the office, he was polite, distant. He hadn't raised his voice once. Even Michael noticed that he was off.

"Whatever his weekend plans were, obviously, they didn't work out," he muttered at one point. "He's worse than usual this way. I'm waiting for the explosion."

I had to agree.

I slipped the file into my case and waited for Jaxson to speak. To give me a clue. I looked around the small antechamber. There were many of them in the courthouse. Places where lawyers could meet with their clients in private. The rooms were simple, equipped with a table and chairs, soundproofed for discretion. This one was tucked into the back, close to the exit. I hadn't been in it until now since Jaxson usually chose one close to the courtroom instead.

Jaxson closed the folder and screwed the cap on his pen. He loved expensive pens and had a small collection of preferred ones. He set it carefully on top of the folder and sat back, his hands folded together on top of the table. His posture was tense, his shoulders set back, rigid and straight. I found myself mirroring his posture, unease winding up my spine. He lifted his gaze, his blue eyes calm and vacant.

"Jaxson?" I asked.

"Grace," he began, the tone of his voice sending a shiver down my spine. "I doubt what I'm about to say is going to come as a shock to you."

I knew that tone. I'd heard him use it with judges. Fellow lawyers. Clients. It was removed, cold. Final.

"Jaxson," I whispered. "No."

"We're done."

Those two words cut through me, piercing my core with an intensity that burned. I was stunned.

"Done," I repeated numbly.

He drummed his fingers on the table. "We should never have begun. It was a mistake."

"Mistake," I echoed, unable to process any other words but the ones he was stating.

"Yes. I let my baser needs cloud my judgment."

There was a beat of silence. "I don't understand."

"Yes, you do, Grace. You're a beautiful woman. I wanted you. Sex with you was epic. But—" he waved his hand in a dismissive action "—now it's complicated. I don't do complicated."

I found my voice. "You're saying all that was between us was sex?"

A fake smile crossed his handsome features. It was as cold and dismissive as his tone. "I admit I was drawn to you. But you're…too much."

"Too much." Once again, I repeated his words.

"The elevator thing. The clinginess. Playing house. Having to look after you. It's tiresome."

My heart broke at his words. Without even trying, he had hit all my weaknesses. I hated my fear of enclosed spaces. I was independent, but I did love to be held. I had especially loved being held by him. I hadn't considered the time we spent together as playing house, and I had thought he wanted it as much as I did.

How had I read this so wrong?

"I told you before I wasn't interested in forever. I don't believe in it."

"Is this because I told you that I loved you?"

"I already knew you thought you did. It's a phase, Grace. You see me as some sort of hero—the same way you do your father. Neither of us is. And with time, you'll see that. You'll find a nice guy to settle down with, and I'll just be a memory."

His casual reference to my father jolted me as much as his opinions. "You think I'm that shallow?"

"No, I think you're that *young*."

His statement hurt. I knew he was more experienced. Older. That had never mattered until this very moment as he sat there calmly, breaking my heart.

"You said you cared. You said you wanted to explore this."

"I've *explored* it as much as I want." He laughed lightly, the sound sharp in the room. "You should congratulate yourself. You lasted longer than most."

My breathing stuttered in my throat. I was only a passing moment to him. He had gotten all he wanted, and now, I was a regret.

"You can go to the partners if you choose. Tell them I've harassed you."

"Do you really think I would do that? Ruin your career out of spite?"

He shrugged, nonplussed. "I would move on. There are lots of firms willing to look the other way to get my expertise on their payroll."

I had seen Jaxson in full lawyer mode. Cold, removed, and dangerous. It was nothing compared to the icy man in front of me. I barely recognized him.

"I wouldn't do that."

"Then I'll ask Lynn to take you on early when she gets back next week. No one will think twice. I've passed on interns and students early before now. I'm sure you'd rather not be in my company every day any more than I want to see you daily. It would be best for both of us."

Somehow, that statement hurt more than I expected. He didn't want to see me anymore. At all.

"Jaxson, don't do this. Talk to me. Please."

His voice was cold. Clipped. "I am talking, Grace. *You're* not listening."

"I don't understand."

He waved his hand in a dismissive gesture. "You were a great distraction, but too much work. You've outlived your usefulness to me—at least personally. How you decide to go forward business-wise is up to you. Does that make it plain enough?"

Distraction. Too much work. His hurtful words bounced around in my head. They echoed and screamed, hitting every insecure nerve I kept hidden, tearing them wide open, flooding my senses with pain.

He stood, indicating his time was over.

My time was over.

"I booked the room until six. You can sit here for a while if you need it. I have to go. I have other meetings."

I was unable to speak. He'd chosen this spot to break it off with me. Somewhere private and secluded, late in the day. If I had gone berserk, no one would have heard. He had planned it well.

"Erase my personal number from your phone," he stated firmly. "I won't be using it anymore."

With shaking fingers, I slid it from my pocket and did as he instructed. It took every ounce of my strength not to fall apart, not to beg him to reconsider. One thing I knew about Jaxson Richards was that once he made up his mind, he rarely ever changed it. I summoned my pride.

"I want my key back."

He regarded me impassively. "I left it on the hook before I went home last time."

Shock tore through me. He'd known even then that he was going to break things off with me. Still, he'd made love to me one last time. One last epic fuck for him. One last time to use me for what he wanted. Because Jaxson Richards always got what he wanted.

He narrowed his eyes and dug into his pocket. He slid a crisp fifty-dollar bill my way. "Take a cab home, Grace. I don't need you collapsing on the street on my conscience."

I stared at the money with distaste. I stood slowly, reaching for my coat. I tugged it around my shoulders, grateful that my hands didn't shake anymore. Anger was replacing the hurt, rage slowly dripping down inside me.

"Contrary to your low opinion of me, Jaxson, I can take care of myself. Fifty dollars for a cab is unnecessary and unwanted."

"Buy yourself something for dinner, then." He pushed the bill closer.

I shook my head. "That smacks of you taking care of me, Mr. Richards. You said you were tired of it. And frankly, I'm beginning to feel like the hooker you insisted I was not. I don't need or want your money."

"Stop being so stubborn."

"Stop telling me what to do. Outside of office hours, you no longer have that right."

"You're making me angry, Grace."

"Really? Then you know how I feel right now. And frankly?" I summoned my outrage, channeling my mother. I met his eyes, the Jaxson I loved gone, and in his place, a cold, uncaring man I didn't recognize.

"You can go fuck yourself, Richards."

I walked out of the room before he could respond and hurried away.

Before I collapsed. I prayed I would make it to the privacy of my own home before that happened.

CHAPTER 17

GRACE

Anger kept my shoulders back and my head high as I hurried from the courthouse. I ignored the cabs lined up outside and headed to the bus stop, refusing to give in to the emotions bearing down on me. I kept my mind blank as I stood, staring out the window as the bus slowly made its way to my stop. I clambered down the stairs at the corner and walked toward my apartment block, my legs beginning to shake as the adrenaline rush faded.

My hands trembled as I tried to get the key in the lock, finally using both hands to accomplish the simple task. Inside, I dropped my coat and kicked off my boots. I looked closely at the key holder, seeing for the first time that Jaxson's key was hanging on the end. In plain sight, yet I hadn't seen it.

I hadn't seen so many things.

I stumbled to the sofa, grabbing the blanket from the arm and wrapping it around my body. I felt ice-cold and out of control, my limbs shaking, my teeth chattering. I knew I was in shock. Filled with disbelief over what had just occurred.

Then anger took over. But it wasn't directed at him. It was toward myself.

I had fallen for the oldest trick in the book. The boss and his assistant. A tawdry affair. His sweet words and kind gestures had all been part of an act. One I had fallen for. I had allowed him into my life, pushed aside the quiet doubts and thoughts that plagued me. Neglected family and friends for him. Let him lead me blindly. I was furious. I knew better. I was smarter than that. My parents hadn't raised an idiot, yet I had acted that way over Jaxson. Given him the power to hurt me. As soon as I told him how I was feeling, he was done. I thought of his hurtful words. He knew me well enough to use the ones that would wound the deepest.

I burrowed farther under the blanket. I thought of his mood swings. The aloof face he presented to the world that I thought was the false one, when really, the one he had shown me in private had been the lie. He didn't care. I had been fun—until I was too much effort to bother with any longer.

I curled up into the corner of the sofa, his words echoing in my head.

Too much work.

Distraction.

Explored as much as I want.

Lasted longer than most.

Hero-worship. Like your father.

I did hero-worship my father. I adored him. But I had never thought about Jaxson as someone to save me. I didn't need saving. I didn't need a hero. I needed him— as a lover, a friend, and a partner.

I had been so blind.

Pain and rejection hit me all at once. I had allowed Jaxson's lies to lull me into a false sense of security. I had actually believed that we had a future.

The truth was we never did. He never planned it. In my naïveté, I had thought what we shared was special.

It turned out to be anything but.

I turned my head into the cushion and let the tears flow.

I woke in the morning, stiff and sore. I had fallen asleep on the sofa and had stayed there all night. I woke several times, my face wet with tears, crying myself back to sleep. I sat up, rubbing my face, traces of mascara showing on my palms. I knew I must look terrible. I staggered to the bathroom, showered and washed my hair, feeling more human once I was dressed. It was just after eight when I called the office, steeling myself as Michael answered.

"Jaxson Richards's office."

"Michael, it's Grace."

"Hey, girl. You running late?"

"Um, no. I have a terrible migraine. I-I won't be in today."

He was instantly sympathetic. "Oh no. Larry gets those. Dark room, medication, and a cold compress is what you need. Want me to bring you some soup?"

His kindness brought tears to my eyes, and I had to clear my throat. "No, I'm good."

"All right. I'll check in with you later." He lowered his voice. "Do you need to talk to the bear?"

My breath caught in my throat at the thought of speaking to Jaxson, but I managed to remain calm. "No. If he needs something, you can email me."

"Okay, take care."

He hung up, and I stared at the phone. I picked up the cup of coffee I had made, sipping it. I grimaced when I realized I hadn't added any sugar, but I drank it anyway. Listlessly, I stared out the window, feeling lethargic and empty. I watched the streets out front get busier, not moving or caring. Until I picked up the cup of coffee for another sip and realized it had gone cold. I glanced at my phone, shocked to see I had been sitting for two hours, staring into space. Instantly, anger tore through me, and I stood.

I wasn't going to allow Jaxson Richards and his selfishness to destroy me. I was Grace-fucking- VanRyan, and I was my father's daughter. He taught me to be strong. To stand up for myself. I refused to let someone else destroy me. With a defiant toss of my head, I straightened my shoulders.

It wasn't that I was too much.

He wasn't strong enough for *me*. *He* wasn't worthy.

And that was how I was going to get through this.

Hours later, I sat down, looking around and feeling pleased. My apartment was spotless. My laundry done. I had caught up on emails, chatted via text to Addi and Heather, smart enough to know if they spoke to me, they would know something was wrong. I made arrangements to meet Heather on Saturday so we could buy items to complete the charcuterie board for Addi and Brayden. I was going to be fine by then. I was already feeling better.

Then I planned my future. Jaxson Richards was right. He was a blip. But he was wrong about one thing. He was the mistake—not me. I wasn't going to allow him to screw up my career the way he messed up my head. If he thought I would allow him to dictate what I did and did not do in that regard, he had better think again.

I smiled grimly as I got ready for bed. I was sure he assumed I wouldn't come in the rest of the week. That he would speak to Lynn and never have to deal with me again.

He had a surprise in store for him. An even bigger one than what he dropped on me.

And he wasn't going to like it.

I was at my desk the next day by seven thirty. I dressed carefully, my hair perfect, my makeup covering up the dark circles under my eyes. I looked tired, but it was easily explained by the migraine I had claimed to have had the day before.

Michael looked surprised to see me when he walked in, asking solicitously about my head. I assured him I felt much better. I indicated Jaxson's closed doors. "Not in yet?"

Michael shook his head. "He texted me last night about a meeting outside the office this morning. I had to rearrange his schedule."

"Ah."

He rolled his eyes. "Girl, you picked a good day for a migraine. He was on a tear of epic proportions. I haven't seen him that bad since…well, I can't remember."

"Sorry I missed it," I stated sarcastically.

"The yelling, the cursing, and the slamming of the door." Michael sighed. "It was constant. He had a fight with no fewer than two lawyers and at least three clients."

I lifted my eyebrows in surprise. Jaxson was known for arguing with fellow coworkers. He was usually more circumspect with clients.

"Must have been having a bad day." Personally, I hoped it was terrible.

"No doubt."

I turned to head back to my desk when the door to the office opened, and Jaxson strode in. His face was like thunder, his eyebrows drawn down, his mouth set in a frown. He startled seeing me.

"Grace."

I walked past him with a nod. I picked up my coat, ignoring him. "Michael, I am going to get coffee at the Hive. You want one?"

"Oh, a latte, please," he replied, answering the phone.

I grabbed my wallet. "Okay." I brushed past Jaxson. "Excuse me."

"Nothing for me, thanks," he snarled, his voice low.

I paused, meeting his eyes. Icy blue irises glared at me. I frowned benignly. "I'm sorry, Mr. Richards. I assumed if you wanted something, you'd have gotten it already. You're good at looking after yourself."

I swept from the office before he could reply. I hurried to the stairs, ignoring the way my heart had picked up when I saw him. I refused to acknowledge the fact that he looked even more tired than I felt. That there had been a flare of something in his eyes when he saw me.

I had to remember that, as of Wednesday, we no longer mattered to each other.

I wished my heart had gotten that message.

I drained my coffee and drew in a deep breath. Michael was busy in the file room, and Jaxson and I were alone in the office. I approached his door and knocked.

"In."

I entered, and he looked up, surprise flitting across his face when he saw it was me. We had been careful to avoid each other all day, using Michael as our unknown intermediary. He was used to Jaxson's whims, so it didn't throw him that suddenly all my work lists were being handed to him first today. He simply rolled his eyes and kept going. I was grateful for his lack of curiosity.

"Yes, Ms. VanRyan?" Jaxson asked, his voice cool. Removed.

I sat across from him, crossing my legs. It was not a fluke I was wearing the pants he loved to despise and the blouse that drove him to distraction. He could pound sand over my wardrobe choices from now on. I matched the tone of my voice to his, keeping it cool and detached.

"I don't want to be transferred to Lynn."

"I beg your pardon?"

"I applied to this firm to work with you. I wanted to learn from you. Despite everything else, you have taught me a great deal, and I want to continue with that."

"Perhaps I don't want to continue."

I lifted my shoulders. "Frankly, I don't care. You agreed to mentor me. I have a short time before I leave on holidays and two months left with you when I return. If I can be an adult and stand being around you, you can do the same thing. As you pointed out the other day—" I smiled without warmth "—you are far more mature than I am. Surely that should be easy for you."

He studied me for a moment. "Are you certain that is what you want?"

I embraced my anger and met his steely gaze with one of my own. "No. I want to be as far away from you as possible. I don't want to see you—ever. But this is my life. My future. You may have fucked me over personally, but I won't allow you to do that to my career. People will talk. Question why you sent me away. I won't have that following me as I begin my law career." I tapped his desk. "You are going to be a professional and treat me the same way. I don't give a damn if you don't want to. You owe me that at least."

His gaze turned even frostier. "You think I owe you?"

"We both know you do. You talk about respect and the law all the time. Show me the same courtesy."

For a moment, I was certain he was going to refuse. Then he nodded. "Fine. I expect you to do your job well."

I stood. "I expect you to be a decent human. I think one of us will have more difficulty in meeting the other's expectations." I strode to the door, turning as I grabbed the handle. I looked over my shoulder. "I'll be using my study time this afternoon. I won't see you again today. Have a good weekend."

Something almost like pride flitted across his expression, then his face once again became impassive.

"Good night, Grace."

I shut the door firmly behind me and gathered my things before I left. I didn't trust myself to stay there any longer.

Heather grinned as she sipped her wine. "That is some basket we got them."

I agreed. "They'll love it."

Heather had picked me up in the morning, and we had gone to a fabulous shop and picked out lots of items for the basket. The company would make it up fresh, along with the small trinkets we added, and deliver it straight to the winery the day before the wedding. I had already contacted them, and they had promised to take care of it for us.

After doing a little more shopping, we went to lunch.

Heather sat back in her seat. "It feels as if I haven't seen you for ages."

"I saw you at the dress fitting."

"That was days ago."

I lifted a shoulder. "I have no time to come into ABC, Hedda. Between the articling and studying, I'm stretched pretty thin. You'll see me every day soon."

"I just miss my sister."

I reached for her hand and clasped it, squeezing her fingers. "I miss you too."

"Ronan finished the plans for the new building. They plan to break ground in the spring if all the paperwork goes through. Summer at the latest, he hopes."

"Wow. That was fast."

She chuckled. "Addi was pretty clear on what she wanted. Her concept was simple, and Ronan used clean lines and made it look great. Party house at the front and very much work house at the back."

I lifted one eyebrow. "I highly doubt anything Addi would dream of would be a 'party house.'"

She winked. "You know what I mean. The offices are awesome, great views, the odd-shaped lot used perfectly. The back of the building is simpler, with lots of bays for trucks and all."

"I guess I'll see the design next time I come to a meeting. Knowing Ronan, it will be amazing." His eye was impeccable. All three Callaghan men had talent, but Ronan's flair for design and style was distinctive.

"How's the articling going?" Heather asked.

I sipped my wine to buy some time. The waiter brought over the sandwich we were sharing and set the divided lunch in front of us. I eyed my plate. "Did this get bigger than the last time we shared it?"

Heather shook her head. "You got smaller."

I rolled my eyes and picked up my sandwich, refusing to acknowledge her statement. I had no appetite, but I wasn't going to give her any ammunition to use against me. If she was worried, she'd tell Mom, who would tell Dad—and that was never a good thing. He would be on a plane faster than I could blink, and I had no desire for him to show up on my doorstep.

"Well?" she asked.

I chewed and swallowed, tamping down the twist in my chest before I spoke. "The articling is good. Challenging. I'm busy from the moment I get there until it's time to go home. It's a hectic place, and I'm working all the time."

"Addi says your boss is hard to handle."

"Demanding," I agreed, not wanting to talk about Jaxson. "But I'm learning a lot, which is what I am supposed to do. He makes sure I get my study time in, so that's a good thing." I had a feeling he was going to make sure I got extra study time added so he didn't have to see me in the office.

She paused, the sandwich partway to her mouth. "Gracie, you okay? You look—" she bit and chewed, swallowed, and set down the sandwich again "—you look sad."

"Sad?" I repeated. "No. Tired and maybe a bit sentimental. Addi getting married, Christmas coming, all that."

That got her going and off the subject of the office. We talked about the wedding and holiday plans. I told her about the glasses I found. She said she ordered a special bottle of scotch for Dad. We discussed what to get Mom and who we had to buy a gift for with the name-drawing for Christmas.

"I got Shelby." I grinned. "I ordered her a bunch of the art supplies she loves and extended her membership to the Art Gallery of Ontario. She was easy."

Heather groaned. "I got Thomas. I have no idea at all. Maybe a stuffed dolphin?"

"He's a marine biologist—or will be. Not six. Why don't you do a meal delivery service for him? I know Emmy always worries he doesn't eat right. He's too busy studying and working."

Her expression brightened. "That's a good idea, sis. Thanks!"

"You're welcome."

I pushed my plate away. "I am stuffed."

Heather finished off her sandwich and all her salad. Not only did she have my dad's lean build, she inherited his appetite as well. She wiped her mouth and regarded me.

"Are you sure you're okay, Gracie? You say you're not sad, but you seem…distracted."

"I'm fine. There's a case that is mind-boggling. And the key is there, but we can't get to it. I have no idea how to figure it out."

"Maybe you need to come at it from a different angle."

"If I could figure one out, I would. But other than that weighing on my mind, everything is good," I lied.

She squeezed my hand. "Okay. I hear you. But if you need anything—to talk, to vent, anything, I'm here."

I fought back the tears her heartfelt words elicited. I wished I could talk—tell her everything. But I couldn't. I couldn't tell anyone. Not yet.

I squeezed her back. "I know."

The next while was a daily lesson in torture. I did my job, worked hard, and kept my head down. Jaxson kept his door shut a lot. There were no more notes with lessons, no interactions unless it was to do with the office. Midweek, he stormed from his office when Helen Fraser once again shut him down, calling him all sorts of names. He threatened to take her to court and force her to disclose the information she had, and she laughed, threw out another dead lawyer joke, and hung up on him. He yelled and cursed, telling Michael to get her back on the line.

"Maybe we need to approach this differently," I said.

He swung around, his gaze cold. "You think you can win her over, Ms. VanRyan?"

"I have no idea. But the two of you spark off each other. Maybe someone else needs to try."

"Good fucking luck," he muttered, grabbing his coat. "I'm going to lunch." He slammed out of the office.

Michael groaned. "That means he's heading to the bar across from the courthouse. He's going to sit and bitch about shit with other lawyers. No doubt, complain about his staff." He lifted an eyebrow. "What did you do to displease 'the God of all he sees'? He keeps calling you Ms. VanRyan."

I shrugged nonchalantly. "I contradicted him in a meeting."

Michael's eyes widened. "And I missed it? Holy shit, I bet he blew a gasket after."

I was surprised how natural my voice sounded. "He wasn't pleased."

He snorted and stood. "He'll get over it. I was Mr. Banks for a month once. It pissed him off even more when I kept calling him Jaxson." He winked. "I notice you're employing the same tactic."

I smiled grimly. Every day it was getting harder and harder to keep up the façade. I thought it would get easier, but it wasn't. I was glad my break was coming up soon. I planned on spending it all in Port Albany with my family, not even thinking about this place. Or Jaxson.

Especially Jaxson.

Michael slipped on his coat. "He'll be gone for a while. Good thing his afternoon is light. I'm heading to lunch. Wanna come with?"

"No. I'm gonna eat and go study."

"Okay, I'll see you tomorrow."

He left, and the office was quiet. I sighed, letting my head drop to my chest. Jaxson's words kept going through my head. *"You think you can win her over?"* Heather had suggested a different angle.

An idea began to form, and with a frown, I dragged my laptop close. Maybe, just maybe, I was onto something.

CHAPTER 18

GRACE

Later that night, I dialed a phone number, holding my breath. The line answered, the raspy voice of an older woman coming through.

"Hello."

"Helen Fraser?"

"Who is this?"

"My name is Grace VanRyan. I work for Jaxson Richards."

"You have my sympathy. Why are you calling?"

"Ms. Fraser, I know you don't like lawyers, but I also know something you dislike even more."

"And what might that be, young lady?"

"Cruelty to animals. Abandoned ones."

"And what does that have to do with your boss? Unless you're about to tell me he was abandoned by his mother when he was a pup—not that I blame her. He's a pit bull, that one. Nasty as they come."

I drew in a deep breath, trying not to laugh. "He's really not, Ms. Fraser. He is trying to help your siblings. Did you know if he can't prove some of these trademarks and copyrights, the money will go to your sister-in-law?"

"Why should I care? I don't like any of them. They can fight it to the death as far as I care."

I knew there was bad blood between the siblings. But at one point, they had all worked together. Surely I could soften her.

"Your siblings are like you. They donate heavily to causes for animals. They support no-kill shelters."

There was a beat of silence. "So?"

"Your sister-in-law was brought up on animal cruelty charges twice."

Helen cursed low under her breath. "I'm not surprised."

"Were you aware they started a yearly bursary in your name in the veterinary program years ago?"

I felt her shock through the phone. I held my breath, hoping that information softened her. All I needed was the tiniest opportunity. The slightest sign of tempering on her part.

"What did you say your name was?" she asked finally, her voice no longer as cold.

"Grace VanRyan."

"Tell me more."

Friday morning, I braved the lion in his den. I knocked on Jaxson's door, waiting for his order.

"In."

I crossed the threshold and sat in front of him.

"What is it?" he asked curtly.

"Helen Fraser has agreed to speak to you at noon. No earlier." I tried not to smile when I remembered her orders. "You keep calling her before she is even out of bed."

He narrowed his eyes. "When did you talk to her?"

"I have spoken with her four times since Wednesday."

"Four times?"

"Yes. She has agreed to give you ten minutes. She will not hang up on you, although I can't guarantee she won't call you names."

He was silent, staring at me for a moment. "What have you done, Grace?"

It was the first time in days I'd heard my name on his lips. Heard his voice without the ice wrapped around it. I had to look down and collect myself. Remind myself I was doing a job for him. Not because of him.

"I smoothed the waters a little." I stood. "Michael will place the call. I got you an opening. How you proceed is up to you." I headed to the door. "Try a little patience, Jaxson. I know you're capable of it."

"Ms. VanRyan."

I turned and met his eyes. For one moment, there was only him and me. The effect he had on me was still there, pulsating and alive. I had to force it down and give him my fake smile. "Yes, Mr. Richards?"

"Good job. Thank you."

I left his office, sitting down on shaking legs. My heart was beating fast, the blood strumming through my veins. Four little words and I was elated. I needed to stop this. He thanked me for doing my job; that was all. I was an employee, nothing else.

I blinked back my tears as a wave of fresh pain hit me. I knew I couldn't stay. I had to get away from this office.

I gathered my things. "I'm going to study, Michael."

He nodded silently. He had a look of pity on his face, and I had a feeling he knew everything. That we'd never fooled him, but that he was too kind to bring it up. His quiet support meant a lot. It also meant I had to be even more careful to hide my feelings.

"Good luck with the call," I murmured and slipped out the door, heading to the library.

I returned to my desk a few hours later. I had tried to concentrate on studying, but my mind refused to cooperate. I read and reread the same case files over and again, but nothing stuck. Finally, I gave up and decided to go back to my desk, clear off anything waiting, and head home.

Michael looked up as I walked in. "Hey."

"How did it go?" I asked anxiously.

"Well, I think. He was on the phone for a while, then he disappeared with one of the partners."

"She didn't hang up on him?"

"Not this time."

"Good."

I walked toward my desk as Jaxson came through the doorway. "Ah, Grace, I was looking for you."

"Oh, I was getting my things and was going to head home."

He frowned. "Home?"

"I, ah, have another migraine coming on."

"I need a moment before you go."

I preceded him into the office and sat across from him. He studied me for a moment.

"You're pale."

"What do you need?" I asked, refusing to reply to his personal remark.

"Helen Fraser has agreed to meet with me. I'm flying to Vegas on Sunday."

"Well, good news, then."

"There's a catch."

"Oh?"

"She'll only see me if you are there."

I blinked. "I beg your pardon?"

"She will meet with me only if I bring you along."

"I can't."

"It's a business trip. Purely professional."

I shook my head. "The wedding is next Friday. I have to be in Port Albany on Thursday."

"We'll fly out Sunday, meet with her Monday, and you can head back that night. I'll stay and finish it off. I've had it approved by the partners."

"I am not going on a trip with you, Jaxson."

He drummed his fingers on his desk. "She will not see me if you don't come. The entire case rests on your agreement, Grace."

The thought of traveling with him, being close to him, made me feel ill. I wouldn't be able to escape. It was obvious the thought didn't bother him, because the bottom line was that I had never meant anything to him. My feelings had been one-sided. I kept my eyes down-cast as I struggled to get through all the emotions I was feeling.

"I know you feel nothing but contempt for me. I promise to make this as easy as possible. I tried to get separate flights, but there was little choice. I did manage separate seating locations on the airplane. You can pretend I'm not even there. We'll share a cab to the hotel, and that is it. Once we meet with Helen, your work will be done." He paused. "I am asking you to please do this. Not for me, for the firm. For the case."

"What time is the flight on Sunday?"

"One. With the time difference, we arrive midafternoon. There is a late flight out of Vegas Monday night you can be on. You can have the rest of the week off, so you won't have to see me again until the new year."

His words, offered in a conciliatory tone and meant to be positive, somehow added to the heartbreak.

But I stood with my shoulders back and my head held high. "Fine. Email me the details, Jaxson."

"Thank you, Grace. You have proven yourself indispensable."

I couldn't help the sharp bark of laughter at his words.

"In this instance anyway," I replied and walked out of his office, not looking at him again. I gathered my coat and laptop, shoving it into my messenger bag and heading out the door.

"Good luck," Michael called, obviously privy to what was happening next week.

I rolled my eyes as I headed down the steps.

I was going to need it.

I woke up early Sunday to a winter wonderland. Snow blanketed the streets, the wind swirling it around the air. I had spent Saturday doing all sorts of errands. Heather dropped over, bringing a small case I could borrow that would fit overhead on the plane. We visited as I did laundry. She shook her head in worry.

"Going away right before the wedding? I don't like it."

I laughed as I packed a few essentials into the small overnight bag. "It's one night, Heather. You're more upset than Addi, and she's the bride."

"That's because Addi is like you—always calm. What if you get stuck in Vegas with the storm?"

I laid a hand on my hip, shaking my head. "It's Vegas, Heather. They don't get snow. And the storm is in Canada. I have a direct flight there and back, so it won't affect me at all. I'll be home early Tuesday morning, and now I have the rest of the week off. I can head to Port Albany and spend some extra time with Mom and Dad."

"When I told you to come at it from a different angle, I had no idea it meant you had to fly somewhere. I know you hate flying."

I did hate flying. I had a window seat, so that helped, although the enclosed space made me nervous.

"I'll be fine."

"Your boss will be with you?"

"He'll be there, yes."

"Maybe he can hold your hand."

The skirt I was folding slipped from my grasp, and I bent to pick it up, hiding my face. I drew in a calming breath before speaking.

"He isn't the type to hold anyone's hand, and I would never ask him. We aren't sitting together anyway."

She snorted. "Typical. You solve the problem and you get coach, while the big shot rides in first class? You should demand an upgrade."

I didn't answer, and she mumbled something about assholes as I tucked a toiletry bag in and zipped the small case closed.

"Maybe a Prince Charming will sit next to you, and you can hold his hand?" she asked, lifting one eyebrow and looking mischievous.

I had to laugh, grateful she hadn't pushed the subject of Jaxson. "Maybe."

The buzzer went, and she leaped to her feet. "Pizza!"

I was glad it had arrived. If there was food, her mouth would be full, and she wouldn't ask any more questions. With a low sigh, I followed her to the kitchen.

My company phone rang, bringing me out of my musings. I was surprised to see Jaxson's name on the screen, and I answered with a quiet hello.

"Grace, sorry to bother you on your personal time. Given the storm, we need to be at the airport early. The car will pick you up at nine."

He was so formal. I knew the company monitored calls and texts, so I matched his tone.

"I planned to take a cab."

"With the snow, it'll be hard to get one."

"Is there a chance the plane will be delayed or canceled?"

"Doubtful. There is enough snow to make things difficult, not shut the airport down."

I withheld my sigh. "Fine. Nine, then."

He hung up.

I had a feeling it was going to be a long day.

The car was there at nine, and aside from a brief hello, we were both silent during the ride. I stared out the window, feeling his glance on occasion but ignoring it. At the airport, we went to separate kiosks, and I was ahead of him in security. I went to get a coffee when he appeared at my side.

"The first-class lounge is open."

"Enjoy it," I replied, keeping my eyes focused frontward.

"You have a first-class ticket," he replied. "You can join me."

I had been surprised to discover that. I also knew I could go to the lounge and that it would be far more comfortable, but I didn't want to sit with him.

"No thank you."

He scrubbed his jaw in vexation. "I want to discuss Helen and the best approach, Grace. I need you with me on this."

"Business," I stated flatly.

"Business," he agreed.

"Fine."

I hesitated outside the elevator door. It was a very short trip up to the mezzanine and I could do it, but still, the fear trembled within me.

"I'm here, Grace," Jaxson said quietly. He stepped in beside me, closer than we had been in days, his warmth familiar and needed. "I'm right here."

I had to turn away, blinking at the tears that gathered. How could anyone be so cruel and still be so kind?

He looked at me as the doors slid open. "Sometimes, we don't have a choice," he uttered then stepped out, holding the door.

I had no idea what that meant.

We sat in the lounge, which was surprisingly quiet. Jaxson made several trips to the buffet of snacks, helping himself to coffee, ordering a drink, sipping water, seemingly at ease. I was barely able to choke down a croissant, although I did have water and coffee.

He frowned at one point. "You've barely eaten. Let me get you something."

"No."

"Don't be stubborn."

"Don't tell me what to do. When I'm hungry, I will eat. Once I'm out of your company, I'm sure my appetite will return."

He glanced over my shoulder, his jaw working. He swallowed deeply then met my gaze. There was a sheen to his eyes that disappeared when he blinked that I must have imagined. He cleared his throat as if to speak, then shook his head. He picked up his coffee cup and finished it off. His phone rang, and he answered it, rising and heading to the coffee station to set down his empty cup. He wandered to the window, looking out over the runways as he spoke. The muted lighting from the outside filtered in, mixing with the overhead lights, casting him in brilliance. His dark hair gleamed. His broad shoulders stretched the fabric of his dress shirt. He rested one hand on the plate glass, the other wrapped around his phone. I recalled how those hands felt on my body. The pleasure they gave. The gentleness with which they touched me. All of it in direct contrast to the words he'd flung at me. I had to look away for a moment as memories swamped me.

Jaxson's voice, risen with satisfaction, drifted to me, and I glanced up again. "I was right? You're certain?" He fist-pumped the air, glanced my way then turned his back and finished his call.

He came back to the seating area, looking satisfied.

"Good news?" I had to ask.

"It could be," he murmured, then flipped open the file, changing the subject. "I'm going to let you lead with Helen. You've built a rapport with her. I need to know what she has, Grace. The documents she claims to have in her possession. If she has what we need to prove that what the family did predates everything before this woman came into Brian's life, then we can nail this shut." He sighed. "And then I can get to work to properly document everything. What a holy mess it is."

"I wonder what broke up the family?"

"According to the younger sister, Gloria, they had a falling-out over one of the inventions. It got ugly, and they bought Helen out of the company at her insistence. She moved away and has refused to talk to them ever since." He lifted an eyebrow. "Gloria told me the sister-in-law was part of the disagreement. Brian was the only sibling ever to marry, and it wasn't a happy union after a while. Gloria thinks she stayed because of the money."

"And now she's fighting for it."

He nodded. "She's banking on the fact that their records are incomplete and they were sloppy about it for so long."

"I can't believe how long they coasted. This was a disaster waiting to happen."

Our flight was called, and Jaxson stood. "I am hoping we put a stop to the disaster now."

I picked up my case and followed him. I hoped so as well.

CHAPTER 19

GRACE

Jaxson followed me on the plane. I slipped into the third row, frowning when he took my case from my hands, slid it into the overhead bin, added his, and sat beside me.

"You said separate seats."

He shrugged. "The booking came from the same office, so they assumed the request was incorrect."

"Did you check if there was another empty seat?"

"Yes. The plane is full."

I snapped my seat belt into place and raised the window covering, taking a deep breath. That was a mistake since Jaxson was leaning over me, and his familiar scent permeated my lungs, filling me with yearning.

"What are you doing?" I hissed.

"Staying close. I'm going to assume flying must make you anxious, and I know having me close helps."

"That was before," I huffed, refusing to meet his eyes.

"Still, I think," he replied.

I twisted my body so that I faced the window, not wanting him to know he was right. In the elevator, his presence helped me. Knowing he'd be beside me during the flight made me relax. I didn't understand it, and I didn't like it. I needed to stop this madness.

But as the plane roared down the runway and I tensed, the feel of his hand wrapped around mine, his thumb stroking soothing circles on my skin, helped to lessen my anxiety.

And the madness continued.

Jaxson moved away once he felt me relax. I was tired and leaned my head back, wanting to sleep. I drifted away, dreaming silly things. I felt his lips on my forehead, heard his voice in my ear telling me everything was going to be fine, felt his fingers running through my hair. All of which I knew couldn't possibly be true. I woke to him shaking my shoulder, telling me we were about to land. I sat up, disoriented. He shut the cover of his Kindle with a snap.

"You slept the whole way."

"I hope I didn't snore."

He rolled his shoulders with a wink. "No, but you were pretty cuddly."

I gaped at him, and he grinned and patted his shoulder.

"I did not."

"A gentleman never tells."

"Then it should be easy for you to speak. You are no gentleman."

He winked. "You would know, Grace."

I turned away, flustered. He was in far too good of a mood. But I refused to be drawn into it. Just because we were away from the office didn't mean I had forgotten what occurred.

He was courteous and helpful in the airport. The drive to the hotel was quiet, although our driver chatted, pointing out landmarks and giving us advice on what to do in the city while we were there. Neither of us bothered to explain we had no interest other than business.

At the hotel, I was surprised when the staff member directed me to the right of the main floor. "Garden-access rooms are down that way. We have confirmed your late check-out for tomorrow. Enjoy your stay."

Jaxson followed me down the hall, passing me. "Enjoy your evening, Grace. I'll be working, but I'm close if you need me."

No elevator. I knew he'd made the arrangements just for me. He liked higher floors for the views they offered.

"Jaxson?" I called quietly.

He turned.

"Thank you."

"Be ready for nine. We can have coffee, and the car will be here by nine thirty. Get some rest, Grace. Maybe have a swim. I hear the pool is great." He disappeared into a room down the hall.

I went inside, glad that Heather had shoved my swimsuit into my case.

"You can't be in Vegas and not swim," she insisted. "I'm sure your hotel will have a pool. It's hot!"

I peeked out the drapes with a sigh. It was hot here. It had felt as if I'd stepped into a blast furnace when we walked outside. The water in the pool beckoned, glinting in the late-afternoon sun. Maybe a swim would feel good. Then I would have dinner and go to bed early. Heather would be aghast that I had zero plans to take in any casinos or shows. She would make the most of every moment she had if she were here. If Reed were with her, she might even follow in Aiden and Cami's footsteps and marry him. That was the difference between us. I had no desire to explore or do anything as clichéd as gamble to extremes, gorge on a buffet, or marry in haste.

I was going to do my job, head home, and hope my heart would stop this incessant yearning for the man I couldn't have. Who didn't want me.

I turned from the window, shaking my head.

Somehow I knew, of all the things I had to do, the last one would take the longest.

The next morning, I waited by the front door, staying under the overhang. Jaxson had sent me a message instructing me to meet him there.

Even though I had slathered on the sunscreen I'd bought in the gift shop, my skin still felt the heat from yesterday's sun. Hardly surprising given my fair skin, but I was glad I hadn't burned badly. My shoulders and back were a little pink, and the end of my nose shone brighter than usual. Thank goodness for aloe. I hadn't seen Jaxson at all since we arrived. I'd walked across the street to a little place and brought a sandwich to the room and ate it sitting under an umbrella by the pool. I read some and was in bed early, although I tossed and turned most of the night. He was close. Right down the hall. How on earth I could feel him with walls and doors separating us, I had no idea, but I swore I could.

A honk made me lift my head, and Jaxson stepped out of a car. I walked over, confused. "I thought you hired a car?"

"I decided to drive. Get in."

I slipped in, grateful for the air conditioning.

"You got some sun." I was shocked to feel his finger touch my nose. "Will you get freckles?"

I swatted his hand away. "No."

"Just asking."

"Keep your hands to yourself."

"There was a time you wanted my hands all over you."

"There was a time I thought you were a decent human."

He chuckled. "Touché, Ms. VanRyan."

He pulled away, and we stopped for coffee. He wolfed down a huge breakfast, frowning at the toast I ordered but remaining silent. Using the car's GPS, we followed the directions, pulling up to a gated house. Jaxson pressed the button, giving his name to the tinny voice.

"Is Ms. VanRyan with you?" the voice asked.

"Yes," he confirmed.

The gate opened. "You may come in, then."

We parked, Jaxson shutting off the engine. For the first time, he showed his nerves, his hands locked on the steering wheel. "If she has a quarter of what her siblings think she has, this case is closed for the wife. I need to win her over."

I studied him, turning in my seat. "You want to win her over? Then be the Jaxson I knew a few weeks ago. Use your charm. You did it once. You can do it again."

"Did what once?"

"Fooled me into thinking you really cared. You can do it to her, too."

I got out of the car, leaving him behind.

At the front door, Helen Fraser waited. She was tall—close to six feet, much like her brothers, who all towered over me. Her younger sister, Gloria, was the odd one, being average height, but that was the only difference. They all looked alike. Thin, almost white-blond hair, and pale blue eyes. Helen's face was clear of wrinkles, her neck tight, no doubt thanks to the skillful hand of a plastic surgeon. She was dressed in silk, her lounge pants and tunic an ivory color. Her hair was in an elegant chignon on her head, and her chin was lifted high. But there was a subtle glint in her eye, and she greeted me kindly. She was cordial to Jaxson and invited us in.

Her sitting room was cool and shaded, and I was grateful. Three cats and two dogs were napping on sofas and chairs. The dogs came over for a sniff and head scratch, but the cats ignored us, too lazy to move. Despite the large size, the room had a homey, lived-in feel about it. I liked it.

She eyed me speculatively. "You should have used more sunscreen," she admonished. "Skin like yours will burn in this heat."

"I used an eighty SPF. They didn't have the hundred. And I sat in the shade." I lifted my shoulders. "It's fine."

She crossed her legs, continuing to ignore Jaxson. "My sister Gloria called me last night. I haven't spoken to her in twenty years."

"I hope you had a pleasant conversation."

"You have siblings?"

"Yes. Four. And even if we had been estranged, I would hope I would accept the chance for reconciliation."

She narrowed her eyes, then sat back with a knowing look. "You are a caregiver, are you not, Ms. VanRyan?"

"I suppose. I'm the eldest. I always liked to care for my siblings."

"A little mother."

I heard Jaxson's swift intake of air, and I glanced over. He was watching us, letting me lead as he promised. I leaned forward, earnest. Helpful.

"Ms. Fraser, I know there is bad blood between you, but they are still your family. If you don't help us, your sister-in-law could take a great deal of the company from your siblings."

"That witch. I always said she was no good. Brian wouldn't listen to me. None of them would."

"They should have." Jaxson surprised me by speaking up. "And they know that now. They know you want nothing to do with them, and they understand. But they, I, am asking for your help."

She pursed her lips. "Why should I trust you? The last lawyer we trusted ripped us off. Tried to steal one of our designs and pass it off as his own."

He nodded. "I understand. I don't blame you. But you allowed me to come and see you. You must want to help. Perhaps this could be the olive branch that reunites you with your family?"

She swung her leg in agitation. She turned her body, facing me once again. "Do you trust him?"

My breathing faltered. She was studying me intently. I felt Jaxson's anxious gaze. I met her eyes. "He will not lead you astray. He is here to help."

"That didn't answer my question."

Images of him ran through my head in fast succession. Helping me on the elevator. Feeding me. Ensuring I had time to study. His closeness on the plane. Making sure I had a ground-floor room here. I spoke the truth. "I trust him with my life."

I didn't add the final thought.

"Not with my heart."

She stood. "Come with me."

Four hours later, my mind was full, and so was Jaxson's briefcase. Documents, lists of the copyrights and trademarks. Which sibling was responsible for what innovation within the company's holdings. So many answers to the myriad of questions. Enough evidence to disprove the sister-in-law's false claims and to ensure the family's legacy. There was even a signed legal document that the company would remain with the siblings unless they all agreed. The sister-in-law's claim that Brian had said she would get his share of the company could be disputed now.

Jaxson smiled grimly. "She'll get nothing other than the life insurance and his personal holdings. He had a lot, so she is hardly destitute."

"What a shame," Helen spat. "She shouldn't get a penny."

Jaxson shrugged. "Not my area of expertise. She married him, so she gets what he had left. At least she isn't getting more." He frowned at her. "You could have made this easier."

She shrugged, not at all put out. Jaxson's charm had worked on her. "It was too fun. And they deserved to sweat a little. I was always going to help them—but on my time. Not theirs."

"Would you consider joining with them again?" I asked. She had taken us to her office. It was full of drawings and prototypes of her own creations. The family members were all talented. Her toys were creative, her games educational, and her eye for detail amazing.

Thank God her filing system was as organized as she seemed to be.

Helen got a faraway look in her eye. "We will see what the future holds. For now, I have done my part." She stood, brushing off her slacks, indicating her time was done.

We thanked her, and I couldn't resist giving her a hug. For a moment, she was stiff, then she relented and hugged me back. "Thank you, young lady," she murmured.

I drew back with a smile. Jaxson got a handshake, then she turned and walked into the house.

He slid into the car and looked at me. "You did it, Grace."

"We did it."

He glanced at his watch. "I thought we'd be at this all day. You have hours until your flight."

The thought of the long hours sitting around the hotel didn't thrill me.

"Oh," I mumbled.

He turned in his seat. "Just for the afternoon, Grace."

"What?"

"Can we call a truce? We have some free time. Neither of us has been to Vegas. Let's see some of the town."

"Together?"

"I hoped so, but I suppose it is too much to ask."

I was as shocked as he was to hear the words that fell from my mouth. "A truce. For this afternoon only."

He grabbed my hand and kissed it. "Great. Let's go."

I tried not to notice how warm my skin was where his lips touched. How his mouth still thrilled me.

It was for the afternoon.

Then we would once again be strangers.

CHAPTER 20

GRACE

I woke up, my head aching and my limbs heavy. I blinked in the darkness of the room, my mouth feeling like the Sahara Desert. The room was unfamiliar, and it took me a moment to recall I was in a hotel room in Las Vegas.

Why did my head ache so badly?

I searched through my memories of the day before. The morning with Helen. The truce with Jaxson. Spending a carefree afternoon in Vegas with him. Having fun at the slots, sampling a couple of buffets. Seeing the sights. Throughout it all, Jaxson was polite, fun, and a perfect gentleman. Then I got a call before we left for the airport to inform me that my plane was canceled due to a mechanical malfunction and the earliest flight I could get out was the next day. I had cursed him, saying I never should have let him talk me into going on this trip. He had apologized. But after that, nothing was clear.

What the hell happened to me after that phone call?

I racked my brain, trying to remember, to grasp some minute detail of yesterday, but nothing appeared. I groaned as I shifted, the pain in my head changing from a dull ache to a constant pounding. As I moved, I stiffened as I realized the weight on my hip wasn't that of the blanket, but of a hand.

My stomach rolled when reality hit me. Someone was in bed with me. I had slept with a stranger. I got drunk in Vegas and slept with a stranger. How clichéd.

Ignoring the ache in my head, I shot out of bed, yanking the blanket with me. I fumbled around, finding the light and switching it on. I squinted as the pain shot through my temples, and I gasped when I recognized the man lying in the bed beside me. Not looking upset at all, Jaxson pulled himself up into a sitting position and had the nerve to smile at me.

"Not a stranger," he said, letting me know I had spoken my thought out loud. "How are you feeling, darling?"

"What the hell are you doing here?"

"Until a few moments ago, I was sleeping. You must need some Tylenol. Let me get it for you."

"Don't bother. I meant, how the hell did you get into my bed?"

He smirked, lifting one leg up to his chest and reclining back with his hands beneath his head. He looked too handsome and far too comfortable for this situation.

"Since this is my room, you're the one in *my* bed."

I looked around, seeing he was right.

"What the hell happened?"

"I would think that was obvious." He indicated the torn condom wrappers. "We had sex."

I gaped at him. "Why did I have sex with you? I don't like you!"

He leaned forward, his blue eyes bright in the dim light. His smile was wicked, and I wanted to wipe it off his face with my fist. "You *really* liked me last night. At least three times."

We'd had sex three times?

"At least," he confirmed. "I'm not counting the orgasm in the car, and I think I missed one other fuck. Against the wall, I think."

I was stunned. I stared at him, horrified. I had slept with my boss. Again.

"I can't believe I did that," I mumbled, gripping the blanket.

"That's not the only thing you did, darling."

"What could be worse?"

He studied me closely. He indicated my hand gripping the blanket.

"You married me."

A thin, too-tight band encircled my ring finger. He held up his hand, showing me a matching ring.

"How about that for clichéd, Mrs. Richards?" He smirked.

The room spun, and my stomach heaved.

The last thing I remembered was his shout before the floor rushed toward me.

Unconsciousness had never been so welcome.

CHAPTER 21

JAXSON

I caught her before she hit the floor. I laid her on the bed and carefully brushed her hair back from her face. She was pale, exhaustion evident under her eyes, and the shock of what I had said to her too much to handle.

Christ, I had fucked all this up.

I hurried to the bathroom and got a cool cloth, a bottle of water, and some Tylenol, then returned to her, wiping the cloth gently over her face.

"Gracie, darling. Come back to me," I murmured, relief flowing through me as her eyes fluttered open. I pressed the bottle to her lips. "Sip."

She swallowed, allowing me to press two pills to her mouth. "Again."

She watched me, her eyes confused and blurry. I shouldn't have let her drink so much. Except it was the one way to get her guard down. To get her to admit to her feelings. To get her to marry me.

My watch started beeping, and I grimaced. "I hate to tell you this, Grace, but we need to get moving. We have a plane to catch."

She sat up instantly, pushing me away.

"Careful," I warned.

She ignored me and stumbled to her feet. She stopped, bent over, and gripped her knees.

"A shower will make you feel better."

"Getting away from you would make me feel better," she snapped.

"Sorry. Not happening."

She brushed past me. "Annulment."

I smirked as she walked away, unable to resist gazing at her ass. It was full and curvy, and I liked how it moved as she walked.

"Sex," I responded. "We had sex. Lots of it."

"It doesn't count if I don't remember."

"I remember."

She spun on her heel and glared at me. Despite her anger and exhaustion, she was gorgeous. "Then forget it. Pretend it never happened. You're a lawyer. You lie. You told me that yourself."

I shook my head. "I was lying."

She frowned. "What?"

"I was lying about lying."

She rubbed her head. "No, you're lying now."

I kept my face straight. "No."

"We're getting a divorce, then."

"No."

"Yes, we are."

"What happens in Vegas isn't staying in Vegas. It's following us home, Gracie darling. You're my wife. You're staying that way."

I was sure the slam of the door hurt her head far more than it hurt my feelings.

She was silent all the way to the airport, holding her head in her hand. We were both unhappy to find the flight was delayed but had no choice but to hang around the airport. In the lounge, I gave her some more Tylenol. She was only able to choke down a few sips of her coffee, and I finished it off for her when she pushed it away.

"Tastes great." I smacked my lips, hiding my shudder. I really didn't want any, but frankly, I needed it.

"I'm surprised a coffee snob like you is drinking airport swill."

I leaned close. "Your lips touched the cup, Gracie. It's almost the same as kissing you." I took another sip. "Sweet."

I was certain I heard a muffled scream as she pushed past me and headed to the ladies' room. I met the eye of an older woman and grinned. "My wife is displeased with me."

My own words made me grin harder. Gracie. *My wife.*

The woman patted the seat beside her with a lewd wink. "Come over here, sugar. I'll share your coffee."

I was still laughing when Gracie came back. I didn't share why since she'd probably lead me by the hand and give me to the woman. Instead, I smiled and let her ignore me.

Once finally on the plane, Grace was tense. It was a smaller model, with no first class, and it was full. I could feel her tension mounting, and I slipped my hand under her hair and massaged her neck muscles.

"I'm right here. I won't let anything happen to you. Hold on to me."

I would be lying if I said I didn't enjoy the fact that she was scared enough to bury her face into my chest and let me hold her until after takeoff. I kept stroking her neck until she fell asleep, still exhausted and hungover. I eased up the armrest and wrapped my arm around her. The death grip on my shirt lessened, but she never let go. She slept the entire flight, and I hated waking her. She stumbled through the next airport, letting me guide her on to another short flight. The long hours ahead of us were a lather, rinse, repeat. Delays, engine failures, missed connections—everything that could go wrong did. She looked better as we finally began our descent into Calgary hours later, moving away from me as she woke up.

"One last flight." I glanced at my watch. "Two-hour layover here, then four hours until we land in Toronto. We'll be home around three."

"We'll be home? You mean I'll be home. You'll be at your place."

I lifted my eyebrows in silent refusal.

"Jaxson." She leaned close, hissing under her breath. "I don't know what's going on, but what happened last night was a mistake. We were drunk."

"You were drunk. But not drunk enough not to agree to marry me. Not drunk enough not to attack me in the car or have sex as often as we did."

Her eyes grew wide with shock. "I attacked *you*?"

"You did. You were quite insistent, darling." I stroked her cheek. "Very passionate. How could I resist?"

She slapped my hand away. "I hate you."

"Ah, the fine line between love and hate. Last night, love. Today, hate." I waggled my eyebrows. "Hate sex is awesome, too."

She turned away, refusing to look at me. I tried not to laugh.

Neither of us was laughing when we found out the plane to Toronto had been canceled.

"There was a delay, and the plane is stuck in BC," the desk agent explained. "We can't fly tonight."

"What about another flight?"

"Not to Toronto." She leaned forward, her voice low. "I doubt, given the storm that is bearing down on us from up north, that any airline will fly out of here tomorrow either."

Gracie stiffened. "What about Thursday?"

The woman shrugged. "If it's as bad as they say it is going to be, maybe not until Friday. I can book you out on the plane tomorrow, but my advice is to get a hotel room. If you can find one."

I glanced out the window behind her, noticing the wind was picking up and snow was beginning to fall. I withheld my curse about flying in Canada during the winter.

"Book them," I requested.

Gracie wandered over to the window, and I met the woman's eyes.

"Tell me honestly. Not as an employee. As a person. Do we have a snowball's chance in hell of getting out of here before Friday?"

She pushed the tickets toward me. "Not even that good. This weather system is going to spread. It will hit us then move east. We might be able to fly west, but not the way you want to go, because we won't be able to land."

I made sure the airline had my cell number, then I moved away. I checked my weather app, wanting to hit something. If Gracie's flight hadn't been canceled last night or I had gotten her on an earlier flight instead of getting her drunk and marrying her, she'd be home now instead of at an airport thousands of miles away with the potential of missing her best friend's wedding. She had already been upset about having to come on this trip, and now she was going to be even angrier.

I headed her way, reaching her as she hung up the phone. "I told Heather I was delayed. She says this system is going to head east."

"I know."

Her lip quivered. "What if I miss the wedding?"

"You won't, Grace. I'll figure this out. I am so damn sorry about this."

She furrowed her brow, surprising me with her retort. "Um, Jaxson, your God complex is showing again. Not even *you* can think you could control the weather."

My lips quirked. "No, Grace, I meant that I should have come alone. I would have figured it out."

She sniffed. "I doubt it. You needed me."

I shocked her when I wrapped my arm around her, dragging her close and kissing her hard. "You're right. I need you on lots of levels."

For a moment, our eyes locked. Then she pushed me away. "We need a plan. I guess I had better try to find us a place to sit. I scrolled through some close hotels—they are all booked up. I'm surprised they didn't say something on the plane. An announcement."

"Well, you were snoring away, so you wouldn't have heard it," I drawled. "I had my headphones on to shut you out, and I might have missed it."

She slapped my arm. "I do not snore."

I leaned close. "You do, Mrs. Richards, when you're exhausted. It's rather cute, like tiny little snorts."

She glared at me. "Take that back."

"The snoring comment? But it's true."

Gracie stepped in and poked me with her index finger. Her surprisingly strong index finger. "I am not Mrs. Richards," she hissed.

I grabbed her hand and kissed the tip of her finger. "That part is true as well."

"Not for long."

Her phone rang, and she glanced down. "Damn, that's Addi. No doubt Heather called her."

Movement outside caught my eye. A truck driving slowly toward the terminal, its snow tires sticking to the tarmac easily. An idea formed, and I did some fast calculations in my head. "You tell her you'll be there. I'll get you there, Grace. I swear it. Wait here."

I hurried away, searching for the sign I needed, hoping my idea would work.

I returned in about thirty minutes. Gracie was sitting, staring out the window. She looked resigned, sad. Tired. I went to her side and handed her a tray of coffee, then reached for the bags. "Let's go."

"You found a hotel?"

"No. We're leaving."

"What?"

I held up a set of keys. "We need to get ahead of this storm. We're driving."

She gaped at me. "Jaxson, it's thirty hours or more driving time!"

"Thirty-six without breaks. But if we leave now, we can get ahead of it. I'll drive until I need to sleep for a bit, and we'll pull over." I gripped her hand. "I'll get you there, Gracie."

"I am not sitting in a car with you for that length of time."

"Then you'll sit in an airport. You're stuck with me."

"Until I get the legal papers saying otherwise."

"Not happening," I retorted. "So, here are your options. Sit here and miss the wedding. Or let me drive you and give you the best chance to get there."

She was quiet, and I felt her silent fuming. She knew there was one option to take if she wanted to get to the wedding.

Me.

"Fine."

"I'm sorry, you said something? It was something 'you,' but I am certain it was polite and not fuck you this time."

"Thank you, Jaxson," she snapped through tight lips.

I waved my hand airily. "No thanks are needed, but I want something. Two things, actually."

"What?" She ground out between clenched teeth.

"I don't want to hear the words divorce or annulment again. Not once during this trip. Am I clear? No talk about our marriage."

"It's not—"

She stopped talking when I glared at her, then she grimaced. "Fine. I'll be thinking them, though."

I rolled my eyes.

"And the second?" she asked.

"I'll tell you in the car. We need to go. We need to get out before it hits." I tugged on her hand. "Now."

I felt a sense of satisfaction when she followed me.

The next few hours were tense. The SUV was equipped with the latest safety features, but even with winter tires, four-wheel drive, and driving in low gear, the roads were hazardous. It was going to take longer to get there than I had thought unless we cleared the storm. I had to admit to myself, even then, it was iffy. Grace was quiet, sitting in the passenger seat. The cab was warm, the snow and wind outside ferocious. Luckily, the highways were mostly deserted. I kept the speed slow, deciding safety was the main priority. Grace had our phones charging, and the radio was playing, weather updates coming in frequently.

"Maybe this isn't a good idea," Grace murmured.

"It's the only option, Grace. No flights are going to go out tomorrow—or now today, I suppose," I said, glancing at the clock. "Chances are not on Thursday either."

"But if they are flying on Friday, I could get there if a flight left first thing in the morning," she said hopefully.

"If the storm hits east by then, we'll be stuck elsewhere if it's not a direct flight. With the time of year and the backlogs? Driving is the best option."

She sighed, and I reached over and patted her knee. "We'll get there."

"I told Addi it might not be until the day of the wedding. She was disappointed, but she said all that mattered was me getting there safely."

"She's right."

I peered through the fast-falling snow. I prayed I was strong enough to make that happen for her.

"Jaxson."

I grunted, shifting. My bed wasn't very comfortable, and something was sticking me in the back.

"Jaxson." The soft voice was sharper. It was a familiar voice.

Grace.

My eyes flew open, and I looked around, confused. I wasn't at my place but in an SUV that was stopped in a rest area on the highway. It was cloudy and overcast, and the snow was still swirling. I sat up, rubbing my hand over my face. I had driven for ten hours and finally had to admit defeat. We pulled over and crawled into the back seat for a short nap. I had woken up at one point to find Grace curled into me, the blanket we had purchased on our rush out of the airport wrapped around us. I had fallen back asleep, holding her tight.

I looked at my watch and cursed. We had slept way longer than I planned.

"I have no cell signal."

I glanced around, not surprised. "We're sort of in the middle of nowhere, Grace." I stretched and rolled my shoulders. "We need to get going."

"I think we're close to a small town if I remember from the GPS earlier. Maybe we can get coffee."

I nodded. "And food. I need to eat."

She frowned but agreed. "Okay."

"I have to keep up my energy to drive."

"I know."

I crawled up front, stretching my sore neck.

"We'll make up the time. I promise."

Grace only nodded.

CHAPTER 22

JAXSON

We found the town, which luckily had a little restaurant that was open. We ordered food, plus some sandwiches to go for later. I had to press on fast to get her there.

"Why are they getting married on a Friday?" I asked as I ate the huge omelet the waitress brought over. "Isn't Saturday the usual day for weddings?"

Grace smiled. "Addi and Brayden never do anything normal. The winery is owned by ABC. The wedding is the first event it is hosting. And because we're doing the Christmas thing as well, they wanted a couple of days to themselves between the two events. They aren't traditional, and they didn't care about the day, just getting married."

"I want to go."

"What?"

"To the wedding. That's my second thing. I want to go to the wedding."

She blinked. "Why?"

"Because I do. You said you wanted to thank me. That's how you can thank me. I'll be your plus-one."

"Maybe I already had a plus-one."

I narrowed my eyes. "Do you?"

"No." She set down her fork. "You are not announcing yourself as my husband."

"Of course not. I simply want to go to the wedding. See the winery. With all this trouble, surely you can't deny me that?"

"You'll have to sit wherever. If Addi has room."

I didn't care where I sat as long as it was in the same room as Grace. "That's fine."

"Stay away from my family."

I took a long swallow of my coffee. "I will be a perfect gentleman, Grace."

"You'll be my *boss*." She emphasized the word.

"Of course."

We drove endlessly. Grace called ahead and tried to get a flight out of Winnipeg, with no luck, so we kept going. Late in the hours of Thursday afternoon, I glanced at her. "No party, Grace." We were getting close, but not close enough.

"I already figured that. I texted Addi and Heather. My mom knows too."

"I need some sleep."

"Okay."

I had been awake for too long, and my eyes were beginning to fall shut of their own accord. The roads were too treacherous and the vehicle too big for Grace to drive comfortably. I had no choice but to keep going.

"If we find a place, we could stop, get a room, and sleep for a while. Have a shower. I'll have you there by eleven tomorrow."

She sighed. "Okay."

She had been quiet for several hours. We had been running on adrenaline and nerves, and both were fading. Talk was sporadic. I turned on Christmas carols; she turned them off. She switched on some classical; I had to change the station before the music lulled me to sleep and we ended up dead. We found a classic rock station, and the heavy beats help keep me awake. As did the horrid coffee at the gas stations. My gut was rotting from the bad food and hot liquid I kept sipping.

There was so much I wanted to say to her, so much to talk about, but this was not the time. Silence was the best option.

"I'm sorry you're missing the party."

She shrugged. "Really, it's okay. I'll see them all at the wedding and on Christmas, and I'll catch up. The ones I want to see the most are Addi and Heather, and they'll be busy with their other halves. As long as I'm there tomorrow, it's good. Really, Jaxson."

I nodded.

"Jaxson," she began, then trailed off.

"No." I shook my head, knowing what she was about to do. "We'll discuss the future in private, not in a moving vehicle while I am trying to concentrate on not crashing."

"There is no future," she mumbled, looking outside the window.

I spotted a small motel light ahead, and I slowed down, putting on the blinker.

"That," I said, pulling into the parking lot, "is where you are wrong."

I got out of the SUV before she could reply.

It was closer to one before we arrived the next day. As we pulled up behind the building where she directed me to go, she reached for the door handle eagerly. The sleep and food we'd had the night before helped restore her pallor. She had been quiet at the motel, not objecting to me sliding in beside her since there was one bed in the small room. As usual when I woke, she was nestled close and my arms were around her. I knew she would refuse to admit her body knew where she belonged even if her pride screamed against it, so I moved away carefully and grabbed the first shower.

I followed her, handing over her bag. She began to turn away when I called her name. "Grace."

"What?"

"If you really want to keep our marriage a secret, you need to remove that." I indicated her hand with a tilt of my chin.

She glanced down at the thin band on her finger. "I can't get the damn thing off. It's too small."

"It was the only one they had that didn't fall off your hand. Mine too. They'd been busy."

"Too big would have been easier to get rid of."

I lifted one eyebrow but didn't tell her she'd never be rid of me. Instead, I held out my hand and drew her close. I picked up a handful of snow and put it in my mouth, then sucked her finger inside, swirling my tongue around the digit. Her pupils grew large as she stared, transfixed.

Slowly, I sucked, caught the ring with my teeth, then released her finger, the metal disc sitting on my tongue.

I held it up. "Ta-da!"

I wasn't prepared for her fast movement. One second, she was in front of me; the next, her lips were on mine and her arms looped around my neck. I took full advantage of the situation and kissed her hungrily. Our tongues slid together, and I groaned deep in my chest. She whimpered, her hands tightening on my neck, and I yanked her as close as I could. She broke away with a gasp, and I buried my face into her neck, nipping at the skin, knowing I was leaving a tiny mark.

I wanted to mark her. Remind her she was mine even if the ring was gone from her finger.

She pushed away, her color high, her breaths coming out in sharp gasps. Her hair was a mess from the short time my fingers spent in it, and she was beautiful. Glowing. Enraged.

"I hate you."

"I know."

She turned and ran.

"See you soon, darling," I called, licking my lips, still tasting her.

Love and hate. How often she mixed up the two. I would have to remind her of that soon.

I watched the ceremony from the back of the room. The attendants were lovely, the bride beautiful, but none of them held a candle to Grace. Stunning in her gown, she was elegant and sexy. The muted gold suited her, casting her skin in a soft glow. Her hair was gathered away from her face, cascading down her back in a mass of curls and waves. She wore only earrings, allowing the dress to shine on its own. She took my breath away, and my determination to keep her solidified. I wasn't allowing anything to come between us again. Simply the thought made me angry.

I got some curious stares, and I had to remind myself not to glare at people. I wasn't used to social interactions of this sort. Family gatherings. They were a complete mystery to me, but they were important to Grace, so I knew I had to get used to them.

In the receiving line, Grace stepped forward, introducing me as her coworker, stumbling over the words as she lied. I lifted one eyebrow in amusement and congratulated the couple, thanking them for allowing me to attend. Addison Riley, the new bride, Grace's best friend, and pseudo cousin, waved her hand.

"Nonsense. Grace told us how you drove nonstop to get her here. We are indebted to you and thrilled to have you with us." Her new husband, Brayden, distracted her, and she turned to the next guest, so I was able to move on.

I stood in front of Grace, smiling. She could have told them it was my fault. She could have made up any story about why she had missed the event the night before. Instead, she made me the hero. Still, I couldn't resist teasing her.

"Coworker, Grace darling? A bit more, I think," I whispered close to her ear as I bent, pretending to kiss her cheek.

She smiled, a wide, fake smile that made me want to laugh. "Not discussing it, Mr. Richards. Those were the rules you laid out. I believe you've been placed at the back of the room. Do try to behave."

Unable to help myself, I winked at her. "I'll try. Not promising anything."

She pressed her hand to my chest in an unknowingly intimate gesture. "How did you get a fresh suit?"

"Michael met me at the Port Albany Motel. I had a shower, changed, and here I am."

She lifted an eyebrow. "The Port Albany Motel? That place is a dive. Addi's been trying to convince them to sell for over a year."

I shrugged. It was old and run-down, but the room was clean and all I needed was a close place to change and clean up. It was deserted at this time of year, so they were happy to get a full night's price for a couple of hours.

"How low you have sunk, Mr. Richards. Staying in *motels*."

I leaned close. "You'd be shocked how low I would sink for you, Gracie." I brushed my lips close to her ear. "Right to my knees if you wanted."

She pushed me back, looking around to see if anyone was watching. There were too many people and too many conversations going on. No one was looking our way. The focus was on the couple of the day, nowhere else.

"Stop it."

"Fine. I'm going to get a scotch. It'll perk me up."

"Feel free to leave anytime."

I shook my head. "Nope. The night is young. I look forward to a dance."

"Don't hold your breath." She turned away, dismissing me. I went through the rest of the line, shaking hands, murmuring stupid salutations. I memorized each face, putting them with the names I'd had Grace tell me about on the long drive. It had helped pass the time and would come in handy. Her sister Heather was easy to spot since their facial features were similar. She was far more outgoing than Grace, sipping a glass of champagne, giving me the once-over, then dismissing me, far too busy having a good time to ask any questions. It reminded me of Grace's earlier action, and I decided it had to be a family trait. Bentley Ridge was easily recognizable, as was Maddox Riley. I shook their hands and received a kiss on the cheek from their wives, both of them exclaiming over the efforts I had made to get Grace to the wedding. I murmured the appropriate response, sighing in relief when I reached the end of the line.

I approached the bar and got a double scotch, turning to find a tall man wearing a kimono and slacks eyeing me speculatively. Between his outfit and presence, he was an event unto himself.

"Grace's last-minute addition, I presume," he stated.

"Jen," I replied, grateful for all the things Grace had told me in the car. He was easy to remember since she'd described him perfectly. "The man himself. Can I buy you a drink?"

"I never drink on duty. I need your name."

"Grace didn't supply it?"

"Unless you wish to be referred to as 'the pain in my ass' all evening, no."

My lips quirked. Apparently, I wasn't painted as a hero to all. "Ah."

"Oh, he smiles," Jen quipped. "Tell me, does that angry, intense look work with women?"

"I don't have a *look*."

"Oh, darling. *You do*. Trust me. Now, name?"

"Jaxson." I spelled it out for him.

"Well, that suits. Now, Jaxson, although Grace suggested a chair by the kitchen, or perhaps a dinghy in the water, I have put you at table four. You're with Grace's family. Given the situation and all, I thought it appropriate."

"Situation?"

"Grace," he said knowingly. "Your *date*."

"I'm her boss," I stated firmly. "I wanted to see the winery."

"Uh-huh. You could have arranged a tour. But you stick to that, young man. A word of warning. Be careful around Richard—he is a protective daddy, and Gracie is his baby. And he bites."

He turned and walked away.

I took a long drink of scotch, then got a top up. I had a feeling I was going to need it. I found table four and hesitated. There was a woman sitting at the table, sipping a glass of wine. I cleared my throat. "Is this seat taken?"

The woman glanced up, smiled, and indicated the chair. "No, please."

I sat down, and she laid a hand on my arm. "Jaxson, I presume?"

I turned in my chair and was able to see her clearly. There was no doubt who she was. Her warm blue eyes and lovely smile were identical to Gracie's.

"Mrs. VanRyan. Yes, I'm Jaxson Richards."

Her smile grew. "Thank you for getting our Gracie here. She told us how difficult a task it was. You must be exhausted!" She glanced over her shoulder. "Richard darling, come meet Jaxson!"

A good-looking man extricated himself from a group and came closer. He was tall, with broad shoulders. His gaze was intense, and I stood to shake his hand. His grip was firm. "Gracie's boss," he stated. "The hero."

I laughed and shook my head. "Hardly. Your daughter did me a great service accompanying me to solve a tricky situation. The least I could do was get her home for an event that meant so much to her."

He regarded me for a moment, tilting his head. There was a frown pulling at his lips. I hastened to add. "She talked a lot on the drive to keep me awake." I indicated the festive room around us. "It made me curious to see the winery, and she graciously extended me the invitation." I smiled in what I hoped was a sincere expression. "A good meal and some company other than my own seemed like too good a prospect to refuse."

He inclined his head. "Of course. Grace is very thoughtful."

He sat beside his wife, his arm going around her. I sat as well, unsure how to proceed.

Grace's mother leaned in. "You live alone, Mr. Richards?"

"Jaxson, please. And yes, Mrs. VanRyan. Just me. I have no family. At all," I added, not sure why I let that tidbit fall from my mouth.

Her eyes widened. "None?"

I shook my head.

She laid a hand on my arm. "It's Katy. And I'm glad you're here with us tonight. I hope you're prepared for this family."

I had to chuckle. "I've heard a lot about them."

Her father's gaze cut to me again. "Oh?"

I lied smoothly. "Michael, my PA, and Grace talk a lot. Plus, the car ride."

"Right."

"You must be very proud. Grace will be an amazing lawyer. Her mind is sharp, and she is focused and intelligent. It's been a pleasure having her in the office and watching her learn. One of the best articling students I have ever worked with." I offered another grin. "I think my PA wishes she'd stay so he could go work for her. She is far more pleasant, he tells me."

"It sounds as if your assistant keeps you in line," Katy said with a grin, looking at her husband.

"He does. The right PA makes all the difference."

Grace's father laughed and pressed a kiss to Katy's head. "That they do."

I had a feeling there was a story there. I would have to ask Grace about it.

I took a sip of my scotch, savoring it.

"Great scotch."

Richard lifted his glass. "One of my favorites. Bent's too. Addi made sure the bar was well stocked."

"Excellent taste, Mr. VanRyan." Remembering Jen's warning, I was careful not to seem too forward.

He eyed me for a moment, then lifted his own glass. "It's Richard." He surprised me by winking. "That should be easy for you to remember, Mr. Richards."

We all laughed, and I relaxed. So far, so good.

CHAPTER 23

JAXSON

Grace's family was loud. Boisterous. Demonstrative. By the end of the meal, I had been slapped on the back, hugged, and exclaimed over far too much. The food was excellent, as were the spirits, the speeches mercifully short and amusing, and finally, I was able to walk around the room and try to find my wife.

I had chosen a good chair to sit in. It gave me an unobstructed view of Grace. She sat beside the bride, glowing in her gold gown, looking more beautiful than anything I had ever seen in my life. It was hard not to stare at her, but luckily, most everyone's attention was on the head table, so my gaze directed that way caused no suspicion. She, on the other hand, looked away every time our eyes met. I knew she wasn't happy about my being here, but I couldn't stay away. Not anymore. I'd made that mistake once. We'd both suffered.

Grace's mom, Katy, was warmth personified. She spoke with me a lot, pointing out people, sharing funny stories. More than once, she asked about my personal life, and I answered as best I could without lying or giving away too much. She seemed very upset over the fact that I would be alone at Christmas, although I assured her it didn't bother me in the slightest.

"But Christmas is a time for family and being close, Jaxson," she insisted in her soft voice.

"When one has never had a family, then it's a moot point," I replied, trying to keep my voice even.

"You've never had a family Christmas?"

"No."

I was shocked to see the glimmer of tears in her eyes. She turned to her husband, who pulled her close and kissed her head. "The holidays are important to my wife," he said.

I could only smile in silence. I had nothing to offer in the way of a reply.

Much to my surprise, I found I liked everyone. They were all friendly, welcoming, and real. Despite the wealth that surrounded them, they were down-to-earth, and the love that enveloped them caused a strange yearning inside me. One I couldn't explain.

Long after dinner, I was standing in the corner, trying to find Grace. I was tired and I knew I had to leave, but I didn't want to do so without seeing her. She had been very successful at avoiding me. She danced with her cousins, father, and brothers, yet magically disappeared every time I approached. I searched the room for the flash of gold, just as her mother stepped in front of me.

"Katy." I nodded my head in greeting. She had been my one dance of the night. The woman I wanted to hold was proving to be too adept at hiding.

"Jaxson," she replied. "How are you holding up?"

"I'm leaving shortly. I admit the exhaustion is beginning to catch up with me."

"Will you be all right to drive? You could stay with us."

I was touched by her thoughtfulness. "I'm fine, but thank you for the offer."

She laid her hand on my arm. "I want to ask you something, and I want you to think it over before you refuse."

I had a feeling I would find it hard to refuse this sweet woman anything. She reminded me too much of Grace. "Of course."

"I would like you to join us for Christmas Day."

"I beg your pardon?"

"We celebrate it together, as you know. As a family."

"Of which I am not a member," I reminded her, even though, technically, I was now.

"You did us a great service getting Grace here. Making sure she was with her family for such a joyous event." She paused. "I cannot fathom you being alone when you could join us. We're very relaxed. We play games, have dinner, and enjoy the day. Please join us."

Suddenly the thought of being close to Grace for another day was too much to resist. I wasn't sure how she was going to feel about it, though.

"It would be my honor. Thank you for your gracious invitation."

A flash of gold disappearing down the back hall caught my eye. "I'll come get the directions in a moment. If you would excuse me?" I asked, already moving. Grace wasn't escaping me this time.

I caught her in the hall as she came out of the ladies' room. It was deserted, and as I suspected, she didn't look overly happy to see me.

"Why are you still here?" she demanded. "You got what you wanted. You saw the winery and the wedding."

"Why should I leave, Gracie? I'm enjoying myself." I ran my fingers down her soft cheek. "You are stunning this evening."

She slapped my hand away and ignored my words, even as color crept into her cheeks. "Stop calling me that. It's Grace."

"All your family calls you Gracie."

"You aren't my family."

"Hmm. I beg to differ."

She crossed her arms. "You shouldn't be here."

"You're here. I belong at your side."

"No, you don't," she hissed.

"I imagine the law would agree with me."

"Fuck the law," she snarled, her fury making me want to laugh. I leaned down, my mouth a breath away from hers.

"I would rather fuck *you* again, darling. Far more enjoyable."

She gasped as I covered her mouth with mine. For one brief moment, she responded, then she pushed me away and turned, running back into the ladies' room. I contemplated following her, then decided to leave her alone. For now.

"Run, Gracie, my darling. I'll catch you, regardless."

I walked back into the reception room, noticing Addi sitting alone in the corner. I had no doubt she had heard us, but I decided to play innocent. Aiden was on the dance floor, a large man out of control with his wild moves. I lifted my eyebrows with a smirk and bent close. "Your boss is funny," I said, referring to one of his jokes during his speech.

"He's not just my boss," she stated knowingly.

I tilted my chin toward the direction I had been with Gracie. "I'm not just her *boss* either."

Leaving her gaping, I went to get another drink. I got the information I needed from Katy, and I waited.

It didn't take long. Grace appeared from the back hall, her gaze sweeping the room and finding me. This time, she didn't ignore me, instead heading right in my direction. She stopped in front of me, anger emanating from her. She was even more beautiful.

"My mother invited you for Christmas?"

"She did," I said, sipping tonic water, trying not to grin at her indignation.

"You said no, of course."

"How could anyone say no to your mother? She is as charming as you are, darling. Of course I said yes." I couldn't help my smile. "She even offered me a bed tonight. Maybe I should say yes and sneak into yours? I could stay until after the holidays. Would you like that, Gracie?"

Her eyes widened to the point of hilarity. Her small hands fisted at her sides. "I just uninvited you, Mr. Richards. Do you understand? You finish your drink, and you leave. I don't want to see you until after my holidays." She lifted up on her toes, as if adding an inch to her height would scare me. It only made her more adorable, but I kept my expression neutral.

"And you had better have those annulment papers ready."

"Sex. We had sex. The marriage was most definitely consummated. In fact, I remember one other—"

She cut me off. "Then file the divorce papers. It. Never. Happened."

She turned and stomped away, heading right to the bar. I hoped she didn't drink too much again, but I knew I couldn't do much to stop her.

I felt the glances from the table I had been sitting at. Katy was watching us, her comrades beside her. Cami, Dee, Emmy, and Liv were with her, and their eyes were focused on the little exchange between Grace and me. Luckily, the father of the bride came into the room, bringing with him the frigid air and the smell of expensive cigars. He spoke to his daughter, swaying slightly on his feet, then stopped at the table filled with women to say something, making them all laugh.

I took the opportunity to disappear.

I had a lot of plans to make.

Michael's eyes were wide with shock when he opened the door the next morning to find me on his doorstep. He looked me up and down. "Was the suit I brought not acceptable?"

"I need your help again. Or Larry's, really."

He stepped back, allowing me in. "This should be interesting."

I followed him to the kitchen, the domestic scene in front of me making me smile. Larry, in a robe, feeding their daughter, coffee cups on the table, a half-eaten yogurt cup sitting beside one.

"Jaxson," Larry drawled. "How good to see you."

"He needs your help," Michael said, sitting down, tickling Abby under the chin.

"My help? I don't know anything about lawyers, except they are difficult to work for," Larry deadpanned, winking at me. "And they disappear for days on end."

I laughed, accepting the cup of coffee he handed me. "Don't remind me. What a ghastly way to spend a week."

"Yes, horrid that," Michael teased. "Days alone with Grace."

I threw him a look, which he ignored. I turned to Larry. "I've been invited somewhere for Christmas. It's a family event. I can't arrive without gifts."

Larry grinned. He owned an online boutique that specialized in pampering products for women.

"How many?"

"Twenty-one men and twenty-one women. No children."

His face went slack. "What?"

"I can take care of the men. Liquor. But the women, I have no idea."

"That's all one family?"

"One blended family."

Michael regarded me. "Grace's family."

I nodded. "They insisted I come for Christmas as a thank-you for getting Grace to the wedding."

"Which you attended," Michael said.

"Yes."

"I have worked for you for years. You have never once attended a co-worker's social event outside the office. Now in the span of three days, you're at two family-oriented events?" He smirked.

"The invitations were hard to resist."

"Or Grace is."

I met his knowing gaze and sighed. "Or Grace is."

"You're playing with fire, Jaxson."

"I've already been burned, Michael. Scarred for life."

His eyebrows shot up. "Well, then."

I looked at Larry. "Can you help? Do you have the inventory?"

He grinned. "Oh Jaxson, you should know me better than that." He stood. "Michael, you need to take over our daughter. My bottom line is about to get a major upswing."

Christmas morning, I brewed a pot of coffee and sat in my silent apartment overlooking downtown Toronto. The streets were quiet, the city not yet awake. There was nothing different about the day for me—yet. But the large bag of gifts and the Santa suit I had procured promised a very different day. I wouldn't be catching up on work, reading, or eating Chinese takeout this year. Instead, I would be spending the day with a large group of people that called themselves a family. And at the center of it would be Grace. I wondered how she would react to seeing me. Somehow, the subject of Christmas had come up on our wild Monday together, and she had told me how, every year, her Uncle Aiden dressed as Santa and appeared at some point in the day, handing out small gifts and making everyone laugh.

"He stopped eventually," she confessed. "But I still miss it. It was the highlight of the day for me."

I planned on giving her that highlight back. Larry had helped me with small gifts for all the women, and I had braved the crowds yesterday, procuring bottles of liquor for the men and a special box of chocolates for Grace. Her real gift was tucked into my coat pocket, and I planned to give it to her in private. I had spent hours wrapping the gifts, my fingers uncoordinated at using tape and scissors, adding bows. But it was important to me, and I did it.

Part of me couldn't believe what I was doing. That I could care enough about another person to want to brighten their day. That I would dress up as Santa Claus in front of a group of people in order to make one person happy.

It was the same part of me that still had trouble believing I could love someone. I cared for Grace—of that, there was no doubt. But love was another thing— and something I was certain I wasn't capable of feeling.

I sighed as I set down my mug and reached for the ridiculous Santa hat. I refused to wear the beard, but the coat and hat would be sufficient.

I hoped the gesture would be enough to soften Grace.

CHAPTER 24

JAXSON

I stepped from the SUV, pulling the hat firmly into place. I stood for a moment, looking over the vast expanse of land, houses, and water. The "BAM Compound," as it was called, was impressive. Well-placed homes with great views and totally private. I had enjoyed the drive out, the roads mostly empty with the threat of the storm Grace and I had madly driven through now finally reaching this area. The air was thick with fog, and the snow was beginning. In case it got as bad as they predicted, I had packed a small bag, planning to take Katy up on her offer of the spare room. And hoping Grace might let me sneak into her room once everyone was asleep.

We all had Christmas wishes. I knew the chances were I would end up back at the Port Albany Motel by myself if the storm was bad. But I could hope.

As I approached the door, my nerves kicked in. Maybe it was a bad idea. Somehow, between the wistful tone in

Grace's voice and the unexpected invitation, the insane idea seemed like a good plan. A chance to make Grace happy. Remind her I was the man she had fallen in love with. Now, in the glaring light of day and with a houseful of strangers, it seemed stupid.

But before I could change my mind, the door was flung open, and Aiden was framed in the entry.

"Santa!" he shouted, far too exuberantly for a man of his age. "Come on in!"

I hoisted the bag of gifts higher on my shoulder.

Too late.

I entered the building they called the Hub, once again impressed. Vaulted ceilings, accentuated with wooden beams, soared high. Large windows faced the water, showing the astounding endless view of water. Hard-wood floors gleamed. A massive tree was in the corner, gifts piled high underneath. Enticing aromas tickled my nose. Warmth surrounded me, not only from the heat of the huge fireplace, but the welcome that greeted me.

My gaze immediately found Grace standing behind Aiden. She looked befuddled. Amused. Angry. Her hands were clenched into fists at her sides, yet her mouth quirked at the corner. She had no idea what to think. I had, indeed, surprised her.

I winked at her, not at all perturbed by her lack of warmth or greeting.

I cleared my throat and put my hands on my hips after lowering the bag to the floor. "Ho ho ho."

My effort was poor, and I tried again. I lifted my arms high, bellowing, "Merry Christmas!"

I was shocked at the chorus of Merry Christmases that greeted me in return, and I felt a real smile cross my face.

"What's in the bag, Santa?" Ronan yelled.

"I hope it's booze!" Thomas added.

I blinked and looked at the bag by my feet. "Some of it," I said, sounding doubtful.

Aiden laughed and clapped me on the shoulder. "Some is good. Let's get this party started."

Everyone, it seemed, loved Santa.

I made my way around the room slowly, distributing gifts, shaking hands, getting hugs. Using my odd gift of remembering details, I called each person by name, never once faltering. My gaze found Grace sitting with Addi and Brayden, the happy couple glowing and angled close together. Grace looked shocked. Annoyed. Bewildered. She watched me, our eyes locking several times as I worked the room.

I took my time and spoke to every one of her cousins, aunts, and uncles. Her grandparents. I still found it amazing that these families were joined together, not because of blood, but with what seemed to be a much stronger bond. It made me curious and, strangely enough, made me want to be a part of it.

I made my way to where her parents were watching the entire spectacle. With Richard and Katy stood Bentley, Aiden, Maddox, and their wives. I could feel the heat of Grace's stare as I handed them their gifts, once again thanking Katy for the invitation. She looked delighted with her bath bombs and the chocolates I had added, wanting her gift to be a little special. Richard turned the bottle of scotch I had given him in his hands, then clapped me on the shoulder. "Welcome," he said.

"I appreciate being included."

Katy patted my arm in a motherly fashion. "Christmas is for family and sharing. We're thrilled you're here with us. We're even more thrilled that Santa joined you." She winked. "Santa's visit was always Gracie's favorite part."

Aiden clapped me on the back, his cigars clutched in one large hand. "You can take up the tradition now. My gifts were never this good."

I wondered if next year I would even be part of Grace's life, but I didn't express that thought out loud. I handed out the rest of the "parent" gifts and turned to the last grouping waiting for me. Gracie was still sitting with Brayden and Addi, looking tense as I approached. She and Brayden appeared to be having some words before I arrived, but they were quiet as I sat down across from Gracie. I pulled off the hat and ran my fingers through my hair with a rueful grin.

"This being Santa is tiring stuff. No wonder it only happens once a year."

Gracie shook her head. "There was no need for all the gifts, Jaxson. Or to risk your life to drive here. You should probably head back before the storm gets worse."

I ignored her rude tone with a smirk. "Your mother and aunts were kind enough to invite me here today so I wouldn't be alone on Christmas. I still have the four-wheel drive, so I was perfectly fine on the roads, although I appreciate your concern. And to show up empty-handed would have been rude."

"A bottle of wine would have sufficed. This—" she waved her hand "—is a little overboard."

"There, I beg to differ. I recall being told that Santa's visit made the entire day magical. How can one ignore a chance to do that?" I paused, lowering my voice as our eyes locked. "Especially for you, Gracie."

She sniffed, turning her head as if she could ignore my presence. I tried not to grin as I gave Addi a box of chocolates and Brayden a small bottle of his favorite whiskey. I had heard him comment about it at the wedding, so the choice was easy.

Addi stood and kissed my cheek. "Thank you. How on earth did you know these are my favorites?"

I smiled. "I listen." I glanced at Gracie. "I'm always listening." I reached into the bag and withdrew a box of chocolate caramels—Gracie's favorite. The box was larger than the others had been and decorated beautifully. I handed them to her. "For my favorite articling student."

"I'm your only articling student."

"Yes, you are. You are both."

She took the box, touching the lovely bow. I noticed the way her fingers trembled.

"Thank you."

I folded the bag. "I guess my work is done." I stood and pulled off the heavy Santa coat and removed the padded stomach, grateful to shed them since they were far too warm. I had dressed casually for the day, wearing a white shirt and navy cardigan with my dress pants. I was still overdressed compared to some others, but for me, it was casual. I reached into the pocket of the Santa jacket and handed Addi an envelope. She frowned in confusion.

"What is this?"

"For you and your husband."

She opened it, scanning the donation receipt to the local no-kill shelter they supported. Gracie had told me they had asked for donations to that charity in lieu of gifts. It was an amazingly unselfish gesture—something I was beginning to realize ran deep with this family.

"You didn't have to do this."

I shook my head. "I enjoyed being at your wedding. Meeting your family. Being welcomed so warmly—" my gaze drifted to Gracie, then back to Addi "—by your family. I wanted to contribute to a cause so dear to your heart."

Addi hugged me. "Thank you. I'm glad you're here today, Jaxson."

I ignored Gracie's muffled gasp of outrage. Brayden stood and shook my hand. "Thank you. We're happy you're here. Up to a game of air hockey?"

"Sounds like fun."

"I'm going to help with dinner preparations. You coming with me, Gracie?" Addi asked.

She pursed her lips. "I would like a moment with Jaxson first."

Brayden indicated the stairs. "Okay. See you downstairs shortly."

I nodded, my eyes on Grace. "If I survive."

She waited until Addi and Brayden left. The room was still full, small groupings sitting around talking. The mothers were making lots of noise in the large kitchen area, the fathers by the window, cups of coffee in their hands. Everyone was busy, but I had a feeling we were still being watched. I faced Grace, smiling.

"Yes, darling?" I asked quietly. "You wanted a moment?"

"Don't call me that."

"No one can hear us."

"I am not your darling."

"What did you want then, Gracie?"

"How did you do all this?" she asked, surprising me. I was certain she was going to tell me to leave.

"Larry."

"Larry?"

"Michael's husband. He runs an online store. He makes these bath bomb things, handmade chocolates, organic oils."

"Oh. Michael said something about Etsy once, but he never elaborated."

"He has a good business. After yesterday, it was a good year."

"You didn't have to do this."

I met her gaze. "Did it make you happy, Gracie? For one brief moment, did I make you happy?"

She smiled, but it was a sad one. "That's the problem, Jaxson. You do these things that make me happy, but then I remember you broke my heart."

"Maybe I can fix that."

"It's not that easy." Then she sat up, making me realize how close we'd been leaning to each other. "Marrying me only complicated the situation, and it needs to be fixed."

I sat back, shaking my head. "Marrying you was the start of our road to recovery."

She stood, looking down on me. "That road is a dead end. And no one here will be the wiser, do you understand?" she whispered furiously.

"I don't think so, darling. I don't believe in divorce."

"You don't believe in love either, and I won't be trapped in a marriage of convenience."

"How *convenient* is it then that we can't keep our hands off each other?"

Her eyes widened and her fury grew. "I would like to punch you," she said, a false smile on her face. "But my family is watching, and it's Christmas. Enjoy the day, Jaxson. Stay away from me."

She turned and walked away, her head high. I noticed Katy watching us, the rest of the crowd seemingly occupied. I smiled at her and waved, hoping I looked relaxed.

I wasn't sure I was fooling her, though.

I had never experienced anything like a Christmas Day with Grace's family. The love that surrounded them was astonishing to me. They all got along. They all *liked* one another. There was laughter and joking. Teasing and fun. And they included me in all of it. Even the gift exchange.

When Addi announced it was time, I felt the pang of being the outsider. The unexpected person sitting on the edge of this enormous, loving group. I had waved her off, telling her I planned to take the time to read, but she had refused my excuse, pulling me along with her.

"No, you have to come join us."

"This is for family. Your gift time. I'm quite fine on my own," I protested.

She leaned close, smiling at me. "It's Christmas, Jaxson. Santa visits everyone here." She tugged on my arm. "*Everyone.*"

A reluctant smile tugged on my mouth. "I don't wish to intrude. It wasn't my intention."

"You aren't intruding. And you have to come."

She was as hard to resist as Grace. She pulled me along, refusing to take no for an answer. Brayden watched us with an indulgent look on his face, his love for her written all over him. I understood his infatuation totally, although I wasn't allowed to express mine.

When I was handed my first of many gifts, I was dumb-struck. I had no idea how to explain to any of them that I had never once had a Christmas. Never been part of a family. That I had never sat beside a tree and held a gift, the unknown contents exciting. The scarf the box contained was handsome and soft. A simple gift to many, but to me, quite profound. There were some other thoughtful gifts for my desk, even a bottle of scotch from Grace's grandparents. Nothing, of course, from Grace, but I didn't expect it.

We ate lunch, and I stayed as close to Grace as I dared. It was interesting for me to see the family dynamics as they gathered. Watching the parents with their offspring, once again marveling at the affection between them all. After the gifts and cleanup, people began separating, drifting to various activities, or for many—a nap. Taking advantage of a lull in the storm, a small group went skating on the frozen ice close to the beach. Aiden planned to build a fire and went to seek out sticks to whittle for a marshmallow roast later. Some went to play more games in the large area downstairs. I wandered the building, taking in all the thoughtful details. The small library. The pool. The worn-in furniture. Despite the size, it was homey and obviously a well-used building. Now that I had seen the little community they had, I understood Grace's desire to live here. As I stood looking out the window at the homes surrounding the area, I felt a strange yearning once again tug in my chest.

Grace appeared beside me. She had been exceedingly polite since our talk, not wanting to draw any attention to us, no doubt.

"Enjoying your day?" she asked, playing the part of hostess. "Can I get you anything?"

"Yes, actually."

She frowned, obviously expecting me to say no. "Coffee? Wine?"

"No. A walk."

"Pardon me?"

"I want to take a walk. With you. Outside. Somewhere private."

"Is that completely necessary?"

I met her gaze, lowering my voice. "It's Christmas, Gracie. I'm asking."

"Fine," she huffed. "I'll meet you outside."

CHAPTER 25

JAXSON

Ten minutes later, Gracie led me down a path away from the Hub. In the distance, I could hear echoes of laughter coming from the lake as the skaters chased one another. I could smell the fire Aiden had started, the smoky aroma filling the air. We walked into the trees, stopping in a clearing.

She whirled around, a frown drawing her pretty mouth down.

"Okay, Jaxson, we've gone far enough. You wanted privacy, you got it. Now, say whatever it is you want to say."

I glanced down at the tracks in the freshly fallen snow and wondered if they had been made by Aiden scouring the brush for twigs or someone else. Grace crossed her arms, tapping her boot-covered foot in the snow, not even noticing there was a chance we could be overheard.

"Is it wrong for a man to want a few moments alone with his wife on Christmas Day?" I asked mildly.

"I'm not your wife."

"I have a certificate that says otherwise," I pointed out dryly.

"Stop it, Jaxson. It was a mistake."

"I disagree."

She huffed a deep sigh, grimacing. Silently, I withdrew a small package from my pocket, extending it to her.

"What is *that*?" she said, sounding horrified.

"A Christmas gift for you."

She backed away. "I don't want a gift."

"Too bad, my darling. Take it."

"You said you didn't buy gifts."

I stepped closer, refusing to let her run. "Which proves, once again, you are the exception."

She didn't move, and I lowered my voice. "Take it now, or I'll hand it to you in front of your family."

She grabbed the box, flipping open the lid and gaping at the contents. The thick platinum band was set with pavé diamonds. It was elegant, timeless, and beautiful. Much like Grace.

She met my eyes, hers panicked and incredulous. "*What* have you done? This is not necessary, Jaxson."

"Our rings didn't fit. I wanted you to have a real one. One as beautiful as you."

"I am not your wife!" She almost snarled.

"Yes, you are."

"We both know I married you drunk and out of my mind. We're getting a divorce."

I stepped close, my response a one-word growl. "No."

"Give me one good reason why not," she shot back, not backing down.

I yanked her into my arms and covered her mouth with mine, kissing her ferociously. All my pent-up frustration went into that kiss as I claimed her mouth, sliding my tongue inside. I wrapped my hand in her hair, holding her tight, crushing her to my chest, refusing to let go. She stiffened for a second, then slid her arms around my neck, kissing me back and making the most erotic sounds low in her throat. I grew hard, my cock pressing against the seam of my pants. I wanted to carry her into the woods and take her. To hell with her family, the day, or anyone watching. I wanted to make love to her until she knew she belonged to me and would stop fighting this. For a moment, with her in my arms, her mouth on mine, everything was perfect.

But she pushed away, gasping. "Stop doing that!"

"Why?" I demanded. "Give in, Gracie. Admit you feel something, and let's work on it. Tell your family. I'll stand by you."

"I am *not* staying married to you."

"Yes, you are."

Glaring, she lifted her arm and let the ring sail over my head and behind me. I shut my eyes, gathering my patience. I had called in a favor to get that ring. Waited for it to be engraved. She hadn't even tried it on. And the damn thing was expensive.

"That's what I think of your gift and this marriage," she spat. "It's not happening, Jaxson. Keep your gifts and your lips to yourself!"

"Gracie," I admonished gently. I had hurt her; I knew that. But I wanted to explain, to start anew.

"I mean it, Jaxson. I will be polite because my mother and aunts invited you. You will leave as soon as dinner is over, and I don't want to see you until I return to the office. And the first thing we're going to do is file for divorce."

She stomped away. I watched her leave, knowing not to follow her right now. I waited a moment, hanging my head on my chest.

"Please tell me you found the ring," I muttered to our silent audience.

Addi's voice responded. "We did."

"You knew we were here?" Brayden asked, standing, pulling Addi up beside him.

I shrugged. "If Grace hadn't been so irritated, she would have noticed the footprints as well. She was determined not to go farther, so I let her speak."

"She's not usually so…" Addi trailed off.

"Angry? Hurtful?"

"Yes."

I held out my hand, and Addi dropped the ring into my palm. I studied it for a moment, then slid it into the pocket of my cardigan. I had no idea where the box had gone.

"I hurt her first. I need to make it up to her." I paused. "I was correct, then, when I had assumed she confided in you, Addi? She told me how close you are."

"She did," Addi confirmed, her voice low. "She's determined to end this marriage. She insists it was a mistake."

I frowned, feeling the sadness weigh me down. I had a lot of work ahead of me. I shook my head firmly. "It was not. And I am as determined to keep her as she is determined to be rid of me."

"Why?" Brayden asked, looking confused.

I spoke the truth. "Because she is the only warmth in my life. Without her, the cold will destroy me."

They both looked shocked at my words. I studied the newlyweds. "Thank you for keeping our secret. One day, you will no longer have that burden."

I turned and left, my footsteps feeling heavy.

I spent most of the rest of the afternoon in the library, reading. Once I went to grab a cup of coffee and saw Grace across the room. I hated the anger in her expression and wanted to do something to erase it, but I knew there was nothing I could do at this moment other than leave her alone. She had a glass of wine in her hand, and I worried she was drinking too much again. I hated knowing I was the cause.

Christmas dinner was something out of a book, the food unending, the wine flowing, and the noise level almost deafening. Aiden's triplets could outeat an entire army, given the chance, and despite the massive amount of food on the tables, most of it was consumed. After dinner, the men did the cleanup, and it was good to stay busy, even if I had little to add to their conversations. I felt like one of them, and I enjoyed it, even if it was only for today.

People were scattered around, dozing, talking, playing board games when I entered the main room again. A glance out the window told me if I was going to leave, now was the time. I could see the snow was getting heavier, and soon I would have no choice but to stay. I knew Grace didn't want that, and I didn't want to force my hand. I sat briefly, enjoying one last cup of coffee, covertly watching Grace as she sat with Richard, laughing over something on his phone. It was obvious the love he held for his daughter, and I wondered if we would ever get to the point we could be friendly. If Grace and I could work things out between us. Richard was intelligent, and I had enjoyed my conversations with him as well as the other "BAM boys," as they called themselves. They were a great bunch of men. Luckily, I was pretty sure he was too caught up in the day to have noticed anything between Grace and me, although I wasn't certain others hadn't observed.

I stood, announcing my decision to leave, waving aside the protests and explaining I had work to do, it was a short drive, and the SUV I still had in my possession would be fully capable of handling the slick roads. I kissed all the mothers, shook the hands of the fathers, and made a point of wishing Grace's beloved Nan and Pops all the best.

Then I headed toward *her*. I couldn't leave without at least a goodbye. I saw Grace tense as I got closer, and I noticed Richard glance between us, suddenly picking up on Grace's reaction. I wasn't watching where I was going when it happened. I tripped over the edge of a throw rug, my arms flying out to break my fall. The sudden jerk caused the ring in my pocket to sail out, the light catching the glint of the diamonds as it soared through the air, landing on the floor and spinning. The sound was loud on the hardwood, and everyone's eyes were glued to the movement until it slowed and stopped, lying there like a beacon.

I tried to get to it, but Richard reached down and picked it up, frowning.

"Pretty ring." He narrowed his eyes. "Why is it in your pocket?"

"I forgot it was there." I held out my hand. "If I may have it back, please."

Richard held out the ring, then pulled back, squinting as he noticed the inscription. I felt the blood drain from my face, knowing my misstep had now blown the secret Grace tried so hard to hide wide open. One look at her and I knew she realized it as well.

"*My Saving Grace?*" Richard snarled. "Why does this say 'My Saving Grace?' Are you..." His eyes widened. "Are you having an *affair* with my daughter?" His voice rose. Behind me, I heard people moving, and to my right, Addi and Brayden stood, wary and alert.

Richard's gaze swung to Gracie. "What is going on?"

"This is why I don't drink," Gracie said, then, once again, burst into tears.

"Are you screwing with my daughter?" Richard bellowed. "You're her *boss*!"

He stepped toward me, and I shook my head. "No. Absolutely not."

Richard shook his hand, the diamonds catching the light. "Explain this!"

I sighed in defeat. There was nowhere to hide anymore. "We're not having an affair, Richard. We're married."

For a moment, only the sound of Gracie's sobs filled the air.

From behind us, one of the Callaghan boys muttered, "Well, holy…*night*. I wasn't expecting that."

Then it happened. Richard's fist shot out so fast, I had no time to react or deflect his punch. I felt the crunch of bone meeting bone, and I stumbled backward, the ring once again hitting the floor. It rolled under the sofa.

Suddenly, Maddox was there, wrapping his arms around Richard to hold him back. Richard was raging—yelling and cursing, trying to get to me. Oddly enough, Gracie stood, blocking his way as I straightened up, holding my jaw. The man knew how to throw a punch. A glance to the side showed me Katy, standing mute and confused across the room, watching the scene unfold in front of her. Dee stood beside her, wrapping her arm around her shoulders in comfort as Katy covered her mouth.

"Talk about decking the halls," another voice spoke up.

"I told you this wouldn't stay secret," Brayden muttered to Addi.

Richard's wild gaze turned to him. "You knew?" he yelled. "You knew about this?" He struggled harder against Maddox's grip. Maddox looked startled then lifted his eyebrows, indicating the door, silently telling Brayden to get out. Others began to file from the room.

It was like the proverbial sinking ship. The rats were deserting.

Brayden grabbed Addi's hand. "Time to go."

Maddox met my eyes. "Go with them. *Now*." Blindly, I followed them outside. Brayden grabbed the keys from my hand for the SUV, and the next thing I knew, I was sitting in their living room. I had no recollection of the short drive over.

"I should go," I muttered.

"You can't drive in this, Jaxson. It would be suicide," Brayden protested.

I barked out a laugh. Grace was probably wishing me dead right now anyway.

Addi went and got the ice pack, pressing it to my rapidly swelling cheek. The cold startled me, and I shook my head to clear it.

"Gracie," I breathed. "I need to go back."

"No," Brayden insisted. "You need to stay right here and let Gracie figure this out with her family. You'll be involved soon enough."

"What happened?" I asked in a daze.

Brayden clapped me on the shoulder. "Welcome to the family, Jaxson. Brace yourself. It's gonna be a bumpy ride."

He sat down, pulling Addi to his lap. "Enjoying your honeymoon?" he quipped, trying to lighten the air. "What's a family holiday without a secret being leaked and fistfights happening? I mean, usually, it's the triplets and eggnog is involved, but at least this one was different."

"This is awful," she whispered.

"Christmas took an unexpected detour," he agreed and hugged her close. "It's going to be okay, Addi. Somehow, it will be."

"What are we going to do?" she asked quietly.

I felt his sympathetic look. His reply was low.

"They need to figure it out, Addi. It's their story to tell. Their future to decide."

He was right. It was our story. One we hadn't finished yet.

And the biggest question right now was—did Grace and I have a future?

CHAPTER 26

GRACE

I made my way toward Addi's house in the early hours of the morning, dawn barely having broken. I carefully picked my way through the piles of snow and ice that had accumulated overnight, planting my boots firmly between each step and holding tight to my overnight bag I was carrying. The five-minute journey took three times as long as usual. I wasn't convinced it was totally due to the snow as to how tired my footsteps were.

There was a light shining in the early morning dimness, and I knew Addi was waiting for me. I had texted her earlier, and she had responded that she was awake and had coffee ready.

I paused outside, noting that Jaxson's SUV rental was still outside. I was grateful he was safe.

I slipped in the door and found Addi in the kitchen, the promised coffee on the table. She was dressed casually, her hair up in a ponytail. She stood as I came in and hugged me tight. I returned her embrace then sat down, accepting the coffee.

"Bray still asleep?"

"Yes. So is Jaxson. I heard him pacing most of the night, but he finally became quiet around four. He probably exhausted himself."

"He does that when he's upset. Paces and thinks. I swear the carpet in his office must need replacing often."

"You know him well for someone who claims not to care."

"I never said I didn't care. That right there is the problem."

She cocked her head. "Talk to me, Gracie. What the hell is going on?"

I sighed. "I don't know what to say. I'm so sorry I ruined Christmas."

She laughed softly. "Ruin is a strong word. The boys will talk about this one for years. But I don't care about that. You *married* Jaxson, Gracie. Why?"

I met her concerned eyes. "I don't know, Addi. I got drunk. I did something stupid."

"Is it stupid? He certainly doesn't seem to think so."

I took a sip of coffee. "That's what's so confusing. He ended things between us. He was hateful. Told me I meant nothing to him. I don't understand." I thought about the hours I had spent trying to recall what happened in Vegas. *How* we ended up married. *Why* Jaxson was so determined not to end the marriage.

"You haven't discussed it?" she asked, shocked. "All that time in the car and you never brought it up?"

"He refused. He said he couldn't concentrate on the road and the conversation. I thought we'd separate once we got here, and my foggy memory would clear. That we could sit down like adults and figure out the next step. I hadn't planned on the wedding." I snorted. "Or the fact that my mother would invite him for Christmas and my entire family would adopt him."

She frowned at my words. "Well, I understand not wanting such a deep conversation while navigating a storm, but you've been home for a few days."

"We haven't spoken since he left the wedding."

"I see. And you didn't expect to see him on Christmas."

"No, I didn't."

"A bit of a shock, I suppose."

I didn't reply. Shock was one word to describe how I felt when I saw him. There were other words such as relieved and elated—which made no sense to me given how he had hurt me.

Wearily, I relaxed back into the comfy chair. Addi and I always liked to sit in the kitchen and talk. Our moms did as well. It was an unwritten rule the chairs had to be well padded, cozy, and big. It felt right.

"What happened after we left last night?"

"Things broke up pretty fast. Heather went home with Reed. Penny, Gavin, and Liam went with Maddox and Dee. Mom, Dad, and I stayed at the Hub for a while. Arguing." I looked at Addi, the memory of the prior night bringing tears to my eyes. "My dad was so angry. I have never seen him like that. He was yelling and cursing. Furious at what I did, but even more so that I hid the fact that I had gotten married. When I told him that Jaxson and I had been seeing each other secretly, I thought he was going to come here and hit him again."

"And your mom?"

"She was calmer. Still upset with me, but not in the same way. My dad and I argued, and he refused to listen to anything I had to say. Then they started fighting." I scrubbed my face, brushing away the tears. "My dad is furious with me and irritated with my mom. Mom is angry with Dad and not speaking to him. She is disappointed in me and hurt. They are both upset." I looked down, a tear splashing onto the table. "I never meant to disappoint them. I thought I could handle it and no one would ever know—or not find out for a very long time."

"That wasn't a very logical thought, Grace."

"I know. I haven't been thinking clearly." I looked at her, meeting her sympathetic eyes. "I don't know what to do, Addi."

She reached across the table and squeezed my hand. "Your dad will forgive you. He loves you too much. Your mom and dad will make up. What you need to do is stop hiding, talk to Jaxson, and figure out your shit, my friend. You can't hide from this. You have to decide what you want and stand up for it."

"The repercussions of this marriage…" I trailed off. "I don't understand why Jaxson is insisting on us staying together."

"Then you need to ask him. And be honest with yourself about your feelings."

"He hurt me."

She gazed at me in silence. When she spoke, her voice was quiet but serious. "And is this your way of hurting him back?"

"What?" I asked, surprised.

"I know you, Grace. I know your heart. If you were involved with him, you must have had feelings. You're not the sort of woman for dalliances."

"I loved him."

"Loved, as in past tense?"

"I don't know. He was so terrible, and he hurt me so badly. I was so alone and scared. I had no one I could talk to."

"Why didn't you tell me?"

"Because you were happy. Getting married. And part of me was ashamed. I felt as if I had been a dirty little secret, and then, I was cast aside. I guess I felt as if I deserved to be alone."

She shook her head, looking upset. "I'm your best friend. No matter what is going on in my life, you always come to me. And you are no one's secret. He was as much a part of this as you were." She stood and hugged me, her embrace tight. "Don't ever shut yourself off from comfort, Grace. Especially from me. Do you understand?"

"Yes," I sobbed.

Her grip tightened. "Figure this out. Be honest with yourself. Don't think today. Think next week, next month. The rest of your life. Is this man the one you want to wake up with every morning? Does his smile make you happy? Is he worth the fight?"

She pulled back. "I love you, Gracie. I want you to be as happy as I am. If Jaxson is that man for you, I will support you. If he isn't, then I will help you. But you need to decide. And more importantly, you need to talk to him and see what he's thinking, how *he* feels." She shook her head. "You know, lawyers are known as big talkers. The two of you need to learn to *communicate*." She met my eyes. "Big difference between those two things."

I sniffled and wiped under my eyes, her words making me smile. I knew she was trying to make me feel better. "I know."

I heard movement down the hall, and I stepped back. "Go see your husband. I'm sure he's wondering why his bride is chatting over coffee with her friend instead of in bed with him."

"Best friend," she corrected. "And he knows." She winked, looking ludicrous as she attempted to be lewd. "I already made sure he was *taken care of* before you arrived."

"Ew. TMI, Addi."

She pushed me toward the door. "He's in the guest room."

I paused and wiped at my face. "Thanks, Addi."

"Love you."

I smiled. "Love you right back."

I slipped into the guest room and made my way to the bed. Jaxson was asleep, but even in repose, he didn't look relaxed. His jaw was tight, his brow furrowed, and his cheek bloomed dark with the bruise my father's fist had caused. I had never known my father to react in such a violent manner. Nor heard him yell the way he did last night. I knew if he found out, he'd be angry—exactly how angry, I had no idea.

Carefully, I sat at the foot of the bed, looking at Jaxson. I still didn't understand. I couldn't remember our night in Vegas. Tiny details floated through my head, blurred images, snippets of conversations, but nothing tangible. Nothing to grab on to and help clear the fog. The strongest images were of him and me together. His hot breath on my neck, his body meshed with mine, his burning, drugging kisses. Wanting more. Needing more.

But how had we gotten there?

And why did our physical connection always come into play? Even now, sitting close to him in the midst of all this hurt and chaos, I felt…better. Calmer.

I sighed, and his eyes flew open, the ice-blue irises meeting mine. He sat up, dragging me into his arms. And like a fool, I went willingly.

"Gracie, darling." He pressed a kiss to my head. "Tell me you're all right. I'm sorry. So fucking sorry."

For a moment, I basked in his strong embrace. Relaxed into his warmth. How he continued to have this effect on me, I would never understand. I pushed him back, studying his face in the dull light. I traced my fingers over his cheek.

"Does it hurt?"

"It's fine. What happened? Are you all right?"

"It was awful. My father is furious, my mother upset. There was lots of yelling. Not my usual family Christmas."

He gripped my hand. "Anything else?"

I frowned. "It's my parents, Jaxson. What do you think they would do?"

He looked away, his jaw flexing as he swallowed. "I don't know."

"You don't really think they'd hurt me, do you?" Understanding dawned, and I gasped quietly. "Did your parents hit you?"

"We're not talking about that right now."

I pushed back my hair. "No, we never talk about anything when it comes to you, do we? Your past, your reasons for breaking it off, why you insist on staying married to me. You expect me to simply agree and follow you blindly."

He caught my hands as I began to rise. "No, Gracie, it's only—"

"Only what?"

"I don't know how to talk about it."

"You pick a word, and you start."

"Not here. Not now."

He was right. Sitting in Addi's guest room wasn't the place to hash this out. But Addi was correct. We had to talk and be honest.

I extricated my hands from his grip.

"I want to go home, Jaxson. I need to sleep and clear my mind. Then we need to talk."

"Okay. I'll drive you." He swung his legs off the bed and stood, towering over me. "Will you come home with me?"

"No. I need to sleep. I need to organize my thoughts and try to sort out my head. If I'm with you, I can't. You-you overwhelm me."

He smiled sadly. "I guess I'll hold on to that, at least."

I paused at the door. "I'll be in the kitchen."

His eyes were troubled, but he nodded. "Okay."

JAXSON

I entered the kitchen, my gaze finding Gracie immediately. She sat at the table, a cup of coffee in front of her. She looked exhausted, her eyes red-rimmed from crying, her shoulders hunched as if she was holding herself in. I hated I had a part in her looking so torn. That I had caused this rift between her and her parents.

Brayden and Addi were nowhere to be seen, but Grace held out a cup of coffee and I drank it quickly, wanting to get her home so she could rest. I picked up her bag, and we left quietly, heading to the SUV. The sight of a large man leaning on the fender made me stop.

Ronan, one of Aiden's triplets, stood as we approached. He was massive, much like his father—tall and strong. His dark hair was tucked under a knitted cap, and his green eyes were piercing as he looked at us. I wondered if I was about to get a matching bruise on the other side of my face.

"Ronan?" Grace asked. "What are you doing here?"

He had a surprisingly soft voice when he was alone. "I wanted to make sure you were okay, Gracie. I saw you out walking earlier. I figured you would be heading here, and I wanted to check on you."

She smiled as she stood next to him, looking tiny beside his large frame. "I'll be okay."

He glanced my way. "You're really married?"

"Yes."

"You gonna treat her right?"

"If she lets me."

"She's my favorite."

Grace had once told me Ronan was her favorite as well.

"I don't think I'm supposed to have a favorite," she confessed. "But Ronan is special. He has a way of caring for people. Looking after them without being asked. We have great conversations, and he always listens to me." She smiled. "He's a jokester when he's with the other two, but on his own, he's quieter. More reflective. If I needed him, he'd be right there."

"I'm glad she has you," I said.

"You won't be so glad if you hurt her."

"Noted."

He bent and lifted her in his arms, hugging her tight. Her feet rose off the ground and swung slightly as he swayed. "I'm right here, Gracie. I can get to you fast if you need me."

She patted his back. "I know."

He put her down and grinned evilly in my direction. "I know where to hide bodies. We have lots of land."

She laughed. "I don't think that will be needed, but thanks."

"Okay." He looked at me. "I'll be watching."

"Right."

He dug into his pocket and opened his palm. Inside was the ring, glittering in the light. "I found this. I thought you'd want it back."

I took it, the metal warm from his hand. I knew better than to try to give it to Grace right now. "Thanks."

"Sure." He grinned and winked. "It's pretty. Drive safe."

He sauntered past me, stopping. "If she decides to keep you, I'm okay with that. You're good at air hockey, and I kinda like you."

"Thanks," I said dryly.

He walked away, and I put our bags in the SUV and opened Grace's door.

"High praise," she said.

"Does it sway your decision?"

She shook her head, not answering.

CHAPTER 27

JAXSON

The drive was silent, the roads bare, and the miles passed quickly. I pulled up to her building, letting the SUV idle at the curb.

"Are you sure you won't come with me?"

She turned to me with a tired smile. "I can't take the elevator today, Jaxson. Even with you."

"I could come up to yours."

"I think we need a little distance."

"I don't want distance from you."

"That's not what you said a few weeks ago."

"Grace, I—"

She cut me off. "I can't. Not right now, Jaxson. I'm exhausted. Emotional. I'm confused and upset."

"I want to hold you."

She opened the door, pausing as she turned.

"I needed you to do that weeks ago. You sent me away."

She shut the door, pulled open the back door, and grabbed her bag.

"Can I at least call you?"

"I thought you got rid of your personal cell."

I shook my head. "No." I paused. "Please let me call you."

She hesitated. "I'll call you."

"You remember the number?" I asked.

"I remember everything."

"Will you?" I asked, frustrated. "Will you call?"

"When I'm ready."

She shut the door and trudged up the steps to her building before I could ask her if she ever would be ready.

It took all I had to drive away from her.

I couldn't settle, no matter how hard I tried. I paced my apartment constantly. Physically, I was exhausted, but mentally, my mind wouldn't shut off. I was worried about Grace. I wanted to talk to her. Make sure she was all right. I thought about her father's reaction. His anger. The shocked look on her mother's face. The odd way that, for the first time in my life, I had felt part of something—connected with a group of people. It felt strange that it should sadden me when I thought of not seeing them again.

I used the gym in the building and worked out. Swam laps. Caught up on emails and correspondence. I had booked time off weeks ago, thinking I could spend it with Grace, and now I regretted it and thought perhaps I would return to the office the next day.

I sat down and turned on the TV, deciding to catch up on the news. I switched to a local channel, half listening to the reports of the usual muggings, shootings, and random feel-good stories they inserted, when the anchor announced a breaking story. A suspected gas line explosion had occurred not long before in a small area off Jamison, causing severe damage to the building as well as neighboring structures. The back of my neck prickled when they said the name. They cut to a live report, and the instant I saw where the reporter was standing, I was on my feet. I recognized the area and the building behind him.

Grace's building.

I was out of my apartment in a flash.

The area was blocked off, but I found a cop and explained my wife had been in the building and I had to get to her. Something about my pleas must have resonated, and he allowed me to duck under the tape. My usual calm had dissolved the second I realized the blast had been in her neighborhood—possibly even her building. I had no idea if she was all right. Hurt. Worse. In the car, the worst-case scenarios played out in my head. I called her cell phone repeatedly, slamming my hand on the steering wheel when she didn't answer. Fear tore at my throat, making it hard to swallow. Sweat beaded on my neck as uncertainty crawled its way up my spine.

Frantically, I searched for Grace, calling her name, my voice shaking. Her building stood, but smoke poured from some windows, and the brick was crumbling in places. Firefighters, police, and paramedics milled around, orders were being shouted, and more than once, I was told to get out. I ignored them all, focused on locating her. Finally, I found my way to where ambulances were being loaded. One helpful man told me there were buses where occupants with minor injuries were being taken to stay warm until they could be transported to the hospital. I pushed my way through the crowds and found the yellow school buses they had brought in. I boarded the first bus, calling Grace's name, only to be met with a sea of strangers. I hurried to the other bus, my anxiety reaching new levels when she wasn't there either.

I began searching crowds, showing the picture I had of her on my phone that she had no idea I had taken. Describing her to people, my voice getting louder, my apprehension reaching epic proportions.

Then I heard my name. I spun on my heel, and she was there. Standing by a gurney, holding an older woman's hand, looking confused to see me. A blanket was draped over her shoulders, her hair was a mess, and soot and dirt were smeared on her face and arms. She held a cloth to her head, the blood a vivid crimson on the white. She had slippers on her feet. Her pants were torn.

She had never looked more beautiful.

I shook with the force of emotions coursing through me.

Relief, terror, anger.

I covered the ground between us, my long strides eating up the distance fast.

I swept her into my arms, holding her tight, repeating her name.

She reeked of smoke, and she shook violently. I pulled off my coat, wrapping her in it, and lifted her.

"What are you doing?"

"Taking you to the hospital."

"Mrs. Nelson—"

I cut her off and yelled for the paramedic. He came over and told me they were taking the elderly woman to the hospital shortly.

"I'm taking my wife."

"Sir, she's been triaged. She can get on the bus—"

I almost snarled. "I am taking her."

He stepped back, holding up his hands. "St. Anthony's," was all he said.

I turned and carried Gracie away.

I ratcheted up the heat in the car. Handed her a bottle of water. Refused to let her talk. I had to keep one hand on her at all times to make sure she was with me. At the hospital, I parked the car illegally and didn't give a flying fuck if they towed it. I refused to let her out of my arms. When they discovered she had come from the explosion scene, I was given a lecture I ignored. The entire time, Gracie was nestled in my arms, silent, except for her hoarse breathing.

"She needs oxygen. Can we skip the damn lecture and get to helping her?" I snapped.

"Jaxson," Gracie rasped. "Please."

It was hard to release her into their care. In the waiting room, I paced. It seemed forever, but it was really only a short time when I was allowed back in the cubicle. An oxygen mask was on her face, the soot on her cheeks emphasizing her pallor. A butterfly bandage was on her forehead, and her arms had been cleaned and ointment applied.

"She'll be fine. We're going to give her some oxygen for a bit." The doctor smiled and patted Gracie's hand. "She's a brave one, going in to rescue her neighbor."

It clicked. "Mrs. Nelson," I murmured, my voice tight. Grace had risked her life to save someone else.

"Yes. She is going to be fine too, thanks to Ms. VanRyan."

"Mrs. Richards," I corrected.

He frowned and looked at Grace. She blinked slowly and nodded.

"We just got married," I said smoothly. "None of her paperwork has been changed."

"Well, my congratulations." He looked at Grace. "You were lucky. So was your neighbor. You rest a bit, and I'll be back. You can go home in a couple of hours, I think."

He looked at me. "I assume there is somewhere else she can go?"

"Yes." I met her gaze directly. "My place—where she belongs."

She sighed and closed her eyes.

MELANIE MORELAND

But she didn't argue.

I sat beside her, holding her hand. She coughed a lot at first, then she settled. Her neighbor's daughter came in, tearfully thanking Grace, who smiled and pulled off her mask long enough to talk for a few moments. After the woman left, I put the mask back in place.

"No more talking."

She shut her eyes, once again not arguing. I couldn't take my eyes off her face. I watched her chest rise and fall. The doctor came in and checked her vitals. "She can go home. If her breathing gets bad, bring her back. Keep the bandage dry. Use this ointment on her cuts." He handed me a slip of paper. "She might cough. It's good—let her get it out. But if it keeps up…"

"I'll bring her back."

A nurse came in and gave Grace some scrubs so she wouldn't have to wear the torn, wet clothing she'd arrived in.

As I was shoving her clothes into a plastic bag, her cell phone fell from the pocket of her sweater.

I saw all the missed calls from me, then six missed calls from "RvR-Dad," and I suddenly realized if I had seen the news, so had her parents. As I held the phone, it buzzed again and I answered it.

"Hello?"

"Who the hell is this?" snapped a voice I recognized all too well.

"Richard," I said patiently. "It's Jaxson."

He let out a string of profanity. "Where is Grace?"

From behind him, I heard Katy's anxious voice. "Is she okay? Tell him about the apartment!"

"I already know. I am with Grace at the hospital—but she is fine," I hastened to add. "She inhaled some smoke, and they were watching her. I'm taking her home."

"Her apartment is gone. Where the hell is home?" Richard snarled.

"With me."

"The fuck it is."

I wasn't going to argue with him. "I will text you my address. You can meet us there if you want."

"What hospital?"

"St. Anthony's, but we'll be gone by the time you get here. She'll be at my place."

I hung up and looked behind me. Grace was clutching the doorframe, looking upset.

I smiled at her, not wanting her worried. "Guess my in-laws are coming for a visit. This should be fun."

CHAPTER 28

JAXSON

I should have expected the punch. I knew Richard was furious. He had called again, cursing me for not getting in touch with them and telling me they were on their way. I let him rage, knowing he was right. I hadn't thought to call her parents. I hadn't thought to call anyone. Never having family, I hadn't given it a thought until I saw his name on her phone.

I opened the door, and Richard led with his right hook. Luckily, something inside me was prepared, and I stepped away, his fist glancing off my chin. It still smarted, but this time, it would fade fast.

Katy gasped and grabbed his arm. "Richard!"

He glared, anger rolling off him. "He deserved that. Not calling us and telling us what was going on. You selfish prick. Do you have any idea how worried we were?"

"No. To be honest, you never crossed my mind. I was focused on Grace. She was all that mattered."

That brought him up short. He looked at Katy, then found his anger again and pushed past me. "Where is she?"

I was about to kick him out. Tell him off and push him out of my place until I saw the glimmer of tears in his hazel eyes. I recognized the wild fear—the same one I had been feeling when I couldn't find her. This was her father, and he was out of his mind with worry.

I pointed down the hall. "In the bedroom."

He rushed away, leaving me with Katy.

"Jaxson."

I looked down at her. "Mrs. VanRyan. Please come in. If you want a swing as well, could you aim for the left? The right side is already sore."

"It's still Katy—not Mrs. VanRyan." She sighed. "As for my husband, he isn't himself."

"I hope not. This will be a long, painful relationship for me if it is."

A smile tugged on her lips, then she frowned. "Is she really okay?"

"Go see for yourself. I was making her a cup of tea. I'll make a pot."

She laid her hand on my arm. "Are you all right? You look shattered."

I captured her hand and squeezed it. "I will be. It-it was a scare for all of us."

She studied me as if making a decision. "All right, then. Tea would be lovely. I'll go see my daughter now."

I watched her walk down the hall, wondering what else could happen today.

I finished making the tea, hearing voices in the living room. I frowned as I walked in and found Grace settling herself on the sofa. Her hair was still wet from the shower, and as I got close, I could still smell the smoke. I knew it would take a while to be completely rid of it. Richard looked calmer, although he was scowling.

"Don't you have some decent clothes?"

"I'm covered up, Dad."

She was wearing one of my shirts, a pair of my boxers, and thick socks. I plucked a blanket from the linen closet and brought it to her, tucking it around her.

"There, perhaps your delicate sensibilities will be assuaged, Richard."

"Mr. VanRyan."

I scoffed. "I don't think so. You're in my home. I'll address you as I see fit."

"We aren't staying. We're taking Grace back to Port Albany."

I stood in front of her. "Like hell you are. She's my wife, and she's staying here with me. I know what she needs."

"I doubt that." Richard ran a hand through his hair. "Jesus, you live on the twenty-third floor. If you knew my daughter at all, you would know she is terrified of elevators," he spat. "I'm sure she's hiding that from you—"

I interrupted him. "I know about what happened to her as a child. I know about the elevator. I know how to help her."

"And how exactly do you do that?"

He opened the door—I simply chose to step through it.

"Usually, I kiss her senseless and make her forget. But holding her close does the trick too. As long as I'm close, she's calm."

He blinked. Looked at Katy, then back at me. "Do you *have* a death wish?"

"You asked."

Grace spoke, her voice still rough. "Stop. Please just stop. Both of you."

Katy huffed in annoyance. "Yes. Behave—both of you. May I remind you Grace is the reason we are here?"

We eyed each other warily and sat down.

I handed Gracie a cup of tea. "I added some honey and lemon to soothe your throat. Drink it, please." I looked up at Katy. "Your tea is in the kitchen. I didn't know how you took it."

"Thank you."

"None for me, thanks," Richard grumbled.

"I thought you might prefer a scotch. God knows I need one."

"Oh. Well… Fine."

I got us each a glass, and for a moment, we were quiet. Richard leaned forward. "If you think we're going to stand by and watch as you force Gracie to stay married to you, you have another thing coming."

"I'm not forcing her."

"She said she wants a divorce."

I sat up straighter, wrapping my hand around Grace's. "Once my wife and I have a discussion and decide our future, I am sure she'll let you know the decision. Until then, kindly fuck off, Richard."

"Listen, you—"

Katy shocked me when she set down her mug with a resounding slap. "Enough, both of you." She pointed a finger at me. "Show some respect." Then she turned to Richard. "And enough out of you. Grace is a grown adult. Who she marries or divorces is her own business. Her *life* is her business."

"I don't want her pressured."

Katy laughed. "Will I remind you of our start, darling? The way you blackmailed me into marrying you? The horse's ass you were when I worked for you?"

"Katy," he hissed. "This is not the time to bring up the past."

I looked at them, my eyebrow lifted. Grace had told me once her parents had an unusual start, but she never elaborated.

"I think this is the perfect time," I said.

Richard glared and Katy sighed. "Long story short. I worked for Richard as his PA. He needed a wife, and he blackmailed me into marrying him. It was all on paper. No feelings." Her voice softened. "Until we fell in love."

For a moment, they smiled at each other, then Richard frowned. "This is totally different."

"Yes, it is," I said. "I didn't blackmail Grace. I asked, and she said yes. We didn't want to wait."

Richard made an odd choking noise. Katy lifted her eyebrows in surprise. "Well, I suppose then we need to let them talk."

"Katy," he objected, but she held up her hand.

"Richard, I believe the expression is 'let he who is without sin cast the first stone.' I suggest you shut up."

He drained his scotch. "She's my daughter."

"My wife."

"I trump you."

"In your dreams."

He glared. "You'll understand when you have kids."

I smiled. "Looking forward to grandkids already? Hey— does this mean I get to call you Dad?"

"Not in this fucking lifetime," he snorted.

I turned to Grace, shocked she was so quiet, only to find her asleep. She was so exhausted—despite her father's and my bickering, she had fallen asleep, her hand held within mine. I felt a rush of tenderness as I looked at her. She looked vulnerable and young. I drew a finger down her cheek and turned back to her parents. Katy was watching me, and Richard was staring at Grace. We exchanged a glance, a moment of shared gratitude flowing between us. She was our link—our common denominator. She was here and she was safe. The rest was just noise.

I removed the mug of tea from her other hand and sat back, wrapping my arm around her. She hummed and nestled closer, burrowing into my chest. A feeling of ease stole through me, knowing how my touch soothed her even in sleep.

The room was silent, and I looked toward her parents. Richard was watching me closely, his shoulders not as tense as they had been.

"I will look after her," I assured them. "Her well-being means everything to me."

Katy stood. "We'll go and let her sleep. But we're staying in a hotel, and we'll be back tomorrow."

I nodded, unable to take my eyes off Grace. "See yourselves out. I don't want to disturb her."

Katy leaned down and brushed a kiss to my forehead. It was an unexpected motherly gesture, and I met her kind gaze with a confused smile. I had never received an act as sweet.

Richard remained uncharacteristically silent.

GRACE

There was smoke. It billowed and swirled all around me. I couldn't find the door. I knew I had to get out, and my movements became more frantic as I searched for a way to escape. I was trapped all over again. There was a voice calling my name, and I tried to locate it in the heavy gray mist that was overtaking me. I knew that voice. If I could find that voice, I would be safe.

It came closer. "Gracie, darling. Open your eyes. I'm right here."

My eyes flew open. Jaxson was hovering over me, his expression concerned. I heard an odd noise, and it took me a moment to realize it was me. I was gasping for air, crying, clutching at him. He wrapped me in his arms, enclosing me in his embrace.

His voice washed over me, low and gentle.

"It's all right, Gracie. You're safe. I'm here, darling. I'm right here." He pressed a kiss to my head. "It was a dream."

"There was a fire," I gasped. "I couldn't get out."

"Yes," he confirmed. "There was a fire. But you did get out. You got your neighbor out, too. It's over now. I have you."

I inhaled deeply against his skin. His warmth sank into me, banishing the shivers, his scent surrounded me, driving away the acrid smell that lingered in my nose. His closeness erased the lingering terror.

He eased back, wiping my cheeks. "Better now?"

"Yes." I cleared my throat, grateful when he handed me a glass of water. The cold liquid felt good on my throat. I looked around in surprise. I was in Jaxson's bedroom. "How did I get here?"

"You fell asleep while your parents were here. After they left, I brought you in here."

I recalled the visit. "My father was rude."

He lifted one shoulder. "It's fine. He was upset."

I searched his eyes, seeing only concern. "You came for me. You found me."

"I saw the live report on the news. I recognized your building. I had to come find you." He cupped my face. "Tell me what you remember."

I frowned as I thought about it.

"Say it, Grace. Get it out so it doesn't lurk in your mind. They said on the news there was a gas explosion."

"That makes sense. I was napping in my chair, and the next thing I knew, there was a loud boom, and the window beside me blew out. The explosion threw me from the chair. I hit my head."

"That explains the cuts on your arms and the gash on your head."

"I knew I had to get out. Smoke was filling the hallway, and I got to the back steps. Then I remembered Mrs. Nelson. I had to go back. I knew if I didn't help her, she would die." I gripped his arm. "Is she okay?"

"Thanks to you, she is."

I breathed a sigh of relief and took another sip of water. "I don't remember much. Somehow, I got her, us, outside. I think I half carried her. There were people and fire trucks. Lights. Someone gave me a blanket. A bottle of water. Told me I had inhaled a lot of smoke. I stayed with Mrs. Nelson." A long, shuddering breath escaped my mouth. "I was cold and scared. Confused." I met his eyes. "And then you were there."

"Thank God," he breathed out. He leaned his forehead to mine. "I have never been so scared in my life, Gracie. I couldn't find you. I kept thinking you were still in that burning building, and I couldn't get to you."

"But you did."

"Yes. Once they released you, I brought you home, and your parents showed up. You were so exhausted, you fell asleep."

I touched his chin in gratitude, noticing his grimace. I looked closer and saw a bruise.

"Did my father hit you again?" I asked, aghast.

"He was upset. Luckily, his aim was off this time."

"He needs to stop this!"

"I know." He leaned close, a smile playing on his lips. "If he doesn't stop giving me facers every time he sees me, I'm going to begin to think he doesn't like me."

"Don't make light of it."

"Given everything else, it doesn't matter, Grace. Besides, thanks to your mom, I think he might ease off a bit."

"Why?"

"She told me about how she and your father got together. Or at least, the gist of it. I think there was way more to the story than she told me."

"She told you?"

He chuckled. "Your father was harping at me, and she got mad. Told him he needed to remember how they started. Then she dropped that bombshell. Your dad shut up pretty fast."

"Oh."

"You have to tell me the whole story one day." He took the bottle from my hand. "But not tonight. You need some rest. Do you think you can sleep?"

"Will you stay?"

He pressed a kiss to my forehead. "Yes. I'll be right here, Gracie. You won't be alone."

"Okay."

He lay beside me, pulling me into his arms. There was a dim light on in the corner, casting the room in a cozy glow. I shut my eyes, but the images from earlier kept coming back, and I was unable to relax. I turned in Jaxson's embrace, and he kissed my head as he ran long, lingering passes up and down my back.

"Sleep, Grace."

"I can't." I paused. "Why was my father upset at you? You came and helped me."

"Because I never called him to tell him you were okay. They saw the news a little while after I did. They called you, but there was no answer. They, like me, were terrified you were trapped in the building. When I answered your phone at the hospital, your dad cursed me out, and frankly, he was right." He tightened his grip on me. "I never thought to call him. To call anyone. I have never had that sort of responsibility before. A family. A group of people that would care."

I studied his face. There was pain in his eyes, a longing in his voice. "What about your family, Jaxson?" I dared to ask.

"I don't talk about them."

"You know my parents' sordid beginning. We can't go forward without dealing with the past. Without it lurking in your mind," I quoted him.

He was silent, and I was about to give up when he suddenly spoke.

"My parents were awful people."

I started but didn't say anything, shocked he was talking. I squeezed my arms tighter so he knew I was listening.

"They were drug addicts and liked to use me as a runner. I was fast, cute, and a kid isn't your usual suspect to be carrying drugs."

"Jaxson," I breathed out, unable to stay silent.

He kept talking, his voice detached, as if he were reciting facts in a case.

"They didn't care where they sent me. How dangerous, what sort of assholes might prey on me. As long as I was useful, they kept doing it. When I was successful, I got to eat. When I wasn't, well, let's just say, your father isn't the only man to have used his fists on me." He swallowed, the movement of his throat hard. "When I was ten, I got caught. My parents were charged with reckless behavior, endangering a minor, and some drug-related offenses, and they went to jail. I was sent to foster care."

"You didn't have any other family?" I asked quietly, my heart breaking at his words.

"No."

"Were they, ah, nice?"

He laughed, the sound humorless. "I was a cash cow. That's all. When I was too much trouble, they sent me back. I went somewhere else. Same story. Rinse and repeat." He was quiet for a moment. "My parents got out of jail. But they weren't interested in taking me back. I wasn't useful anymore. They severed all ties and disappeared. I was told they died when I was about fifteen." His hand tightened on my arm. "By then, I no longer cared. I was used to not eating, not having a proper bed. Being disregarded."

I felt tears gather in my eyes. I could imagine him as a young boy, his dark hair and blue eyes. Alone. Abandoned. Scared.

He still was. Only he couldn't see it.

He spoke again. "I ran away. Lived on the streets. Got caught. Sent back. I ended up in a group home. I learned to be responsible for myself and myself alone. The one thing I knew for certain was that everyone had a use and a purpose. Once that purpose is done, the person is no longer needed. I was never useful to anyone for very long. I went from place to place, thrown away like yesterday's garbage—useless and unwanted. I learned at a very young age that love was fickle and unreliable."

I couldn't look at him. I felt his pain, no matter how much he denied feeling it.

"But love does exist," I whispered. "*Real* love does."

"In some people's worlds, yes. In mine, no."

"But—" I began, but he cut me off.

"Enough, Grace. You've been through enough tonight, and I'm tired. I shouldn't have told you."

"How did you become a lawyer?"

He sighed but answered. "Always wanting more information. I buckled down, finished school. I worked and saved, then went to university. I held down three jobs, got my degree, passed the bar, and never looked back."

"Sometimes you need to look back in order to move forward," I whispered.

He sat up, pushing himself off the mattress. "Go to sleep. I'll be back."

I had to ask the burning question.

"But if you don't love me, why did you marry me?" I challenged.

He stopped at the door, not turning around. "Because it was the only way I could keep you."

He walked away from me, his footsteps heavy and measured.

I wiped at the tears in my eyes.

I was more confused than ever.

CHAPTER 29

JAXSON

Until Grace had entered my life, the only other person who had ever been in my personal space was Michael. And his presence was always short and due to business. She had been the first and only person I had ever brought here.

Today changed all that. From midmorning, the apartment had buzzed. Grace's parents arrived, bringing with them new clothes for Grace. Her sister Heather was there, her partner, Reed, along for the ride. There was a video call from her other siblings, who were in Port Albany, with promises to visit the next day.

"They didn't want to overwhelm you," Katy said with a smile.

I wanted to tell her it was too late, but I refrained.

Soon, Addison and Brayden joined the group. Then Ronan appeared, representing the triplets. He engulfed Gracie in his massive arms, saying nothing, but the look on his face was enough. He brought Sandy and Jordan with him. They were emotional—her entire family much the same. Everyone wanted to touch her, talk to her. There were hugs, tears, whispered words of assurance from Grace. When the BAM men and their wives showed up, the apartment seemed too small. Their presence filled the rooms, their loud voices echoing off the normally quiet walls.

Grace sat in a single chair, close to the window, quiet but happy to have her family gathered around her. My gaze found her often, checking to make sure she was okay. Something flowed between us each time our eyes met. I had the feeling she was comforting me, and I wondered if she knew the emotions this gathering stirred up. Having told her about my past last night had been disconcerting enough. Add in this ensemble, and I was on edge.

My kitchen was suddenly full of food; there were flowers on the table for Grace. More toiletries, clothes, and other items were piled in the bedroom and on the table. The subject had come up about her apartment, and her visceral reaction to the idea of returning to it was evident. Her already pale complexion became pasty white, and her eyes grew round. Ignoring everyone else in the room, I crouched in front of her.

"You never have to go back," I promised her quietly. "Your dad and I will look after getting your things out. Whatever is salvageable, we will retrieve." I knew, despite our differences, on this matter, Richard and I would be in full agreement.

"I'll help. We all will," Ronan added.

"BAM will arrange it all." Aiden spoke up. *"The movers, the storage, the cleanup. When you're ready to go through your things, they'll be there."*

Gracie's eyes filled with tears. "Thank you."

I squeezed her hand and leaned close. "Do you need to rest?"

"No," she replied. "Everything I need is right here."

I stood, meeting the intense gaze of her father. He had been almost conciliatory all day. Polite. Not a single facer or even a snarl. I wondered if he was under warning from Katy or Grace. Maybe both. But he had watched me closely and stayed near Grace.

I wandered into the kitchen, needing a cup of good coffee and a moment's peace. I filled the French press and waited. A voice from behind me made me turn my head.

"Hiding?"

I turned my head to look at Katy. "I needed coffee."

"There's a full pot."

"I prefer this."

She pulled herself up onto a stool at the island. "Gracie said you had a favorite type of brew. A coffee snob, I think she said?"

I had to smile, because Gracie was right. I lifted a cup. "Would you like one?"

"Yes, please."

She took a sip and closed her eyes. "Delicious."

"I agree." I swallowed a mouthful of the hot, rich coffee, enjoying the taste and aroma.

"I guess it's all a little much?" Katy asked. "All of us here in your space."

"I'm not used to it," I admitted. "But I knew it would be important for Grace to have her family around, and for them to see her and know she was okay."

"You don't have a relationship with your family."

"I have none."

"But earlier in your life?" she urged gently.

"No. I did not," I said through gritted teeth. "And the subject is closed."

She took another sip, not at all perturbed by my tone.

"You care for her very much."

I shifted on my feet, wondering if I could ask her to leave the kitchen. My sanctuary had become far too crowded. I had a feeling, though, that Katy would only refuse and keep talking. Probing. In her own way, she was more dangerous than Richard could ever be.

"Of course. I married her."

"We both know marriages happen for many reasons."

"I didn't blackmail her."

"I know that. She loves *you* very much."

I had no idea how to reply. She smiled and finished her coffee. She leaned her elbows on the island and rested her chin in her hands.

"Gracie tells me you are not much for expressing feelings."

"Ah…"

"Neither was Richard. Even after we fell in love. It was hard for him."

"Some of us are simply not capable," I said, hoping she would take the hint that I didn't want to have this conversation.

She didn't.

"He grew more comfortable with words. Showing his feelings." She tilted her head. "I think that is how you express yours, Jaxson. You show them."

"I'm sorry?"

"The way you care for Gracie. You watch her. Antici-pate her needs. You played Santa for her to make her happy and give her back a memory. You were there yesterday, searching for her." She indicated the full room behind the wall. "You let her family overtake your space even though it makes you uncomfortable." She paused. "Because of your past history with your own family."

"She needed to see them," I said stiffly.

"And you needed her to be happy."

"Yes." The word was torn from my throat.

"That's all we want, Jaxson. For her to be happy. If it's you who makes her so, then we're good."

I met her brilliant blue gaze that was so like Gracie's. "And if I don't?"

"Then let her go." She slipped from the chair. "It's very simple. Showing love and feeling love, they go hand in hand. But if you can do one and not the other, then it will never be enough."

"It's only a word," I argued. "Four letters."

"No, Jaxson, that is where you are wrong. It is a spoken vow. A promise. Those four letters can encompass our entire world and change it." She paused. "You know, when Gracie was born, it changed Richard. It was as if she had unlocked something in him, and all the love he had kept deep inside him exploded and he couldn't contain it anymore. She had that effect on him as a baby." She smiled and patted my cheek as she went by. "Maybe she can do that again."

And she left me alone, the thoughts in my head now chaotic and loud.

I cared for Grace. More than I had ever cared for another person in my life. I wanted her in my life. I liked being with her. But love? Was I capable of that? A few months ago, the answer would have been an emphatic no.

But now?

I had a feeling peace wouldn't find me again for a long time.

GRACE

"It killed me to do it, Grace."

"She saw us."

"Protect you."

"Anything. I would do anything for you."

I opened my eyes, confused, and looked around. I was in Jaxson's apartment, in his bed. Alone. I rubbed my head, wondering what I had been dreaming about. More snippets of conversation played through my mind.

"Always been alone."

"I can't love, but you make me want to."

It was Jaxson's voice in my head. His words pushing through the memories. But when had he said them?

Vague images pricked at my mind.

Jaxson in front of me, holding a glass high above my head. "No more, Grace. You're drunk."

"I like being drunk. I don't have to care then."

"Care about?"

"Saying the right thing. Doing the right thing. I can do what I want."

"And what do you want?" he asked, an indulgent look on his face.

"To kiss you."

I touched my mouth, somehow feeling the possession he had shown when he had yanked me close and kissed me.

That was in Vegas. It was the first time I had remembered anything from that night. Was it starting to come back?

I sat up and glanced at the clock. It was late afternoon, the sun already setting. After everyone had left, Jaxson had insisted I lie down. I was exhausted, so I didn't argue much. I had a shower before I did, the scent of smoke still lingering in my hair. I slid from the bed and padded down the hall to the kitchen where I could hear Jaxson moving around. He looked up as I walked in.

"Hey."

"Hi. Something smells good."

"Since your family brought the equivalent of a grocery store with them, I thought I would make dinner." He slid a tray into the oven. "Feeling better?"

"I think so. The nap was good, and the shower I had got rid of the last of the smell, I think."

He tossed the oven mitt on the counter and came closer. Bending low, he slid his fingers through my hair and buried his face into the waves, inhaling deeply. I shivered as he glided his lips along my ear and down my neck, darting out his tongue and brushing it along the sensitive skin.

"You smell like Gracie," he murmured. "Light, sweet, perfect."

Then his mouth was on mine, his lips gentle, seeking, and warm. With a sigh, I opened to him, and he pulled me closer, kissing me. He tasted of wine, decadent and delicious. It was different from other kisses we had shared. There was an underlying tenderness to his mouth, a slow, sensual drag to his tongue. He caressed the back of my head with his fingers, his other hand splayed wide across my back. He kissed me until I was breathless, clutching at his shirt and trembling in his arms. He drew back, his eyes shining in the light.

"You taste perfect too. I love your hair like this—wild and out of control. The way you make me feel."

"Jaxson," I whispered, overcome with longing.

"Tell me what you need, Gracie."

"You."

He lifted me off my feet, settling me on the counter and stepping between my legs. I could feel him, hard and ready.

"Then you get me."

Jaxson grinned at me around a mouthful of his delicious pasta. He chuckled as I dropped my eyes, taking a sip of my wine. He had kissed me again earlier, his hold on me tight, until a timer sounded on the stove. He drew back and touched the end of my nose. "Enough of that. I need to feed you."

I watched him walk away, disappointment pooling inside. I had felt better in his arms. I always felt better in his arms. I had wanted him to take it further, but he didn't.

As if he knew what I was thinking, he smiled, his dimple deepening.

I took a bite of my pasta, trying to ignore the burning in my cheeks.

After dinner, we cleaned up and sat in the living room. I looked out the window, the city a blanket of white. Jaxson sat across from me, silent, sipping a scotch. It occurred to me he'd drunk quite a bit. Wine before and with dinner, and now scotch. I wondered why.

"Thank you for putting up with my family today."

"They needed to see you. I understand that."

"Why did you come yesterday?" I asked. "You were frustrated with me."

"How could I not?" he replied. "At best, your home was burning. At worst…well, I can't even put that into words. I had to go find you." He was quiet for a moment. "I was terrified, Grace. Terrified you were hurt

371

—or worse." He closed his eyes. "I couldn't begin to fathom that."

His confession startled me, and I decided to seize on his openness.

"Yet a few weeks ago, you tore us apart. Why, Jaxson?"

He drained his glass. "I wondered when you would ask that question."

"I'm asking it now. I didn't understand then—I still don't. What did I do so wrong that weekend that you ended it?"

"You didn't do anything, Gracie. I did."

I frowned in confusion.

Jaxson sighed, leaning forward, resting his arms on his thighs. "I was arrogant. We'd done a good job hiding our relationship, and somehow, I thought the weekend would be the same. The moment I ran into the couple from the firm, we should have stopped."

"You were tense the rest of the weekend, but I still don't understand."

He scrubbed his face. "I know. It was the elevator, Grace. When we were heading to our room and the drunk kid pressed the buttons. And it was the slowest fucking elevator every time the doors opened. You remember?"

"Yes. You held me."

He stood and began to pace. "When the doors opened two floors from ours, someone was waiting for the elevator. It was Sabrina Wells. She saw me. She saw you. Your face was reflected in the mirror behind you. I was holding you. She saw us together."

"That's the lawyer you despise."

"Yes. She has been trying to get me to sleep with her since I started with the firm. She's a vindictive, selfish bitch. She saw us, lifted her phone, took a picture, and smiled. I've never seen a smile so malicious. I knew right then, we were done."

I stared at him, shocked. *He knew we were done?*

"She called me on Sunday. That was the call you saw me on when I was angry. She insisted we meet that day. She threatened to go to the partners."

"Why didn't you tell me? We could have figured something out. I know your position at the firm is important, but together——"

He cut me off. "I don't give a shit about my position at the firm. She could have gone to the partners and told them, and if they let me go, I would have a job at the end of the day."

"Then why?" I cried. "Why did you break us? Break me?"

He threw up his hands. "She was going after *you*, Grace. She despises me, and somehow, she knew I cared. She knew you were different. It infuriated her that I chose a law student over her, and she wanted to make me suffer. She was going to the partners to tell them what she saw. And to add a bunch of lies about you. She was going to slander you. End your career before it even began. She would have tainted your reputation so badly that it would have followed you, even to BAM." He tugged a hand through his hair. "And when she told me what she was going to do, I tried to call her bluff. Told her that you meant nothing. I thought she'd buy it, but she didn't. I hadn't kept my feelings as well hidden as I thought. She said to keep her quiet, I had to break it off with you. I tried to figure out another way, but she had me in a corner."

"Why did she do this? Did she think you'd sleep with her then?"

"No, she knew that would never happen. But she liked to see me miserable. She knew seeing you every day would kill me, and she loved that. To have something over me. That's how she works. She is well known for her tactics—in and out of the courtroom."

A small flicker of anger lit within me. "You never thought to talk to me, Jaxson? That maybe between us, we could have figured out something? Pretended a breakup, or I could have gone to another firm?"

"It wouldn't have worked. She was watching too closely."

"So, you thought breaking my heart was the best thing."

"I thought you'd get over it."

"I can't believe you just said that. Do you think I'm that shallow?"

"No, I think love is."

My anger kicked up a notch. "So, you dump me to protect me, then you marry me. How does that make sense? Doesn't that give her more ammunition?"

He sat across from me. "I read and reread my contract. Had a colleague who specializes in employment contracts confirm it. I found a loophole. She can't touch you. Or me."

I blinked. "What?"

"It meant we could be together." He frowned. "I missed you. I missed being with you."

"You married me because you missed me?"

"Among other things."

"Other things?" I prompted.

"Our physical connection is strong. Fucking you is a pleasure," he admitted. "I enjoy your company as well."

"Fucking me is a pleasure," I repeated slowly, unable to believe he said those words.

Exactly how much had he had to drink?

I cleared my throat. "Do any of those other 'things' include love, Jaxson?"

"You know how I feel about that. I care for you, but…" His voice trailed off, his silence saying it all. He cleared his throat. "Nothing lasts forever. I told you that."

"So, now we're married, and you don't miss me anymore. What's next?"

"We'll figure that out as we go along. However long we have together, we can enjoy it."

I had to grip my hands to stop from shouting at him. "Let me get this straight. You broke up with me because some vindictive bitch threatened to ruin my reputation, then you married me because you found a loophole and you missed being with me physically. You expect me to stay married to you because you enjoy fucking me, and basically, as long as it lasts, it lasts?"

He scratched his head. "When you say it like that…" He trailed off again, then cleared his throat. "I married you because I didn't want to be without you, Grace. I missed you for a myriad of reasons." I waited for him to say something else, to add more to his words, but he didn't.

"Sabrina can still go to the partners. She can still make trouble. Have you thought of that?"

"Yes. I have a plan."

"Care to fill me in?"

"Not yet. But I'll protect you, Grace. Being my wife affords you that as well." He lifted his arms. "And you get me."

I knew he was trying to lighten the atmosphere. Make me smile. But I was far from smiling.

"You've been reading too many of my historical novels, Jaxson. I don't need your protection. I'm a grown woman capable of taking care of myself. I certainly have no desire to be kept in the dark and fed bullshit like a mushroom. Because that is what your idea is. Bullshit. Marriage is a partnership. Not one person deciding what is best for the other. Not one person changing the other's future without consulting them."

"I did what I thought I had to do. She would have destroyed you."

I met his gaze. "So, you did that instead."

"It killed me. I had no choice."

"No, you did. You simply decided on your own. And you decided wrong. I want out, Jaxson."

"No. Stay with me. We'll get a place together—one where you are comfortable. We could have a lot of fun. We could travel and explore. We get on well. The marriage doesn't have to end."

"Until you get tired of me."

He stepped forward. "Grace—"

I held up my hand, stopping him. "No. I will not be trapped in a loveless marriage, Jaxson. I want it all. I want what my parents have. Love. Laughter. Children. A real family. A lifetime. If you can't give me that, then give me a divorce."

"I can't do that. But I don't want to lose you."

I shook my head. "You already have."

I turned and walked away, pausing at the door. "My parents asked me to come stay with them for a couple of days before they leave. I'll go in the morning."

This time, he didn't argue.

CHAPTER 30

GRACE

Snow crunched under my boots as I wandered down the trail. I stopped in a small clearing, recognizing the place where Jaxson and I had spoken on Christmas Day.

I sat down on an overturned log, gazing up into the sun. I wondered what he was doing. I hadn't heard from him since I left his apartment. In fact, we hadn't spoken since that night. I left the next morning, Ronan picking me up and driving me to Port Albany. I was too numb to even worry about the elevator, not even blinking as I stepped inside on my own. The last thing I saw was Jaxson, watching me from the end of the hall. He looked exhausted, but he didn't say anything. Our eyes locked and held for a moment, then I pressed the button, closing the door on him.

On us.

I was too tired to fight with him anymore. To fight with anyone. Since my arrival in Port Albany, my parents had been surprisingly circumspect. Happy to have me there, fussing over me, but not bringing up the subject of Jaxson, except once.

This morning, my mother found me at the kitchen table, sipping tea and watching the sun come up. She poured herself a cup and sat beside me.

"You're up early."

"Still on my usual schedule."

"Or not sleeping," she guessed.

I only shrugged.

"Gracie," she began, covering my hand on the table.

"Don't," I pleaded.

She sighed. "All I was going to say is sometimes a person is broken beyond repair."

"That's what you think Jaxson is? Broken?"

"He cares. In fact, I think he more than cares, but he has no experience with love. Family. From what he said, and you told me, he has never had either."

"I know. But he insists we have no future, only a right now."

"Your father thought the same way once upon a time. Our time together had an expiry date."

"That was different."

"In some ways, yes. But I've seen the way Jaxson looks at you. The wonder on his face. There is something there, Grace. Something profound."

"It's lust," I stated dryly.

She shook her head, even as she smiled. "I have no doubt there is a lot of that, but there is more. Even your father saw something."

"Is that why he stopped punching him? If I had known what he had done, I might have let Dad have another shot or two."

She sipped her tea. "What did he do, Gracie?"

I told her the whole story, and she frowned when I finished.

"His words are at such odds with his reactions. I don't think he even knows it." She cupped my cheek. "I'm sorry you went through so much pain, Grace. I wish I had been there for you. I wish you had told me."

"I'm so confused, Mom. I am so mad at him, yet..."

"You still love him."

"I don't know. I shouldn't. He hurt me. He keeps hurting me."

"VanRyans love deeply. You are very much your father, so I am not surprised. But you have to make your own decision, Grace. You need to move forward. Only you can decide if that is with Jaxson or not. You have to decide if he is worth the risk of your heart being broken over and again."

Her words resonated with me. I did have to move forward.

Footsteps made me look up. Addi appeared, carrying a thermos. Her blond hair glinted in the sunlight, and she brushed a kiss to my cheek as she sat down.

"Your mom told me you were out for a walk. She sent me with some hot chocolate."

"How did you know I'd be here?"

"Wild guess." She winked as she unscrewed the lid. "Scene of the crime and all."

"Jaxson told me you were there. Making out with Brayden."

"You did some pretty heavy making out yourself." She frowned. "Only one cup. We share."

I shrugged and sipped the hot chocolate. My mom made delicious hot chocolate. Deep, rich, and laced with cinnamon. I loved it. I handed the cup back to Addi, who drank it, humming in appreciation.

"You doing okay?"

"I'm fine."

"I meant mentally more than physically."

"My mom gossiped to you while the chocolate was heating?"

"She didn't gossip. I asked, she answered. You're in a right mess, aren't you? So un-Grace-like."

I laughed. Addi was always blunt. "Yeah, I really stepped in it this time."

"For what it's worth, what I saw on Christmas Day was a man in love. He watched you, Gracie. He couldn't stop. His heart was in his eyes."

"Pretty sure that was his dick."

She threw back her head in laughter. "Listen to you." She leaned forward. "He *loves* you."

"Well, if he does, he can't say it. I don't think he ever can. To him, admitting love means admitting he can be hurt. Vulnerable. He will never allow that again. His parents hurt him. The system destroyed him."

"Put him back together."

"What if I fail, Addi? If I accept him and we go forth together with no promise of the future, no promise of anything but now. He could walk away and leave me in pieces. Ones I'm not sure I could ever put back together."

"And what if by showing him you're there, with him, despite his ridiculous ideas, it pieces him back together and he is able to admit his feelings? That are already there, by the way—" she snorted "—he is just too much of a man to see them."

"It's a big if."

She drained the chocolate and regarded me. "So is every marriage, Grace. Drunk or not, you must have wanted to marry him. Temporary or not, he wanted to marry you. A couple madly in love this year could be divorced by next year. The words 'I love you' don't heal everything. Just ask Uncle Halton."

"Well, that was uplifting."

"Simply being honest. Jaxson is correct on one thing. Love isn't a guarantee. But the effort you make helps." She grasped my hand. "The night of the cake tasting, Grace. You looked different. I didn't know why, but now I do. You were happy. So happy, it showed. You were with Jaxson. If he makes you that happy, then maybe, just maybe, he is worth fighting for."

"He also made me unhappy. And angry."

A grin played on her lips. "It's called passion. You were like a spitting, angry kitten on Christmas. Yet every time I watched you, *you* were watching *him*. Your eyes tracked him everywhere."

"I was making sure he didn't step out of line."

She frowned as she poured another cup of chocolate. "Be honest with yourself, Grace. It was because you were drawn to him. You *are* drawn to him." She tilted her head. "Did you see how devastated he was the other day when someone would talk about the fire? The what-ifs? He couldn't bear the thought of you being hurt. That is not a man only interested in now. That is a man who needs you to be strong and show him it's okay to open his heart."

I took the cup from her hand. "Jeez, married a matter of days, and you're an expert."

"Damn right, I am. Listen to me for a change. Brayden says I'm the smartest woman he knows."

"Brayden is still trying to get in your pants daily."

She winked. "He succeeds, Gracie. Usually more than once."

I stared at her wide-eyed, and then I began to laugh.

Her phone buzzed, and I lifted one eyebrow. "Speak of the devil."

She grinned. "He is missing me."

"Go."

She paused. "Are you all right? I don't want to leave you alone."

"Really, I'm fine. I need some time to think."

She stood, brushing the snow off her pants. "Gracie, I don't want you to think I'm taking Jaxson's side. I'm not. I don't want you in an unhappy relationship. But if this for-now had a chance to turn into forever with anyone? It would be him. That man exudes love for you. I saw it. I felt it. And he will figure it out." She huffed out a long breath, a white cloud of air swirling between us. "Do you know what he told Brayden when he asked him why he was so determined to keep you?"

"No."

"*Because she is the only warmth in my life. Without her, the cold will destroy me,*" she quoted. "That hardly sounds like a man without love."

I gaped at her. *Jaxson had said that?*

She bent and pressed a kiss to my head, handing me the thermos.

I watched her walk away, her words echoing in my head. A part of me—a huge part—wanted to believe her. Despite everything, the fact was that I still loved him, and I wanted him to love me back. The question that remained was, would he figure it out before it was too late?

At the house, I ran into Ronan. He was coming down the steps, a huge sandwich in his hand.

"Hey, Gracie-girl," he called, using my dad's nickname.

"Having a snack?" I drawled.

"Your mom makes the best bagel sandwiches."

I smiled. "Dad loves anything on a bagel."

He swallowed the giant mouthful and grinned. "I know. I love anything she makes."

"I know."

"I was hungry." He indicated the house. "I dropped off a package for you."

"A what?"

"Jaxson sent you something. He asked me to bring it."

"Jaxson was here?"

He nodded. "I saw him by the gates. I went to see him, and he gave me the package to give to you."

I felt a flash of disappointment. "I see."

"We talked a bit. He asked if you were okay. If you needed anything."

For some reason, my throat felt thick. He had been here and didn't ask to see me. "Thanks for doing that."

He finished the sandwich, wiping his mouth. "I like him, Grace. He seems like a decent guy. A little uptight, but decent."

"It's complicated, Ronan."

He pursed his lips. "Life is. But it must be kind of nice to have someone love you just because you're you."

"You don't feel loved?"

"Of course I'm loved. I know that. But I'm part of a trio most of the time. Having that person love you only because you are *you*. I think that would be great."

I rubbed his arm. "You'll find it, Ronan. Some woman is gonna love you so hard."

"Of course she will. I'm awesome."

I leaned up and kissed his cheek. "Yes, you are."

He began to walk away, then turned. "Hey, I'm staying out here for the next while. So, if you want, we can coordinate our schedules, and I'll drive you in."

"That might work. Thanks."

He nodded. "Anytime. And, Grace?"

"Yeah?"

"Just be happy. Life is too short, you know?" Then he turned and jogged away.

Upstairs, there was a box on my bed, wrapped in brown paper. I lifted it, noting the heaviness of the package. Curious, I opened it, gasping in delight at the collection of Scarlett Scott books inside. I opened the note attached.

Gracie—
I know your books will be something we can't salvage.
I thought I would begin replacing them for you.
I hope they make you happy.
PS – I will always be your protector.
Jaxson

I ran my fingers down the spines. My favorite series—the ones I wanted to suggest we read first for our book club. I picked up the phone and called his number. When he answered, I could hear the subtle sounds of road traffic.

"Grace?" he answered. "Are you all right?"

"Yes. I got your books. Thank you."

"I wanted you to have them. I was sure you were missing them."

The words were out before I could stop them. "I miss you too."

"Fuck, baby, I miss you. I'm sorry, Gracie. I screwed everything up. Even when I tried to tell you, to explain, I fucked it up. I can stand in front of a judge and wax on for hours, but I try to explain things to you, and I become an idiot."

"You hurt me."

"I know. I hated hurting you. I hated being the person who brought shadows into your beautiful eyes. I broke your trust—I know I did. But you still care—I know you do."

"How can you say that? How well do you really know me, Jaxson?"

"I do know you. I know more than you realize."

I huffed a sigh, but he kept talking.

"I know that you prefer cooked apples to raw. You dislike Brussels sprouts with a fiery passion that amuses me. That you sneak a little chocolate every day. That you save a little bit of extra fruit in the bottom of your yogurt because you like the sweet at the end."

"You know those things because you've seen my habits," I protested, even while I was surprised he noticed the yogurt thing.

I could hear the warmth in his voice. "I know that you love fuzzy socks on your feet because they are always cold. Nothing makes you happier than a naughty historical romance and a cup of tea with a cookie." He paused. "You love your family with a fierce devotion, and you would do anything for them. You worship your father and constantly worry you will do something to displease him." Sadness crept into his tone. "I hate the fact that marrying me has caused an issue with the two of you."

"Then give me my divorce, and we'll be fine."

"I don't want to, Gracie," he replied.

"Jaxson—"

He kept talking.

"You're kind and good. Sweet and funny. Intelligent. I love talking to you more than any other person in the world. I treasure our conversations, except perhaps this one." He drew in a long breath. "You're more beautiful than you believe. It's the sort of beauty that lives inside and out. Your soul is pure and wonderful."

His words stunned me. But they weren't the words I needed to hear.

"And yet you still don't love me."

"Gracie, I care. I really care. It's all I have to give."

My heart broke again. "It's not enough," I whispered.

"I know," he replied sadly.

The line went dead.

CHAPTER 31

JAXSON

I straightened my tie and shrugged on my overcoat. It was cold today. I drove to the office on autopilot, the place still mostly deserted given the early morning hour. Since I had spoken to Grace on the phone, there'd been no contact. New Year's Eve came and went without even a text. To stay busy, I had been working, both at the office and home. Grace was in my thoughts constantly, her absence from my life somehow magnified more than I had expected. Considering how short our relationship had been, her impact on my daily routine was astounding. I was anxious to see her today, although I wondered how she would react to the news being announced. How she would take the information I had to give her.

I had to let her go. I couldn't give her what she needed to be happy, and I couldn't stand to be the cause of her unhappiness. It was as simple as it was complex.

Michael walked in, not surprised to see me at my desk so early. He carried a cup of coffee and set it down in front of me.

"Hey, boss man. Happy New Year."

"Not much happy, but same to you."

He frowned. "I thought…" He trailed off. "Grace?" he asked quietly.

"She'll be here soon, I think. Her cousin is driving her in from Port Albany."

He sat down, uninvited. "Is she not here with you?"

"No."

"I thought after the fire and everything else, you'd have worked it out."

I rarely got personal with anyone, but for some reason, the chance to talk grabbed hold.

"We can't work it out. She wants something I can't give her."

"What is that?"

I met his gaze. "She wants what her parents have. What her entire family seems to drown in. Love."

"And you don't love her? I call bullshit on that one. You certainly act as if you do."

"I don't believe in it. I'm not capable of it."

"Not capable—or scared?"

393

I glared at him. "I beg your pardon?"

He crossed his legs, smoothing the fabric. "I knew I was gay from an early age, but I hid it. I tried to be what was considered normal. What I thought was expected of me. Then I met Larry. He was warm, kind, and perfect for me. I could be me with him, and it was enough. For the first time in my life, I *was* enough. We fell in love, but we stayed a secret. He was my roommate, my friend, my wingman. At least that was what I told my family and friends." He cleared his throat.

"Finally, Larry had enough. He told me how much I was hurting him and he couldn't do it anymore. We were living two lives. We were a couple with his family, and friends with mine. He told me he didn't plan on hiding the rest of his life, and it was time to make a choice."

I nodded, waiting for him to continue.

"The day I told my family I was gay was the scariest day of my life. I knew I could lose them, but the thought of losing Larry was even worse."

"How did they take it?"

"They weren't surprised. In fact, they were glad I had finally spoken up. They had suspected it all along, and frankly, they loved Larry. Especially my mom." He smiled. "So, you see, Jaxson, I understand the fear of the unknown. The power those three little words can have." He winked. "The only thing is that mine were 'I am gay,' and yours are 'I love you.'"

"I've tried—"

He cut me off. "Gestures aren't enough, Jaxson. Caring isn't enough. In fact, the words 'I care' are probably the most hurtful ones you can utter. Trust me. I said it too many times."

He leaned forward before I could speak. "Whatever is stopping you, forget it. Whatever it is in your past that makes you doubt love, stop listening to it. Think of her. Grace. What your life would be like without her. Ask yourself if it is really worth it."

I stared at him, silent.

He stood. "As for being *capable*, you aren't giving yourself enough credit. You are far more capable than you know."

He paused at the door. "Good talk, boss man. Try not to fuck it up."

And he walked out.

But his words echoed in my head all morning.

GRACE

By eleven, my head ached. Ronan had dropped me off early, and the morning had been a busy one. Catching up on emails, voice mails, and case files. Meeting with

Jaxson and Michael about ongoing cases and his calendar. Trying desperately to act in my usual calm manner and not to react to Jaxson's unwavering gaze every time I lifted my eyes. I felt him watch me. I knew he tracked me everywhere in his office, his door wide open, his line of vision clear. He was unfailingly polite, professional, and courteous, but his gaze was an icy-blue storm that burned me from the inside out. My tension mounted, and I knew I had been fooling myself, thinking we would be able to work together with this unresolved between us.

I relaxed a little when Jaxson disappeared around ten. He hadn't returned when I followed Michael to the large boardroom for an unexpected meeting called by the partners at eleven. I stood in the corner, pressing myself close to the window as the room filled. It wasn't a large law office, but the room was crammed with associates, interns, other articling students, and staff. The partners walked in, Jaxson trailing behind them. I noticed the partners look in my direction, and I frowned, wondering what was going on.

The senior partner stepped forward, holding up his hand for silence. He smiled at the group, welcoming everyone back from the holidays and expressing his wishes for the new year. Then he dropped his bombshell.

"I wanted to gather everyone together to announce a new partner with the firm. It is no secret how much we hoped this would happen, and I am pleased to confirm it today. It happened last month, but we have decided to announce it now. Please join me in congratulating Jaxson Richards as partner."

I tried not to gape. Jaxson accepted a partnership? He told me he never wanted to be a partner. He didn't want the responsibility. The bond.

Why would he do this? What changed his mind?

I met his gaze across the room. It was entirely focused on me. There was something in his expression. It was open. Pleading.

It hit me.

He had done this for me. Why, I didn't know, but I was convinced that was the reason.

I didn't know whether to laugh, cry, or yell.

There was a flurry as people crowded around to shake his hand. I turned to Michael, who was watching me. "You know?" I asked quietly.

"Yes." He leaned down. "They know too."

The partners knew of our marriage. He had told them.

Again, the word hit me. *Why?*

I didn't respond. The room was beginning to close in around me, so I turned and headed to the door. I slipped into the washroom down the hall, turning on the tap and letting cool water run across my wrists. My mind was going a hundred miles an hour. He told the partners about our marriage. He accepted a partnership.

Why? What was he doing?

The door opened, and Sabrina Wells stepped in, meeting my gaze in the mirror. Her cold eyes swept over me as she approached. She reminded me of a snake, dangerous and silent as she drew close, ready to strike. Planning on leaving me bitten and bleeding on the floor.

I turned, waiting for her, letting the anger and confusion inside me build. She was going to be the one bitten. Thanks to something Addi said, I was armed and ready.

She crossed her arms, regarding me silently. I mimicked her stance, adding what I hoped was a smirk.

"What can I do for you, Sabrina?"

"You can cut the innocent act."

"I have no idea what you're talking about."

"I saw you," she hissed. "I have a dated picture. Jaxson was fucking you long before this supposed partnership deal was made."

It made sense suddenly. The loophole he had mentioned. I shook my head and put on my poker face.

"He was a partner before you saw us, Sabrina. And why you should care, I have no idea." I looked her up and down. "He's not going to sleep with you, regardless of what you do." I paused. "Your desperation is beginning to show."

"You little bitch. I can have any man I want."

I smirked. "According to the rumors, you often do."

Her cheeks darkened, and she narrowed her eyes.

"But unlike the other men you go after, Jaxson isn't interested."

"I can make your life miserable." She snapped her fingers. "You can kiss your career goodbye."

I leaned against the sink. "You should really learn more about the people you threaten, Sabrina. Once my articling is done, I'm working for BAM. You've heard of them, I presume? They're my *family*. My uncles. My future is set, no matter what lies you perpetrate. They wouldn't listen or believe them. So, go ahead and say whatever you want about me. I don't really give a care."

I turned back to the sink and pretended to fuss with my hair. I was pleased to see my hands didn't shake and I looked calm. Detached.

Sabrina, on the other hand, was furious. Her eyes glittered with anger in the light, and her hands were clenched into fists.

"But," I added, giving myself one last look and turning back to face her, "you say a single solitary word about my husband, I will come after you like the devil himself stepped from hell."

She blinked. "Husband?"

"Husband," I confirmed. "Something else you don't know. Jaxson and I are married. So, as his wife, I'm warning you. Back off." I smiled widely. "And one last thing. Another one of my uncles is Halton Smithers. He had a lot to say about you when I talked to him." I grimaced. "Not very nice things."

Halton had cursed a lot when I'd called him. When Addi mentioned his name, an idea had formed, and he was all too happy to be on board with my plan when I told him what was going on. He had come up with an amazing idea. I loved his devious mind.

"Halton Smithers?" she repeated once again.

"Yes. He enjoys destroying you in court, he tells me. Oh, and by the way, one of his new partners is Lisa Thorne. You must know her—she specializes in personal law. She's standing by to help me with a defamation of character suit against you if you so much as breathe a word about Jaxson or me." I laughed lightly, my nerves beginning to overtake me. "Not to mention your harassment of him. She'll be only too happy to dig into your ah, string of 'attachments,' and what they have to say about you. She's a pit bull, that one."

The door to the washroom moved as if someone was about to come in, but no one appeared, so I ignored it.

"I suggest you leave Jaxson alone. Forget about him. Forget about me. I'm no one to you. A law student. I'll be gone soon enough." I tilted my head. "And given Jaxson's new position, he will have something to say if you continue your harassment of him. He's been a gentleman until now, but his, ah, circumstances have changed. You come after me, and he will return the favor. And he is relentless—I promise you that. So is Lisa." I narrowed my eyes. "And I won't let him be subjected to the likes of you. Not to mention how displeased the partners will be when they find out. Do you understand me?"

If looks could kill, I would be dead. Instead, I met her furious gaze with a calm one of my own.

"Do we understand each other, Sabrina? Leave my husband alone. Leave us alone. Move on." I walked toward the door, pausing before I opened it and looking back at her. She was reeling from what I had told her. My threats. Her face was ashen and her posture down-trodden. She looked almost human.

"Get some counseling," I advised. "Life is too short to be angry all the time."

And I walked out.

Michael was at his desk when I walked in, my legs shaking as the adrenaline left me. Jaxson's door was shut, but Michael indicated it with the jerk of his head.

"He wants to see you."

"Ah," I croaked.

"And I have the rest of the afternoon off." He stood. "The outer office door will be locked, and the phone is being answered by the front desk."

I nodded. He stopped next to me and gave me a hug. "Talk to him, Grace. Listen to what he is trying to say, even though he can't use the words," he encouraged.

He walked out, and I heard the lock engage. I shut my eyes and drew in a long breath. I opened Jaxson's door. He was leaning against his desk, as if waiting for me. His shirt sleeves were rolled up, exposing his forearms, and his large hands rested on the wood beside him.

We regarded each other as I shut the door and approached him.

"You told them. You told the partners we were married."

"I was honest, yes."

"You accepted a partnership," I stated without rancor.

"Yes. The loophole I found stated no fraternization with regard to associates, not partners."

"I thought the loophole was marrying me."

He shrugged. "I lied. I married you because I wanted to. The phone call I got before we flew out to Vegas was my colleague confirming the loophole of associates dating. I called Hodges that day and told him I would accept the partnership they kept offering as long as it was back-dated to December first. And they had to wait until after the holidays to announce it. It didn't take long for us to come to an agreement."

I frowned. "If you could just *date* me, Jaxson, why did you marry me?"

"Because even if you agreed to seeing me again, dating you was no longer enough."

I passed a hand over my head, weary and confused. *Would I ever understand him?*

He tilted his head, studying me. "I know you don't remember Vegas. But the fact is it happened pretty simply. We'd had a lot to drink—you more than me— you told me off about hurting you. I confessed to why I did it. You kissed me, and I knew I didn't want to give you up. We were by one of the chapels, and the idea hit me. I asked, you said yes, and we got a license and got married. I knew as a partner I could have dated you and ignored Sabrina and her threats. But the bottom line is, I *wanted* to marry you. I wanted you with me forever, even if I couldn't say it. The bonus was it gave you an extra layer of protection." He held up his hand to stop me talking. "Even if you didn't want it. Sabrina would never dare disparage a partner or his wife. Not even she is that stupid."

I didn't know what to say.

"What I didn't realize—" he smirked "—was that my wife had something up her sleeve far more effective. That of a woman determined to protect what was hers." He leaned forward. "I heard you, Gracie."

"That was you on the other side of the washroom door."

"Yes." He tutted, a smirk tugging at his lips. "You lied. You blatantly lied. You had no idea when I became partner."

I tossed my hair. "It's called a calculated bluff. You taught me that. I assumed a little white lie about a date wouldn't bother you or the partners much."

"I taught you well. You were very passionate. You defended me. Fought on my behalf."

"Yes."

"You're going to be a fabulous lawyer." He winked, then became sober. "No one has ever done that for me." He cocked his head to the side. "Of all the things I knew, this one thing shouldn't have surprised me, but it did. Your tigress hidden inside, protecting the ones you love."

"I guess you didn't know me as well as you thought."

He lifted one shoulder. "I know one thing now I didn't before."

"What?"

"That having you, knowing you—it's changed me, Gracie. I want, *I need* that warmth you carry inside in my life. I need *you*."

I was stunned at his words. They echoed what he'd said to Addi and Brayden, but this time, he was saying them to me.

"I've learned a few other things about us," he murmured, meeting my eyes.

"Oh?" I asked, finding my voice.

"I know you like to be held at night and that I want to be the one to hold you. I know you will never be over your fear of enclosed spaces, and it would be my greatest honor to make sure you never have to face that fear alone. I will hold your hand, hug your body, and be whatever you need to overcome that fear, even if it is only for a moment, and yes, even if it has to happen every single day."

Tears clouded my eyes at his words, the genuine sentiments he was expressing.

"I hate that I hurt you. The things I said. I spoke from fear, Gracie. I didn't mean any of those hateful things I said to you when I broke us up. In my desperation to protect you, I hurt you worse than she ever could have. You never had a time limit. You meant more than anyone ever had or will to me. I saw the pain I caused you that day in your eyes. I knew you really believed me, and I hated myself more than ever for putting it there. I've never lied so much as I did that day." He lifted his head. "But I will never lie to you again."

My breath caught in my throat at his confession.

Our gazes locked—his was as honest and open as I had ever seen. "I love you," he said. "Those are words I never expected to say. Words I never expected to feel.

But I do. I love you. I want you as my wife. I want you by my side. I don't want to be without you. Ever."

I could only blink.

"I want to discover every little thing about you. I want to share your happiness. I want to be the cause of your happiness. I want everything with you."

All I could do was whisper his name. He grimaced ruefully and ran a hand through his hair.

"I don't know how to say this properly, how to do this, Gracie. But with you, I want to try. Please give me the chance to try."

I shook my head in disbelief.

Tears formed in his eyes, gathered in the corners, shimmering in the icy blue of his gaze. Except there was no ice, but warmth, need, and a new emotion I was having trouble believing.

Love.

Did he really love me?

"I waited too long," he said. "I let my fears overpower me, and I stayed silent, which hurt you. But I heard you earlier, and I thought you must still love me—even a little." He exhaled hard.

I struggled to find my words. I was overwhelmed and shocked. Scared to believe what he was saying because I wanted it to be true.

He hung his head, shaking it slowly, then looked up. The devastated look on his face shook me. "I didn't want to do this, but I have no one to blame but myself. I love you, Gracie. I love you so much that, since it's what you have told me you wanted, I will let you go. You can have your divorce if that's what you need to make you happy. Maybe that will prove to you that you come first. That you will always come first." He looked sad. "Of all the things I have lost in my life, losing you will be my biggest regret. I will never stop loving you. I will never stop missing you."

He turned away, his back to me. "I think I need you to go."

His shoulders were bent as if too heavy to hold up. My mind tried to process his words. He was letting me go. Giving me what he thought I wanted. What I thought I wanted.

Except it wasn't. I was with him the day I married him, and I needed to stop blaming him for it. In his own way, he had been fighting for me, for us, this whole time. He loved me. He'd said the words, offered me his heart, and when he thought I refused it, he let me go so I could be happy.

The one flaw with that logic was that it was Jaxson who would make me happy. Because underneath the anger and hurt, I still loved him. I would always love him. Addi and my mom were right. He was worth the risk.

I laid my hand on his shoulder, feeling him flinch. "Jaxson."

He turned, barely having the time to brace himself before I flung myself into his arms. "Hold me every night," I begged. "Never let go."

He held me in an embrace that was tight and hard. His heat wrapped around me, warming my body and sinking inside my skin. "I love you," I sobbed. "I'm sorry."

He kissed my forehead. "No, baby, I'm sorry. I'm sorry for everything. I love you, Gracie. I love you so much."

I lifted my head, meeting his eyes. Now I could see the emotion—real, honest, and open. The love that blazed in the depth of blue. His love for me.

"I love you," I vowed.

He pressed his forehead to mine. "Promise me you'll never stop."

"I promise."

"Stay with me. Work this out with me. Show me how to love you."

"Yes."

"Then, Gracie Richards, I'm going to ask something else of you."

"What?" I sniffed.

"Marry me. I want a real wedding with you. The flowers and the dancing. Your father giving you to me—" he flashed a grin "—hopefully without a facer involved. I want everyone to know how much you mean to me. And I want you to remember our wedding day."

"Yes," I answered simply.

He brought his mouth to mine. "Thank you."

His kiss erased everything else. The past. The hurt and pain. The worry. All that mattered was him and me. His arms, his mouth, his love. I had him, which meant one thing.

I had it all.

CHAPTER 32

A MONTH LATER - JAXSON

I sat back, exasperated. Grace and I had spent weeks making plans. Talking. Figuring out our future. I had meant what I said about marrying her again. I wanted her to have her day. To be a bride and all the memories that went with it.

She was surprisingly lacking in enthusiasm for the idea. She finally admitted she wanted a small event, with family, a brief ceremony, and a party afterward.

"No grand dinner, no large guest list, no bridal party. Addi and Heather. You and me. Whoever you choose to stand up for you. Our vows at city hall." She winked cheekily. *"Rocking Ramen for dinner."*

I had kissed her and agreed to whatever she wanted.

I had never known such profound happiness. I had never shared as much of myself with another person as I did Grace. It was as if talking to her released the poison from my heart, leaving more room to love her.

And love her I did. She was so deep within in my heart and soul, I knew I could never be without her again.

Her parents returned for another visit, and we invited them over for dinner to tell them our plans. Her mother hadn't been surprised, but Richard was being difficult. He wanted to throw a lavish wedding. Give her things she had no interest in. I argued with him because it wasn't Grace's wish, and frankly, he was just too much fun to rile up.

He, in turn, liked to do the same. Ours was a complicated relationship.

"No, Goddammit. Listen, VanRyan. I don't care if you're her father or you have some sort of weird '*I was her dad first*' bullshit ideas in your head. She's my wife, do you understand? Mine. Mine to care for, mine to look after, and mine to love. You need to get that through your thick skull because I'm not going anywhere. And I know what she wants, and a huge wedding isn't it."

"I never got a chance to walk her down the aisle. You never even asked me for her hand!"

"That's what this is about? You want to walk her down the aisle? Fine. We can do that. Name the date, and I'll be there."

A throat clearing made me look at Gracie. She was watching us, her arms crossed, a displeased look on her face.

"If Grace wants that," I amended.

"Pussy-whipped," Richard muttered.

"Your daughter," I replied.

"Shut up, both of you," Katy said, shaking her head. "Can't you two get along?"

"He started it," we both said at the same time.

"And I'm not asking you for *permission*. She's already mine," I muttered.

"I should punch you again."

I glared at him. "Go for it, old man. You wanna punch me? Come at me. But this time, I'm going to return the favor. I'll give you a facer so hard, it will send you back in time."

Richard snorted. "Good. Go ahead. I'll take it if it stops her from meeting you."

"That makes no sense," I replied.

"Neither do you," he snapped.

"Asshole," I breathed.

"Jerk."

Katy stood. "Idiots. Both of you."

Gracie joined her. "Mom is right. You should both go fuck yourself. We'll plan this ourselves." She pointed at her dad. "You can walk me down the aisle, but that's it. I don't want a huge production. And I want it soon."

Then she glared at me. "Stop ramping him up. You get too much enjoyment out of it."

They walked away, disappearing into the kitchen.

"Well, that was harsh," I muttered.

Richard sat back. "Uncalled-for." Then he winked, and I chuckled. We both enjoyed our verbal sparring.

I stood. "Scotch?"

"Is it the good stuff?"

I snorted. "Like I would have any other kind. Only the best." I winked. "Like your daughter."

He took his glass. "I don't wanna hear about it."

"Whatever."

He took a sip. "I don't like you, but your scotch is good."

"You have to like me. I'm your favorite son-in-law."

"You're too old for her."

"She doesn't think so. She likes me just the way I am. Besides, Gracie is an old soul. And she is perfect for me. She'll keep me young."

He grunted. I knew he didn't like the age difference, but I didn't care. Besides, there was nothing I could do about it. I wasn't giving Gracie up. Ever. Finally, he spoke.

"Technically, you're my only son-in-law. Reed ranks higher."

"Reed doesn't give you scotch."

He snorted. "I know. He and Heather and their vodka martinis. He needs to change that."

"See? Young people. Pfft. Favorite."

He waved his hand. "Whatever."

"I don't like you much either, but I love your daughter. And I think you're an okay father-in-law. Arrogant and an asshole on occasion, but okay—especially since you stopped punching me."

"Well, fuck, I have no reply for that."

"Good. Shut up, then."

We were silent for a moment before he asked, his voice serious, "You going to treat her well?"

"Every single day. I love her more than I can say." I met his eyes. "She is my world, Richard."

"I guess you're not so bad."

"So, I have your blessing?"

"I'll think about it."

"Fine."

He leaned over. "What the hell is a facer anyway?"

I laughed. This was going to be fun.

I slid between the sheets with a contented sound. I enjoyed the visits with Grace's parents but was always glad to see them leave. It was going to take me a while to adjust to having family around all the time. It seemed constant. Aunts, uncles, cousins. Someone was always stopping by, or we were invited some place. I had to admit, part of me enjoyed it, but I still liked having Gracie all to myself. I propped myself up on my elbow, studying Gracie. She had been quieter than usual tonight, especially after her parents left. "What is it?" I asked.

"My parents offered me their house until ours is ready in Port Albany." She swallowed, her voice nervous. "I don't think I can take much more of the elevator, Jaxson."

I frowned, reaching up and cupping her cheek. "It's all right. Your dad and I talked about that too. They leave next week, and we can move anytime." I winked. "The landlords will let me out of my lease, no problem—family connections and all."

I was shocked when, instead of laughing, tears filled her eyes. I was fast to assure her. "Don't cry, darling. I know how much you hate the elevator, and you've been so brave."

"I've been emotional," she admitted. "And stressed."

"I know. We'll move. Drive in together every day. It'll be fine."

"Jaxson."

I sat up, something in her voice making me tense. "Gracie, what is it?"

"It's been a while since Vegas."

"I know. A lot of shit has happened." I leaned forward and kissed her. "But life will settle down. We'll get married again in a few weeks, move to Port Albany, and find a new rhythm."

"Sometimes what happens in Vegas follows you home," she burst out. "Not right away but later."

I furrowed my brow in confusion. "Later?"

"Nine months later."

"Nine—what are you…" I trailed off as the meaning of her words hit me. "Holy shit. Are you—are you pregnant?"

"Yes."

I was hit with a myriad of emotions. Confusion, worry, shock. But one other emotion overrode them all.

Wonder.

I was going to be a father. Grace and I would have a family. *Be* a family.

The happiness I was getting used to accepting suddenly squeezed my heart, making my chest ache with the ferocity of it.

I met her eyes. "We're having a baby?"

"Yes."

"Our wedding night," I recalled. "We weren't careful every time."

"No. And I think I forgot to take a pill."

"You were rather drunk."

"Yes, I was."

I lifted an eyebrow. "So, one unused condom and one missing pill make one baby."

"Yes."

I swallowed. "Our baby."

"Yes," she whispered.

"Are you happy, Gracie?"

"Thrilled," she responded. "Scared. Nervous."

"This will change your plans for the future."

"It makes them better."

I kissed her, my touch tender and lingering. "You make it better." I laid my hand across her flat abdomen. "You both do." I kissed her again. "Thank you."

"You're happy?" she asked, tears running down her cheeks.

"Ecstatic. I love you, Grace Richards."

"I love you," she sobbed.

I took her in my arms, rocking her, making hushing noises. When she was calmer, I laid her down and pressed a kiss to her stomach.

"Hi, baby. It's Daddy. We're happy you're on your way, and we can't wait to meet you."

Another tear slid down her cheek. I lifted her hand and kissed the palm. For a moment, neither of us spoke, basking in the warmth of the moment.

Then a thought occurred to me. I looked up, my eyes dancing with glee.

"Do I get to tell your dad? I want to be the first to call him Gramps."

A grin pulled at her lips. "He might give you a facer."

I kissed her stomach again. "So worth it."

Gracie was asleep, resting in my arms. My mind was too alert to sleep.

I was going to be a father.

A year ago, I had been facing another year of being alone. A world filled with work, silence, and regrets. Unable to feel or be involved with people, except from a distance.

Then she entered my life. Despite the ups and downs, and all the pain I put her through, she was here with me. My wife. She had changed me in every way. All for the better.

And now she had given me a gift I never even realized I longed for.

Gracie was making me a father. I would have a child of my own to watch over. To care for. To love. My child would never know fear the way I had. Loneliness or hunger. I would protect him or her with my life.

For the first time in my life, I felt gratitude. A reason to look to the future because thanks to the slumbering woman beside me, it was bright.

I pressed a kiss to her head in silent appreciation and love. She snuggled closer, and I held her tighter. She was love personified, and she was mine.

My Grace.

My saving Grace.

EPILOGUE

A YEAR LATER - JAXSON

Katy appeared beside me, her smile wide. "She's here."

"Okay, great."

"Are you sure you don't want to be at the door?"

"No, let her see everyone, say hello, and hug them. She'll want to hold Kylie when she's done."

Katy lifted an eyebrow. "In other words, you don't want to risk the chance of someone else taking your daughter."

I pressed a kiss to my daughter's head, gazing down at her in rapt fascination. "I have no idea what you're talking about."

Katy chuckled and I grinned. "Go to the door. She'll be so excited to see you. Take Richard with you," I suggested.

Shaking her head, Katy walked away, stopping to take Richard's hand and pull him along with her.

Gracie was going to be so surprised. She thought she was coming here with Addi to meet a new client. She had no idea it was a party to celebrate her passing the bar.

When the envelope arrived last week, she had stared at it endlessly, then looked up at me, holding it out.

"I can't," she said.

I took it from her, opening it right away, no doubt in my mind the news it would contain. And I was right. My brilliant, astounding wife had passed.

She wept, and I held her.

"How could you think otherwise, darling?" I crooned. "You are so amazing."

"I was just worried," she sniffled. "I didn't want to disappoint you or my dad or anyone."

I lifted up her chin. "You never could. The bar is a hard thing. If you didn't pass that time, you would have tried again. No failure." I pressed a kiss to her mouth. "But you passed."

And I went directly to my ace in the hole.

Jen.

He already had the winery on hold for several dates. Her parents on standby. The caterers ready. The guest list on speed dial. As soon as I knew she passed, everything went into motion, and today, the room was filled with Gracie's family and the few people she considered friends from outside it. All to celebrate with her.

I owed that man the biggest damn bottle of champagne I could find. He would love it.

As long as it was expensive and rare.

Just like him.

The doors opened, and she walked in, talking to Addi, stopping short when she saw the group of people waiting for her, shouting congratulations. Her eyes widened, sweeping the room, and I held up Kylie, showing her we were there. Grace was lost among well-wishers, and I grinned, watching her hug and accept their felicitations.

"Your mommy is so amazing," I cooed to Kylie. She looked up at me, blinking in the light, her eyes the perfect replica of Gracie's. Her hair was as dark as mine, little fluffs of curls on her head, and she had my dimple in her chin. Otherwise, she was a blend of both of us—her own perfect little self.

A small fist waved in the air, and I lifted it, kissing it. "Your mommy finished her articling, wrote the bar, and gave birth to you." I shook my head. "No easy feat any of them—but to do all three in such a short time period? Pretty damn spectacular."

"Of course," Richard's amused voice stated. "She's my daughter after all." Then he tutted. "You're holding my granddaughter wrong. Give her to me."

"No."

"You get her all the time. Give her to me," he repeated, reaching for her.

"Nope." I pointed to my chest with my free hand. "*Dad*. I trump you."

He huffed. "Hardly. Grandpa trumps Dad."

"Ha. You always change it up to suit you. Dad trumps Grandpa."

Katy stepped forward, sliding Kylie from my arms.

"And Grandma trumps both of you." She walked away, heading toward Gracie, who was slowly making her way over.

"Well, damn it, now neither of us has her," I griped.

"Your fault," he growled.

"Whatever."

He blew out a long breath. "Might as well have a scotch while we wait. You got our brand at the bar?"

"Of course."

"I'll go get us one."

My father-in-law headed to the bar. Ours was a complicated relationship of constant battle. We loved to squabble.

Trade shots. One-up each other. But the bottom line was I respected him, even liked him, and on the rare occasion, he admitted to feeling the same way. If I plied him with enough scotch and no one else was around to hear him.

He was a good man who loved his family deeply, and I followed his example daily.

I simply never told him that.

The memory of the day he found out he was going to be a grandfather still made me grin.

Richard and Katy were leaving to head back to BC. Gracie and I were moving in to their house in Port Albany so Gracie no longer had to contend with the elevator. All of my things were going into storage, and we would be in her old room. There was no way I was sleeping and making love to her in her parents' bedroom. I ordered a new, bigger bed than the double it currently contained, and we would live there until our new home was ready. She loved it there, and I had to admit it would be a great place to bring up a child.

She was nervous about telling her parents, and I took her hand in mine as we sat at the table having coffee before they left for the airport.

"Aiden says your place will take priority. With the crew they have, the house will be ready by the summer," Richard mused.

Gracie nodded. "Yes."

"We'll be back in a couple of weeks for the wedding, then you'll be on your own. I'll be back and forth as usual, but I'll stay in Toronto." He cleared his throat. "Newlyweds like their privacy."

I chuckled, and Gracie sputtered over a sip of coffee.

He frowned, looking between us. "Gracie, you're pale." He narrowed his eyes. "What did you do?" He aimed his glare at me. "Keep it up, and I'll withdraw my blessing."

I rolled my eyes. "You realize, Richard, that our legal wedding date is in December. That we are, in fact, already married. We're doing this for the family."

He sat back. "Your point?"

"You can't withdraw your blessing. I'm already her husband."

"Uh-huh."

I turned slightly in my chair so I could see the expression on his face. "The father of her children."

"Not yet."

I drew in a deep breath. "Soon enough." I pulled Gracie close. "Sooner than we expected."

Katy's breath caught, and she covered her mouth, looking between us as my words lingered in the air.

I looked at Richard. I expected anger. Accusations. Maybe another facer. What I didn't expect was the softening around his eyes. How his hand sought Katy's on the table. The glimmer of tears as he blinked.

"You're pregnant?" He addressed Gracie.

"Yes," she confirmed. "And Dad, I'm thrilled." She squeezed my hand. "We're thrilled."

"Your career," he said with a frown. "Your plans."

"*Haven't changed. We're just taking a different route,*" she insisted.

"*And you're happy?*"

"*So much.*"

"*We're both happy,*" I inserted. I met his eyes. "*My wife and child are my number one priority. Now. Always.*"

He was silent for a moment.

"*My baby is having a baby. I'm going to be…*" He trailed off.

"*A grandpa,*" I finished triumphantly.

"*Grandpa,*" he repeated as if testing out the word.

"*The sexiest grandpa I know.*" Katy smirked.

Suddenly, he grinned. "*I beat Mad Dog. And Bentley. They'll be so freaking jealous.*"

Then he stood and took Gracie in his arms, hugging her and talking quietly. I got a hug from Katy and waited until Richard finished his private conversation with Gracie. I extended my hand, shocked when instead I got a fast, hard hug, and he slapped my shoulder. "*Enjoy this,*" he said. "*Nothing beats becoming a dad. Nothing.*"

I met his gaze, sharing a moment of camaraderie with him. It strengthened our rather odd relationship, but I knew he supported us, and that was all that mattered.

"*I'll be around to make sure you don't fuck it up too much,*" he added dryly, making me laugh.

Typical Richard.

I roused from my memories as Richard handed me a scotch with a wink. "Katy loves being a grandma. I guess I'll let her win this one."

I snorted. "You *let* her win a lot."

"I wouldn't talk, Jaxson." He grinned. "My daughter has you whipped."

"Whatever, *Dad.*"

We both laughed.

I listened to the laughter and conversations around me, thinking of the last time I had been in this room.

I had married Gracie. Again.

This time, in front of her family. Watching as she walked the short distance to me, her eyes clear, bright, and shining with happiness. Wearing a pretty lacy dress Cami had made for her, her bare shoulders and neck gleaming in the light. Addi and Heather stood beside her. Ronan and Michael flanked me. I had grown closer to Ronan, discovering his quiet side. We enjoyed spending time together in Port Albany, and he was a frequent guest at the house.

Richard was surprisingly calm, although he had already sat with me and spoken at length about his daughter and what she meant to him. His expectations. I think I shocked him when I listed my own expectations of myself. I divulged my past and my still-unclear concept of family and how I would try to be everything she needed.

He had clapped me on the shoulder in understanding.

"You'll sink or swim with this family," he teased. "No one entering the BAM universe comes out the same as they went in. And they like you after the Christmas thing."

"I want Grace to stay close to her family. The real one and the adopted one."

He frowned and leaned close. "The adopted one is real too, Jaxson. Family isn't a name. If anything, it's even tighter because it grows from the heart." His tone was serious. "You'll understand when your child is born. You want them to know this sort of love." He met my eyes. "You'll need this sort of love." He glanced down, his voice lowering. "I understand you more than you think, Jaxson. I didn't know love until Katy. But once you know it? You will never be the same. Once family gets added, life gets even better."

That was the moment that cemented our relationship. A shared understanding of the pain and loneliness we had lived before the women in our lives opened our eyes to another type of world. Taught us how much we were missing.

Not that we ever let on. It was too fun to wind each other up. But our phone calls and texts, his encouragement when I was worried about Gracie or the baby, were what got me through the pregnancy. And he had been correct. This family was amazing.

I eyed him watching Gracie come closer, now holding Kylie as she greeted people. I needed to make sure she reached me first.

Just because I liked him didn't mean I wanted to give up baby time, though.

Gracie appeared in front of me, a wide smile on her face. She cupped my cheek, bringing me to her mouth, the heavy platinum and diamond ring she had once flung over my head now resting on her finger, marking her as taken. Marking her as mine.

I kissed her thoroughly, partially to bother Richard, partially to take the opportunity to slip Kylie from her arms, but mostly because I loved kissing my wife.

She eased back, her breathing fast. She shook her head at my maneuvers and chuckled. "I love you," she murmured.

I kissed her again.

"I love you back, darling."

GRACE

I knew Jaxson was up to something, but I had no idea he had planned a party for me to celebrate passing the bar. He had made a big deal of making a reservation at my favorite place for dinner on the weekend, and I thought that would be our celebration.

Not gathering as much of my family together as he could. Adding in a few close friends and coworkers. Not flying my parents in to celebrate. Choosing the place we were married in to celebrate. I had been shocked walking in with Addi, thinking we were meeting a client.

I had found his intense stare across the room right away. Saw him holding our daughter with his large hands, cradling her head and holding her close in that protective way that made my heart beat faster. I had never seen a sight sexier than that. Or the expression he wore these days. I doubted he realized the way his lips were curled into a half smile most of the time. Or the gentle softness in his eyes when he was with me. And when he looked at Kylie, I melted. Pure, total love poured from his gaze.

When my mother took her away to bring her to me, I tried not to laugh at his woebegone expression. There was no doubt he and my father were quarreling over her again. They bickered about everything, but my mother and I were both aware of how deep their friendship had become. And we found their bantering amusing.

I made my way over, stopping to say hello to people, getting hugs and kisses, accepting congratulations. Jaxson's kiss hello set my blood boiling. Simply looking at him raised my temperature most of the time. His mouth on mine was like a match to gasoline. Even if he used my distraction to slip Kylie from my arms and reclaim her.

Sneaky man.

"Surprise," he whispered.

"It certainly is. How did you do this?" I asked.

He grinned, his dimple deep. "My secret weapon."

"Ah." I grinned back. "Your biggest fan. Jen."

"What can I say? He loves me."

My dad snorted. "Quit hogging my Kylie." He took advantage of me being close to Jaxson and took the baby away. "It's okay, baby girl. Grandpa's got you," he crooned. "Daddy is always useless when Mommy is around."

Jaxson rolled his eyes but let him keep Kylie. He wrapped his arm around my waist, tucking me into his side.

"I wanted to celebrate this with you. To do something that would make you happy," he said quietly. "And I know nothing makes you happier than your family."

"One thing does."

"Oh?" he asked.

I leaned up close to his ear. "*Our* family. You, me, and Kylie, alone together."

His eyes glistened, and I was rewarded with his widest smile. "Mine too, darling. Mine too."

He was more comfortable showing his emotions these days. At least with me. The rest of the world might still see him as stern and distant, but I knew the real Jaxson.

My Jaxson.

Kylie's daddy—her favorite man on earth. Much to my father's pretend dismay.

I watched Jaxson laughing with my parents, his arm firmly around me, keeping me anchored to his side. The way he kept me anchored.

He had changed so much, barely resembling the man I had first met. He was more relaxed and open. His love was unguarded, and he didn't care. Even at the office where we were on display with colleagues and clients alike until I finished my time there. He had gone to the partners, asking to have me assigned to him the whole time I was articling, explaining that he needed to keep an eye on his pregnant wife, and they had agreed. Sabrina had left after a disturbing incident, which even the partners couldn't ignore, despite her billings. It came to light during a messy case that she was sleeping with both her client and the soon-to-be-ex-husband. She used the information she gathered between the sheets, so to speak, to pit them against each other and drive up her billable hours. She and the firm parted ways immediately. Two new attorneys came in, and her memory dimmed quickly for everyone, especially me. I was glad she was gone from Jaxson's firm and could no longer be an irritant to either of us.

He had been a rock while I was pregnant. Held my hair when I was ill. Immersed himself in my pregnancy, quoting books and facts constantly. Made sure I stuck to my hours at the office. He and Michael fussed over me. Ensured I was eating right. Catered to all my cravings. The day I was to write the bar, Kylie decided to arrive early. My water broke just before I got out of the car. I panicked, and he remained calm, pulling a U-turn and driving to the hospital, holding my hand and helping me with my breathing. By the time I was settled in a room, he'd contacted my parents, gotten word to the right people about the test, and was gowned and gloved, as anxious as I was to meet her. In the hours that passed, the only time he faltered was when the doctor decided I needed a caesarean. Worry and fear passed over his face, but he held my hand and stayed close.

"I'm right here, darling. I have you."

We both wept when Kylie was placed in my arms, pink, wet, and wriggly. Seeing Jaxson hold her for the first time was a sight I would never forget. The wonder and love on his face blazed. She barely left his arms for the next twenty-four hours.

He still hated to give her up.

He had taken parental leave to look after her and me so I could recover. We spent hours with him quizzing me as she slept. He drove me to the test, took me out after, and held my hand as I lamented about questions I thought I got wrong. He was totally amazing.

All this from a man who insisted he could not love. That nothing lasted. Who knew nothing about being part of a family. He now embodied the term.

He often reminisced about our beginning, hated to think about our middle, and lived for our future.

Because now, forever was our mantra.

And he was my always.

BONUS EPILOGUE

TWO YEARS LATER

JAXSON

I pulled up to the house, cutting the engine, the sudden silence welcome. I stepped from the car, inhaling the warm, early-summer air. I could hear the water lapping at the shore, the sounds of the lazy waves relaxing me. I shrugged off my jacket and made my way toward the house, anxious to see Gracie and Kylie.

I paused before entering the house to take in the vista. The late-afternoon sun hit the water in a bright reflection of light. Kylie loved it, clapping her hands in glee when we would walk the sand, and she would pick out sparkles on the water.

I never imagined my life to be as it was these days. Married to a beautiful woman, father to an adorable, if slightly stubborn, daughter. Living in a place that was as beautiful as it was tranquil. Surrounded every day by people who were now my family and who epitomized the word love.

There was only one thing missing, and I hoped what happened today would put that final piece of the puzzle into place.

I paused as the sounds of my wife's and daughter's voices drifted up from the beach, and I set down my briefcase and jacket, hurrying across the deck and down the steps toward them.

Kylie spotted me first, dropping the stick she was carrying as she raced toward me. "Daddy!"

Laughing, I scooped her up, letting her cover my face with her tiny butterfly kisses. Gracie joined her, slipping her arm around my waist and smiling up at me. Her dark hair blew in the breeze, her bright blue eyes alight with happiness. I bent and pressed a kiss to her full lips, then another one to her head. "Hello, darling."

Kylie giggled the way she always did when I would kiss her mother, and I turned my head, meeting her blue gaze that was so much like Gracie's. Warm, vivid, and expressive. "You need a kiss, Kylie Kat?" I teased.

"No, Daddy! I kiss you!"

"Hmm…you did. But you know what? You look good enough to eat…" I teased.

"No!"

Laughing, I buried my face in her neck, pretending to gobble her. She squirmed and shrieked, pushing at me until I placed her back on the sand.

She planted her hands on her hips. "No eat me!" Then she turned and hurried back to her stick and a pile of what I was sure were today's favorite rocks and broken bits of shells.

I turned to Gracie with a leer. "That's not what mommy says," I winked and pulled her into my arms. She slapped my chest, chuckling.

"Incorrigible."

"In love with my sexy wife."

She gazed up at me, a smile lighting her face. "In love with my sexy husband."

"Then we're perfect for each other."

"Yes, we are." She tugged my hand. "I brought a picnic down since it is so beautiful today. Sandwiches and snacks."

"Sounds great."

I followed her to the Adirondack chairs we kept on the beach, far enough back they escaped the water's edge. In front of the chairs was a blanket with a tinier version of our chair for Kylie, not that she'd sit much, except maybe to eat, but even that was doubtful. A basket sat on the blanket, and I knelt beside Gracie to help her unpack the feast she'd brought down from the house.

Kylie joined us, swinging her little legs as she sat in her chair, puzzling over what to eat from the plate I had filled for her. It was hardly a shock when she bypassed the sandwich and began grazing on the carrots and grapes. Those were her favorites.

I tugged off my tie, rolling up my shirt sleeves, and sat back with a hearty sigh of contentment. I caught Gracie eyeing up my forearms, and with a wink, I flexed my muscles.

"All yours once munchkin is asleep, my little wench."

She winked back. "I look forward to it."

I sipped the cold beer as I ate, enjoying the simple food, the warm sun, and the time with my family. I kicked off my shoes, laughing as Kylie tried to tug off my socks. I bent and helped her, knowing she would want a walk by the water once we finished eating.

"You'll ruin your pants," Gracie murmured.

"I'll roll them up. We have a good dry cleaner." I shrugged, not worried. I reached for another sandwich, trying to tempt Kylie with a bite. I always worried she didn't eat enough, even though her pediatrician and Grace assured me she was fine. Kylie shook her head but did accept a piece of cheese to nibble as she began to dig in the cool sand with her free hand.

I smiled fondly, watching her be her busy little self.

I glanced at Gracie, who was observing us with adoration. "I had lunch with the BAM boys today," I announced.

"Oh?" she asked. It was nothing unusual anymore. I enjoyed a good relationship with all the men in her family, and we often met up for lunch. "Any good gossip?"

I chuckled. Despite their protestations, they did enjoy a good story. Especially Aiden and Maddox.

"One tidbit. Bill told them he wants to retire now."

Her eyes flew open. "Now? I hadn't heard that. He was going to stay on for another couple of years."

"Changed his mind."

"Wow. So, they need to find a replacement."

"They offered me the job."

Her mouth opened, but no sound came out.

"Bentley plans on moving the entire operation out this way," I continued. "He wants to spend more time at home with Emmy. All the guys want to be home more. So, they're going to take over the second floor of the ABC building. And they asked me to join them."

"So, you'd give up the partnership and go to BAM?"

I reached for her hand. "I only took that partnership to get you. To keep you. I don't care about it. This would be an amazing opportunity for me." I squeezed her fingers. "I get to be part of something I do care about. Something important to both of us."

"You won't get bored?"

I laughed. "How could I be bored working for them? And being part of ABC? Getting to work with my wife?"

"So, technically, you'd be my boss again."

"In a roundabout way. I'd be there for advice."

"And you'd be in the same building? No more commute?"

"We can drive the ten minutes together." I blew out a long breath. "I can be home more with you and Kylie. See her grow. I feel like I miss so much with the commute and the hours the firm demands."

"You'll see more than you expect."

Something in her voice caught my attention. I studied her, noticing the slight apprehension in her gaze and the way she was holding herself. I had the sudden feeling I wasn't the only one with something to share today.

"Gracie, do you have something to tell me?" I asked, quietly hopeful.

"You're not the only one with news."

I leaned forward, excited, now certain. "Another baby?"

"Yes."

I stood with a loud whoop and pulled her from her chair, swinging her around before embracing her and setting her on her feet. I cupped her face and kissed her thoroughly, ignoring the little hands pulling on my pant leg for a moment. I bent and lifted Kylie into my arms, holding them both close for a moment.

My entire world encased in my arms.

A world I'd never thought possible until the day she walked into my office and set my soul ablaze.

My Grace.

I kissed her again. "Thank you," I whispered against her lips. "Thank you for our life. For giving me all of it."

She wiped away the tears that spilled out of my eyes. "I love you."

"I love you right back, Gracie. So much."

Kylie tugged on my neck. "Walk, Daddy."

"Okay, munchkin. Let's walk."

I set her down and took Gracie's hand. We walked behind Kylie, laughing at her antics, smiling at each other. I could already see the day Kylie would be holding the hand of her little brother or sister.

And a few years later, the next child doing the same.

I thought about what Richard had said. *"Once family gets added, life gets even better."*

He was right.

Not that I would ever admit that to him.

And just the thought made me smile even harder.

Thank you so much for reading MY SAVING GRACE. If you are so inclined, reviews are always welcome by me.

If you would like to meet Gracie's parents, check out Richard and Katy in THE CONTRACT.

If you love to read about Gracie's side of the story during her best friend's wedding, check out A MERRY VESTED WEDDING.

Enjoy reading! Melanie

NEXT in the ABC Corp World
FINDING RONAN'S HEART

"The boys."
"The Callaghan Triplets."
"Three of a kind."
All his life, Ronan Callaghan has been part of a group.

Always looking out for his brothers. Never seen as an
individual or judged on his own merits.
When his brothers veer onto their own path, he finds
himself alone. Restless.
Then he meets her.
Beth.
A waitress who sees him just for himself. None of the
trappings of his wealth or family.
A woman who only wants to know him—Ronan.
She captures his heart, but how will she feel when she
discovers the truth he's holding back?
Can he show her the man he really is?
That he would be rather be hers than anything else?

Available on ebook, paperback and audiobook

ACKNOWLEDGMENTS

As always, I have some people to thank.

Lisa—despite your love of food boxes and flaunting them, you are truly awesome. Thank you for your words of support when I so desperately needed them.

You helped more than you know.

Beth, Trina, Melissa, Peggy, and Deb—thank you for your feedback and support.

Your comments make the story better—always.

Kim—many thanks for all you do. So thrilled you are part of the team.

Karen—you do so much I cannot even begin to thank you for. You are my bookmark in this world and I always find my place because of you. Much love.

To all the bloggers, readers, and especially my promo team. Thank you for everything you do. Shouting your love of books of my work, posting, sharing, making videos—your recommendations keep my TBR list full, and the support you have shown me is deeply appreciated.

To my fellow authors who have shown me such kindness, thank you.

I will follow your example and pay it forward.

My reader group, Melanie's Minions—love you all.

Matthew—my always and forever. I love you.

ALSO AVAILABLE FROM MORELAND BOOKS

Titles published under M. Moreland

Insta-Spark Collection

It Started with a Kiss

Christmas Sugar

An Instant Connection

An Unexpected Gift

Harvest of Love

An Unexpected Chance

Following Maggie (Coming Home series)

Titles published under Melanie Moreland

The Contract Series

The Contract (Contract #1)

The Baby Clause (Contract #2)

The Amendment (Contract #3)

The Addendum (Contract #4)

Vested Interest Series

BAM - The Beginning (Prequel)

Bentley (Vested Interest #1)

Aiden (Vested Interest #2)

Maddox (Vested Interest #3)

Reid (Vested Interest #4)

Van (Vested Interest #5)

Halton (Vested Interest #6)

Sandy (Vested Interest #7)

Vested Interest/ABC Crossover

A Merry Vested Wedding

ABC Corp Series

My Saving Grace (Vested Interest: ABC Corp #1)

Finding Ronan's Heart (Vested Interest: ABC Corp #2)

Loved By Liam (Vested Interest: ABC Corp #3)

Age of Ava (Vested Interest: ABC Corp #4)

Sunshine & Sammy (Vested Interest: ABC Corp #5)

Men of Hidden Justice

The Boss

Second-In-Command

The Commander

The Watcher

The Specialist

Reynolds Restorations

Revved to the Maxx

Breaking The Speed Limit

Shifting Gears

Under The Radar

Full Throttle

Mission Cove

The Summer of Us

Standalones

Into the Storm

Beneath the Scars

Over the Fence

The Image of You

Changing Roles

Happily Ever After Collection

Heart Strings

ABOUT THE AUTHOR

NYT/WSJ/USAT international bestselling author Melanie Moreland, lives a happy and content life in a quiet area of Ontario with her beloved husband of thirty-plus years and their rescue cat, Amber. Nothing means more to her than her friends and family, and she cherishes every moment spent with them.

While seriously addicted to coffee, and highly challenged with all things computer-related and technical, she relishes baking, cooking, and trying new recipes for people to sample. She loves to throw dinner parties, and enjoys traveling, here and abroad, but finds coming home is always the best part of any trip.

Melanie loves stories, especially paired with a good wine, and enjoys skydiving (free falling over a fleck of dust) extreme snowboarding (falling down stairs) and piloting her own helicopter (tripping over her own feet.) She's learned happily ever afters, even bumpy ones, are all in how you tell the story.

Melanie is represented by Flavia Viotti at Bookcase Literary Agency. For any questions regarding subsidiary or translation rights please contact her at flavia@bookcaseagency.com

Connect with Melanie

Like reader groups? Lots of fun and giveaways! Check it out Melanie Moreland's Minions on Facebook.

Join my newsletter for up-to-date news, sales, book announcements and excerpts (no spam). Click here to sign up Melanie Moreland's newsletter

or visit https://bit.ly/MMorelandNewsletter

Visit my website www.melaniemoreland.com

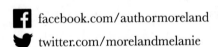 facebook.com/authormoreland
twitter.com/morelandmelanie
 instagram.com/morelandmelanie